PARTNERSHIPS, NEW LABOUR AND THE GOVERNANCE OF WELFARE

PARTNERSHIPS, NEW LABOUR AND THE GOVERNANCE OF WELFARE

Edited by Caroline Glendinning, Martin Powell and Kirstein Rummery

First published in Great Britain in July 2002 by

The Policy Press
Fourth Floor, Beacon House
Queen's Road
Bristol BS8 1QU
UK

Tel +44 (0)117 331 4054
Fax +44 (0)117 331 4093
e-mail tpp-info@bristol.ac.uk
www.policypress.org.uk

Transfered to Digital Print 2006

British Library Cataloguing in Publication Data
A catalogue record for this book is available from the British Library

ISBN 10-1 86134 339 6 paperback
ISBN 13-978 186134 339 0
A hardcover version of this book is also available

Cover design by Qube Design Associates, Bristol.
Front cover: photograph supplied by Third Avenue.

Printed and bound in Great Britain by Marston Book Services Ltd, Oxford.

Contents

Acknowledgements

The biggest thanks must go to Fran Morris, who kept track of the contributions in all their various stages; checked and chased up missing references; worked through the minutiae of copy-editing; and generally chased after us all when we threatened to miss deadlines. Quite literally, this book would never have seen the light of day without her major contribution.

Thanks also to Dawn Louise Rushen at The Policy Press for encouragement and support and to the two anonymous referees who provided helpful comments on the draft manuscript.

Finally, thanks are due to our contributors, who have responded to our requests and increasingly urgent demands with good humour and patience.

Caroline Glendinning, Martin Powell
and Kirstein Rummery
January 2002

Notes on contributors

Correct at time of first printing

Pete Alcock is Professor of Social Policy and Administration and Head of Department of Social Policy and Social Work at the University of Birmingham. He is author of *Social policy in Britain* and *Understanding poverty* and editor of a number of books on social policy. He has recently been involved in qualitative research on voluntary sector organisations with Duncan Scott.

Marian Barnes is Reader and Director of Social Research in the Department of Social Policy and Social Work, University of Birmingham. Much of her work over the past 12 years has been on user involvement and user self-organisation in the context of health and social care. She is currently a member of the national Health Action Zone (HAZ) evaluation team, and is leading a project on public participation and social exclusion in the Economic and Social Research Council's (ESRC's) Democracy and Participation research programme.

John Clarke is Professor of Social Policy at the Open University. His work is concerned with political and ideological conflicts involved in the remaking of welfare states. He has a particular interest in the role of managerialism in the changing governance of welfare, and is the author (with Janet Newman) of *The managerial state: Power, politics and ideology in the remaking of social welfare* (Sage Publications, 1997).

Karen Clarke is Senior Lecturer in Social Policy in the Department of Applied Social Science at Manchester University. Her research interests are family policy, gender roles and work–family relationships. Before working at Manchester University, she worked for 10 years as a researcher at the Equal Opportunities Commission.

Gary Craig is Professor of Social Justice at the University of Hull. Prior to returning to academic work in 1988, he worked in the voluntary sector and in local government, usually in large-scale community development projects. His research interests include poverty and inequality, local governance, community development, and 'race' and ethnicity. He is President of the International Association for Community Development.

Guy Daly is head of the School of Health and Social Sciences at Cheltenham and Gloucester College of Higher Education. His current research interests are in citizenship, local government and public accountability. His recent publications include 'Citizenship and public accountability: older people and community care', in the *Journal of Education & Ageing* (2001) and 'Redefining the local citizen' (2000), in L. McKie and N. Watson *Organising bodies: Institutions, policy and work* (Basingstoke: Macmillan).

Jonathan S. Davies is a Senior Research Fellow at the Local Government Centre in the University of Warwick. He gained his DPhil from the University of York in July 2000. His research interests include British politics, public policy and urban affairs. His monograph, *Partnerships and regimes: The politics of urban regeneration in the UK* was published by Ashgate in October 2001.

Howard Davis is Principal Research Fellow at the Local Government Centre, Warwick Business School, the University of Warwick. For the past three years he has coordinated the monitoring and evaluation of the Local Government Best Value Pilot Programme in England and Wales. He has undertaken a wide range of local government projects in both Britain and the countries of Central and Eastern Europe. He has authored or contributed to a large number of publications, including the evaluation of the Best Value pilot programme and papers in such journals as *Public Money & Management*, *Local Government Studies* and *Policy & Politics*.

Marny Dickson is a Research Officer in Policy Studies at the Institute of Education, University of London. She is a sociologist, currently researching the formulation and implementation of the Education Action Zones policy.

Mark Exworthy is currently a Research Fellow in the Department of Epidemiology and Public Health at University College London, having worked previously at the London School of Economics and Political Science and the University of Southampton. His main research interests are in health policy, particularly in the areas of primary care, managerial and professional relationships and health inequalities. He is the editor of *Professionals and the new managerialism in the public sector* (Open University Press, 1999, with Susan Halford) and the author of a number of articles on partnership working and health inequalities.

Sharon Gewirtz is Professor of Education at King's College London. Her research is in education policy, social policy and the sociology of education.

Caroline Glendinning is Professor of Social Policy at the National Primary Care Research and Development Centre, University of Manchester, where she leads a programme of research on partnerships between primary care and local authority services. Her other main research interests are in the areas of community care, disability, informal care and the interactions of cash payments and services in these areas.

David Halpin is Professor of School Management and Policy at the Institute of Education, University of London, where, in addition to conducting an evaluation of the government's Education Action Zones policy, he is completing a Department for Education and Skills funded study of school leadership development in England.

Brian Hardy is a Principal Research Fellow at the Nuffield Institute for Health (University of Leeds). He has undertaken extensive, government and ESRC-funded research on inter-agency and inter-professional collaboration in health and social care over the past two decades. He is the author and co-author of several books and articles in this field.

Bob Hudson is a Principal Research Fellow at the Nuffield Institute for Health (University of Leeds). He has undertaken extensive research on inter-agency and inter-professional collaboration in health and social care in recent years. As well as being the author and co-author of several books and articles on such collaboration, he is a regular columnist on partnership for the main professional journals in this field.

Gordon Hughes is Senior Lecturer in Social Policy at The Open University. Recent publications include *Understanding crime prevention: Social control, risk and late modernity* (Open University Press, 1998); *Crime prevention and community safety: New directions* and *Youth justice: Critical readings* (Sage Publications, 2002, both co-edited with Eugene McLaughlin and John Muncie); and *Crime control and community: The new politics of security* (Willan, 2002, co-edited with Adam Edwards). His research interests lie in the comparative field of local community safety partnerships and the local governance of crime control, and communitarianism and the contested politics of community.

Eugene McLaughlin is Senior Lecturer in Criminology at The Open University. His primary research interest is police governance. He has written extensively on policing and criminal justice matters and his most recent books are *The Sage dictionary of criminology* (2001) (co-editor) and *Crime prevention and community safety* (Sage Publications, 2002) (co-editor).

Martin Powell works in the Department of Social and Policy Sciences, University of Bath. His research interests include welfare theory, policy evaluation and health policy. He is the author of *Evaluating the National Health Service* (Open University Press, 1997) and is the editor of *New Labour, new welfare state?* (The Policy Press, 1999). He is widely published on various aspects of health policy.

Sally Power is Professor of Education in Policy Studies, Institute of Education, University of London and Co-Director of the Education Policy Research Unit. Her main research interests are sociology of education and education policy analysis. Her research has focused on education and the middle class, private and public schooling and recent reforms aimed at countering disadvantage.

Sally Ruane teaches health policy and the sociology of health at De Montfort University, Leicester. She studied Sociology and Social Policy at Durham University, completing her PhD on *Baby adoption and the social construction of motherhood* in 1990. Her current research interests include public–private boundaries in healthcare and the experience of the private finance initiative in the NHS, and she has published on these topics.

Kirstein Rummery is Lecturer in Health and Community Care, Department of Applied Social Sciences, University of Manchester. Her research interests include disabled and older people's citizenship, access to care and partnership working between health and social care. She is currently undertaking research into the development of partnership working between Primary Care Groups, Trusts and local authorities around services for older people. She has written widely about partnership working in health and social care, disability and community care. Recent publications include *Disability, citizenship and community care: A case for welfare rights?* (Ashgate, 2001).

Duncan Scott is Senior Lecturer in Social Policy and former Head of Department, in the Department of Applied Social Sciences, University of Manchester. He has been a consultant to a wide range of (urban and rural, local, national/international) community groups and voluntary organisations for over 30 years, and a researcher in the fields of the third sector and social policy. Publications include 'Contracting: The experience of service delivery agencies', with L. Russell, in M. Harris and C. Rochester (eds) *Voluntary organisations and social policy in Britain* (Palgrave, 2001); *Moving pictures: Realities of voluntary action* (The Policy Press, 2000); and *Vidas Secas, Lutas Fecundas: Community and development in the Brazilian north-east* with T. Ireland (Whiting and Birch, 1999). He is currently co-directing a research study of social enterprise and the social economy.

Helen Sullivan is Lecturer in the School of Public Policy, University of Birmingham. Her main research interest is in cross-sectoral partnerships and collaboration, with a particular focus on the changing role of key institutions such as local government and the NHS. She is currently a member of the national HAZ evaluation team, and is writing a book on collaboration in UK public services.

Marilyn Taylor is Professor of Social Policy at the University of Brighton. She has been carrying out research in the fields of community development, the voluntary and community sectors and partnerships since the 1970s. Recent relevant publications have covered resident involvement in neighbourhood renewal, partnership between local government and the third sector and neighbour management (all published by the Joseph Rowntree Foundation). She is currently carrying out research on Compacts between local public bodies and the voluntary and community sector, on community involvement in neighbourhood renewal, and on the role of voluntary and community organisations in the democratic process.

Sue Ward is a freelance journalist, researcher and trainer. She is the author of a number of books about pensions, socially responsible investment and communications. She currently writes regularly for a number of pensions journals, including *Pensions World*, *Employee Benefits* and *Professional Pensions*. She was a member of the Good Committee on Pensions Law Reform, and has recently finished a term of office as a Board member of the Occupational Pensions Regulatory Authority (Opra).

Geoff Whitty is the Director of the Institute of Education, University of London. His current research interests are in sociology of education and education policy.

ONE

Introduction

Martin Powell and Caroline Glendinning

Since before its election in 1997, the 'New' Labour government has emphasised a collaborative discourse (Clarence and Painter, 1998; Kirkpatrick, 1999; Painter, 1999; Huxham, 2000; Ling, 2000; Balloch and Taylor, 2001a). This collaborative discourse employs a wide variety of terms; policy documents across a number of fields use terms such as partnership, Compacts, inter-agency working, integrated delivery, joined-up government, coordination and seamless services. However, the term 'partnership' appears to be particularly widely used (Hudson, 1999, 2000; Lewis, 1999a; Fairclough, 2000; Ling, 2000; Powell and Exworthy, 2001; Powell et al, 2001). According to Balloch and Taylor (2001b, p 3), New Labour has tied its colours to the partnership mast, in proclaiming its intention to move from a 'contract culture' to a 'partnership culture'. Partnership represents a 'Third Way' – 'a new model for a new century' – which is distinctive from both the centralised bureaucratic hierarchies of Old Labour and the market of the Conservatives. Moreover, New Labour's collaborative discourse extends beyond simply improving the linkages between government departments and statutory services. It also encompasses government at local, regional and national levels, acting in partnership with the private sector and with agencies in civil society (Giddens, 1998; Powell, 1999b, pp 19-21).

This new discourse of collaboration has parallels with academic debates about changes in the relationship between the state, welfare institutions and civil society and, ultimately, the means by which the state governs. For example, it has been argued that the dominant mode of government has shifted from hierarchies to markets and, most recently, to networks (see Exworthy et al, 1999, for a critical account). Moreover, this governance narrative (for example, Rhodes, 1997, 2000) asserts that networks are interdependent and are characterised by a significant degree of autonomy from the state. Their central coordinating mechanism is trust, in contrast to the commands and price competition that articulate hierarchies and markets respectively.

The aim of this book is to examine critically whether the partnerships advocated and created by New Labour represent a new and distinctive form of welfare governance. The book arose out of a seminar on 'Partnerships', which was held at the University of York in April 2000 as part of a series of ESRC Research Seminars on 'New Labour and the Third Way in Public Services'. The papers presented at the seminar covered a range of different policy sectors and types of partnerships, and revised versions of these papers constitute the core of this book. Some additional chapters were commissioned so that the book as a whole covers the widest possible range of welfare sectors, actors and provision.

This introduction focuses on the 'what', 'who', 'why' and 'how' questions of partnerships. Use of the term has been promiscuous, albeit with positive moral connotations (see Chapters Two and Three). What are partnerships? In what ways do partnerships differ from other types of relationships between organisations? The 'who' question focuses on the different types of agencies and sectors that can be involved in partnerships. For example, public–public partnerships, involving statutory health and social care services, may be characterised by different features and raise different questions for the governance of welfare than partnerships between public and private sector organisations. Similarly, multi-agency partnerships such as Health Action Zones (Chapter Six) and Education Action Zones (Chapter Twelve) may be more complex than bilateral partnerships. The 'why' question involves the rationale of partnerships. Why are partnerships established and whose interests are they presumed to benefit? As partnerships have a long and largely inglorious history in social policy (for example, Challis et al, 1988; Hudson, 1999), will New Labour's partnerships succeed where earlier partnerships have failed? The 'how' question is related to the mechanics of partnership working. How do partnerships work? How can net benefits be increased and net costs decreased?

These questions are critically examined in the sphere of welfare and related social and economic policies. Our focus is largely on partnerships at local and regional levels. We do not consider joined-up government at the centre, partnerships at supranational levels, such as the European Union or International Monetary Fund (see Deacon, 1997), or multi-level social partnerships (for example, McCall and Williamson, 2000). Moreover, with one exception (Chapter Five, which considers the development of partnerships between different professional groups), the contributors tend to focus on partnerships between organisations.

The indefinable in pursuit of the unachievable

This section explores the 'what', 'who', 'why' and 'how' questions of partnership. It shows that although partnership is difficult to define and evidence of success is far from extensive, it has long been both a defining characteristic of social policies in the UK and a key policy objective.

What?

Partnership risks becoming a 'Humpty Dumpty' term ('when I call something a partnership, by definition it is one ...'). The Audit Commission (1998, p 6) claims that many partnerships are partnerships in name only. Simply terming a relationship a 'partnership' does not make it so. This begs the question of what constitutes a partnership. Most commentators emphasise the difficulty of definition. Challis et al (1988) point out that partnership is a word in search of ways of giving it effective meaning in practice. In government circulars and ministerial policy pronouncements, it is largely a rhetorical invocation of a vague ideal. Balloch and Taylor (2001b, p 6) "lay claim to no single definition or model" of partnership. The Audit Commission (1998, p 16) states that partnership is a slippery concept that is difficult to define precisely and Ling (2000, p 82) claims that the partnership literature amounts to "methodological anarchy and definitional chaos". According to the Department of Environment, Transport and the Regions (DETR, 2000, p 37), partnerships are highly contextually specific and come in all shapes, sizes and structures. There are no unique models of successful partnership. Nor is there an easy route to the design of the successful partnership. The document continues that despite a growing volume of research on partnership and a growing literature on collaboration, there are no agreed definitions of partnership, nor is there a clear theoretical framework within which to analyse partnerships.

A minimal definition, however, would require the involvement of at least two agents or agencies with at least some common interests or interdependencies; and would also probably require a relationship between them that involves a degree of trust, equality or reciprocity (in contrast to a simple sub/superordinate command or a straightforward market-style contract). This minimal definition is at the core of the Audit Commission's (1998, p 8) description of partnership as a joint working arrangement where the partners:

- are otherwise independent bodies;
- agree to cooperate to achieve a common goal;
- create a new organisational structure or process to achieve this goal;
- plan and implement a joint programme;
- share relevant information, risks and rewards.

Implicit in this definition, therefore, is the requirement that partnerships are characterised by a degree of autonomy on the part of relatively equal partners to determine and implement a plan or programme. The ways in which decisions are made by and within partnerships therefore distinguish them from contractual arrangements, which, according to the Audit Commission, are characterised by mutually compatible rather than shared objectives (see Chapter Two). However, Mackintosh (2000), in her study of managers involved in setting block contracts for social care services, argues that relational, rather than adversarial, contracts can also create substantial areas of common interest between partners. Most of her interviewees actually used the language of partnership and she concluded that the relationship between these contractors and their contracted organisations was more one of joint policy making than one of public sector 'principals' and non-profit 'agents' (see Chapter Two).

The distinction between partnerships and other types of inter-organisational relationships (such as bureaucratic command or contracts) is therefore clearly problematic; nor does it seem to map neatly onto network (as opposed to hierarchical or market) approaches to governance. This ambiguity is particularly true of partnerships involving private sector organisations, as illustrated by the rather distinctive public–private partnerships discussed in Chapters Eleven to

Fourteen. The extent to which partnerships under New Labour share any distinctive, common characteristics or are simply the products of empty political rhetoric is a key theme of this book and one to which we will return in Chapter Fifteen.

Who?

Partnerships can involve relationships between two or more different sectors within a mixed economy of welfare, including public–public, public–voluntary, public–community and public–private. Such relationships have a long history in welfare and are certainly not distinctive to New Labour. Indeed, the most traditional form of partnership, between the state and the voluntary sector (Brenton, 1985; Finlayson, 1994; Lewis, 1999b), predates the post-war 'classic' welfare state (see also Chapter Eight). Some writers (for example, Rooff, 1957) date statutory–voluntary partnerships from the 1601 Poor Law. Other examples are found in healthcare, with the major legislative milestone in statutory–voluntary cooperation being the 1929 Local Government Act. This led Simey (1937, p 136) to describe the pre-war hospital service as increasingly resembling a partnership between the statutory and voluntary sectors. Such significant statutory–voluntary sector partnerships were described as the 'new philanthropy' (Macadam, 1934). Miles (1948, pp 10-11) added "Maybe it is but another example of the British genius for compromise which enables the public and the voluntary services to develop side by side and in fact to seek and discover a basis for co-operation".

Even Sir William Beveridge (1942, 1948), often termed the founder of the British welfare state, noted that "co-operation between public and voluntary agencies ... is one of the special features of British public life" (Beveridge, 1948, p 8). He was disappointed that the "marriage of 1911 between the State ... and voluntary agencies [in relation to pensions] ... has been followed in 1946 by complete divorce.... The Government of 1911 sought the maximum of co-operation between the State and voluntary agencies in the field of social insurance. The Government of 1946 has divorced the two completely" (Beveridge, 1948, pp 81, 82-3). Indeed, after the Second World War, the voluntary sector came to be regarded very much as the 'junior partner in the welfare firm' (Owen, 1965; Brenton, 1985; Finlayson, 1994; Whelan, 1999).

In the post-war welfare state, the most significant – and enduring – emphasis on partnership has probably been between statutory health and social care services, regardless of their particular organisational configurations. "It has become part of the conventional wisdom to extol the virtues of close co-operation between many public services" (Thomas and Stoten, 1974, p 48; cf Challis et al, 1988; Hudson, 1999). During the post-war period, there was only limited emphasis on partnership between the state and the private and community sectors, although the rhetoric about such relationships increased during the Conservative Governments of 1979-97 (Brenton, 1985; Finlayson, 1994; Johnson, 1999; Drakeford, 2000). However, much of this historical material tends to treat the term 'partnership' as unproblematic – if the relationship is termed a 'partnership' by the 'partners', then it *is* a partnership. In other words, the relationships between the partners are not generally subjected to much scrutiny (see 'What?' discussed earlier, and 'How?' discussed later).

Why?

This concerns the rationale for partnerships – the long search for coordination (Hudson et al, 1999). However, like partnership, coordination is difficult to define (for example, Hudson et al, 1999; Peters, 1998). According to Perri 6 (1997, p 21), "Under every government since the beginning of the century at least, ministers have called for more cross-departmental working and announced grand reform projects". As Peters (1998, p 295) puts it, the administrative Holy Grail of coordination and 'horizontality' is a perennial quest for government and policy makers. Haywood and Wright (2000) claim that the search for 'coordination', 'joined-up solutions' and 'horizontal coordination' is the philosopher's stone of modern government, ever sought but always just beyond reach. Moreover, this search is an international quest. Pressman and Wildavsky (1984, p 133) argue that the most frequent complaint about federal bureaucracy in the US is its 'lack of coordination'.

Writers such as Mackintosh (1992) and Hastings (1996) point to at least three different models of partnership, each with its distinctive rationale. Behind the 'synergy' or 'added value' model is the aim of increasing the value created by a combination of the assets and powers of the separate organisations. The 'transformation' model emphasises changes in the aims and cultures of the partner organisations, with the degree and direction of transformation dependent on the power of the organisations: where they are roughly equal partners, there may be bilateral changes; where one organisation has more power, there may be takeover, isomorphism or virtual integration on the terms of the more powerful. The rationale behind the 'budget enlargement' model is the enhanced budget that can be brought to bear on a policy or welfare problem.

Different partnership models may be appropriate in different contexts. The synergy and budget enlargement models appear most useful where the problem is mainly one of inadequate resources (financial, human and other). The transformation model seems more appropriate where organisations or agencies may have divergent foci and priorities. However, it is not clear whether these models require different preconditions or organisational structures, nor whether there are different routes to moving towards them. The Audit Commission (1998, pp 13-14) suggest a number of rationales for partnerships:

- to deliver coordinated services;
- to tackle 'wicked issues' or interconnected problems;
- to reduce the impact of organisational fragmentation and minimise the impact of any perverse incentives that result from it;
- to bid for, or gain access to, new resources, and;
- to meet a statutory requirement.

This highlights an important distinction, that between 'internal' and 'external' rationales. The first four reasons above constitute mainly internal rationales – local partners decide that there are good reasons to act in partnership rather than in isolation, presumably because it is believed that this will have positive results, with net benefits outweighing net costs. The last reason, on the other hand, reflects an external rationale – agencies form partnerships because they are forced (or encouraged, or incentivised) to do so. No doubt, central government believes that positive results will occur. However, there may be significant differences between the forging of willing and reluctant partnerships. At worst, enforced partnerships may be as successful as the parental wishes of Romeo and Juliet or some of the pairings on the TV programme 'Blind Date'. Indeed, at one level, it might be argued that such compulsion is incompatible with the whole notion of partnership, which is implicitly associated with some degree of choice and autonomous action. In particular, 'compulsory partnerships' may not provide appropriate conditions for the generation of trust in inter-agency relationships, which, as Chapter Four argues, is a key condition of successful partnership working.

How?

Making partnerships work effectively is one of the toughest challenges facing public sector managers (Audit Commission, 1998, p 5). Although there is little dispute about the potential benefits of partnerships, these potential gains are often difficult to realise in practice. According to DETR (2000, p 27), the absence of collaborative or integrated working, although long-standing and obvious to all concerned, is nevertheless culturally embedded, impervious to changing historical circumstances and deeply entrenched in both central and local government. "The history of previous attempts to co-ordinate policy does not suggest that this will be easy" (Wilkinson and Appelbee, 1999, p 1). As Perri 6 (1997) puts it, joint working has delivered less than it has promised.

As suggested above, the mechanisms of partnerships have rarely been subjected to much analysis. This gap has been particularly noted by observers of the voluntary sector over the years. Mencher (in Rooff, 1957, p xi) argued that there has been little investigation into the nature of the relationship between voluntary and state action (but see Simey, 1937; Mess, 1948, ch 13). Brenton (1985, p 31) also concludes that, although relationships between the state and the voluntary sector were often described as a 'partnership', they were "neither systematic nor formalised, most often being left to ad hoc arrangements or chance". More recently, Lewis has pointed out that:

> The voluntary sector has always sought a 'partnership' with the state, but its nature, in terms of funding, terms and conditions and the associated expectations of each party have changed significantly over time.... Neither the specialist third sector nor the generic welfare state literature has been particularly successful in addressing the voluntary–statutory relationship. (Lewis, 1999a, p 256)

Similar conclusions could be drawn about other sectors and partnerships.

In the context of the allegedly distinctive, network-based partnerships of New Labour, a key question is whether current partnership arrangements rely on different instruments and mechanisms from those associated with hierarchy and markets. Literature on hierarchies, markets, networks and wider governance transformations all draw attention to the contrasts between the trust associated with partnerships and networks, and the commands of hierarchies and the price mechanism in markets (see Chapters Two and Three). It is clearly easier for the state to exercise command over public rather than other partners. For example, partnership mechanisms for statutory health and social care agencies have included compulsory Joint Consultative Committees and Joint Care Planning Teams (Thomas and Stoten, 1974). Similarly, the 1977 NHS Act required health and local authorities to become partners (Hudson, 1999). Mechanisms to encourage partnership working on the part of organisations from other sectors might include carrots as well as sticks; Challis et al (1988) suggest the financial incentives of 'crocks of gold'. However, quasi-markets also use financial incentives to promote goals. The distinction between contracts and partnership may be most unclear in relation to public–private partnerships. In particular, it is unclear whether 'relational contracting' belongs to the world of markets or networks (Mackintosh, 2000; also discussed later).

Not only are partnerships generally underspecified, they are also often underevaluated. Many accounts assume that partnerships are necessarily a 'good thing'. There has been a tendency to focus on the benefits of partnerships without examining the costs; to examine 'collaborative advantage' (Huxham, 2000) without looking at the reverse side of the coin of 'collaborative disadvantage'. There are considerable difficulties in evaluating the costs of partnerships, such as time in meetings (Audit Commission, 1998, p 7). Nevertheless it is possible that the full picture (for example, Kirkpatrick, 1999) may show that in certain contexts the process of collaboration can generate more costs than benefits, contributing to governance failure (Jessop, 2000) and to negative synergy or value-subtracted (see Chapter Eleven). These costs may also fall disproportionately on one partner, rather than being shared equally (see Chapters Four, Eight and Nine). The Audit Commission (1998, p 14) notes that there may be times to consider other collaborative options, such as consultative arrangements; networks of personal relationships that do not also require organisational commitment; and contractual arrangements such as Private Finance Initiative (PFI).

New Labour, new partnerships?

The subsequent chapters of this book cover a diverse range of material on the theory and practice of partnerships under New Labour. In Chapter Two, Powell and Exworthy review conceptual approaches to partnerships from both inductive and deductive perspectives. Paralleling the theoretical approach to social policy of quasi-markets, they analyse whether partnerships can be construed as quasi-networks. Clarke and Glendinning examine partnerships through the lens of governance in Chapter Three. They use evidence from the fields of health and social care to illustrate some of the questions that are raised by an uncritical utilisation of the governance narrative for social policy. Hudson and Hardy in Chapter Four discuss how 'successful' partnerships can be measured. Derived from extensive empirical research, again particularly in the arenas of health and social services, they bridge the divide between theory and practice to show how conceptual analysis can contribute to evaluating the 'health' of partnerships.

Chapters Five to Fourteen review New Labour partnerships in a very diverse range of contexts. Chapter Five by Clarke and Rummery examines partnerships at the 'front-line'. They focus on inter-professional partnership working in an innovative project in primary care. Their analysis of the factors affecting the development of team integration complements and underpins the following chapters, which focus mainly on inter-organisational partnerships. Barnes and Sullivan examine Health Action Zones (HAZs) in Chapter Six. As the HAZ initiative was intended to 'mainstream' successful innovations, their conclusions flag up some of the wider lessons for partnership working.

The role of partnerships in the 'regeneration' and renewal of civil society is a theme running through Chapters Seven, Eight and Nine. The partnership agenda for local democracy and local communities is the subject of Chapter Seven by Daly and Davis. They link a general discussion of the topic with a study of partnership working in Birmingham, concluding with a number of key issues for those wishing to construct effective partnerships for local governance. In Chapter Eight, Alcock and Scott examine partnerships between the statutory and voluntary sectors, as do Craig and Taylor in Chapter Nine, where they extend the analysis to include partnerships between statutory organisations and less formal, more diverse and fragmented community groups. At the core of both chapters is the question of whether New Labour's policy of 'Compacts' will succeed in transforming relationships between the statutory, voluntary and community sectors. Although the precise focus and approach of Chapters Eight and Nine differ, it is noticeable that they both identify continuing major inequalities of power and resources in statutory–voluntary sector partnerships and warn that there is still a long way to go before the least powerful and most excluded groups can feel that they are taken seriously as 'real' rather than 'nominal' partners.

Hughes and McLaughlin trace the development of crime prevention partnerships in Chapter Ten, identifying both their long history and their distinctive 'New Labour' characteristics. Like Clarke and Glendinning in Chapter Three and Dickson et al in Chapter Twelve, they warn that externally imposed targets, audit and performance management systems risk undermining the development of strong local collaborations. A similar theme runs through Davies' analysis of economic regeneration partnerships in Chapter Eleven. He argues that the rhetoric of governance and partnership fits uneasily with the centralising tendencies and distrust of local authorities that characterise the current government and forcefully points out that partnerships can 'subtract' rather than 'add' value. Dickson and colleagues discuss the partnership elements of Education Action Zones (EAZs) in Chapter Twelve. Although EAZs are officially viewed as multi-sector partnerships, it is the public–private dimension that has received the most attention. Dickson and colleagues present empirical data from a number of localities and conclude that the fear of those who see EAZs as privatisation has not (yet) been confirmed, as the resources and other contributions of the private sector partners remain marginal. There is little evidence of any meaningful community involvement in EAZs either. Like other contributors, Dickson and colleagues also point to the threats from the wider policy environment, which can distort local partnership activities – in this instance school league tables and competitive bidding for additional central government resources.

Chapters Thirteen and Fourteen focus exclusively on public–private partnerships. Ruane in Chapter Thirteen investigates the PFI in the NHS, drawing on interviews with NHS managers. Her conclusions throw doubt on whether the relationships between private finance, construction and management companies and the NHS really constitute partnerships, as current government policies would claim. Similarly in Chapter Fourteen, Ward largely dismisses the partnership credentials of public–private partnerships in pensions. She presents a detailed discussion of the objectives and strategies of the partners, reaching a critical view of current directions in pensions policy. In the concluding chapter, Rummery draws together the diverse strands from the previous chapters, and moves towards a theory of partnerships.

This summary allows us to return to the main questions outlined earlier. At this stage, the aim is to open up, rather than close down, debate and to pose, rather than answer, questions. The first issue concerns the definitions of partnerships and the models of partnership used by New Labour. Beyond being termed 'partnerships', what – if anything – do the diverse arrangements analysed in this book share? In particular, is New Labour's most controversial type of partnership – the widely advocated public–private partnership – merely an updated and 'rebadged' version of policies previously criticised as Conservative 'privatisation'? Moreover, if New Labour's partnerships do indeed share common, distinctive features, are these features more characteristic of networked governance rather than hierarchies or markets?

A second question is concerned with the types of partnerships and the sectors involved in them. Can different types of New Labour partnerships be discerned and, if so, do these vary according to the sectors from which the partners are drawn? For example, public–public partnerships may differ in a number of important ways from statutory–voluntary partnerships. Similarly, New Labour has promoted a plethora of area-based, total or multi-sector partnerships such as HAZs and EAZs. The requirement on the police, local authorities and local communities to work jointly is now embedded in the 1998 Crime and Disorder Act. Local Strategic Partnerships (LSPs) will introduce further multi-sector partnerships. Are these partnerships inevitably more complex than bilateral partnerships (cf Ling, 2000)? Or is their potential complexity averted by the designation or emergence (by accident or design) of one or two 'lead' partners? While all sectors may be emphasised on paper, in practice it may be difficult to differentiate between bilateral and multi-sector partnerships.

A third question concerns the rationale for partnership. Much of the literature on networks and governance, with its emphasis on self-organising and relatively autonomous partnerships, suggests internal, rather than external, rationales. It is assumed that organisations *choose* to work in partnership because it is the best way of achieving common objectives or 'added value', at minimum cost. However, New Labour places a 'duty of partnership' on organisations. This has been termed 'mandatory partnership working' (Audit Commission, 1998, p 5), or 'statutory voluntarism', in which "partnership, co-operation and collaboration are emphasised and mandated at every turn" (Paton, 1999, p 69). However, earlier legislation – Acts of 1929 and 1977, for example – shows that successful partnerships cannot be created by administrative fiat (cf Challis et al, 1988). To what extent can partnerships be enforced, particularly between partners whose power and command over resources is very unequal? What is the relative importance of the horizontal and vertical relationships within which partnerships are enmeshed? Is the external environment of New Labour partnerships different in these respects from previous collaborative endeavours? If so, what are the implications for the autonomy and self-regulation that are assumed to characterise networked forms of governance?

The fourth question focuses on instruments. In particular, it examines the mechanisms of order, price and trust as regulating mechanisms for, respectively, hierarchies, markets and networks. Again, important questions must be posed about public–private partnerships in particular. For example, the Audit Commission's (1998) definition of partnership excludes contractual arrangements between public and private sector bodies such as PFI projects. It argues that although such contractual arrangements are sometimes referred to as partnerships, they are different because they stem from mutually compatible, rather than shared, objectives. However, mutual compatibility (rather than complete synonymity) of objectives characterises many of the partnerships described in this book; moreover, contractual arrangements may also have partnership characteristics. In any case, a 'contract' is, like partnership, an essentially contestable term; if it is interpreted as an 'agreement', then there seems to be no reason why public and private agencies could not make a partnership agreement. This is essentially the rationale behind the introduction of Compacts between the statutory and voluntary sectors, to replace contracts for delivering services.

Drawing on the work of Challis et al (1988), Hudson (1999) argues that New Labour is moving from an optimistic to a realistic view of collaboration, with simple exhortations replaced by a panoply of sanctions, incentives and threats. More broadly, what range of carrots and sticks to achieve partnership are now available; to what extent are these distinctive and different; and in what circumstances, in relation to which types of partnerships, are these mechanisms likely to succeed?

The fifth point is that while there is a growing body of literature on definitions, concepts and theories of partnership (to which this book makes a modest contribution), evidence of the impact and outcomes of partnership is somewhat less easy to come by. Yet, at the same time as advocating closer inter-agency and inter-sectoral collaboration, New Labour discourse also advocates a pragmatism based on evidence of 'what works'. The promotion of evidence-based policy and practice is itself far from problematic and sidesteps major epistemological issues such as what constitutes 'evidence', or the extent to which 'evidence' from one sector of welfare is relevant or applicable to others (see Davies et al, 2000). It is even more problematic in relation to partnerships, as the evidence that is available on their effectiveness, impact and outcomes – their capacity to transform the experiences of welfare users – is particularly sparse. What difference would we expect partnerships – whether between statutory, voluntary, community or private sectors – to make to the experiences of those who use, and provide, welfare; and what evidence is there that these expectations are actually being met?

In conclusion, and more broadly, how do New Labour's partnerships fit within wider policy contexts (Exworthy et al, 1999)? In sectors such as health, New Labour has reduced and refined, but not abolished, the Conservatives' quasi-market reforms (Powell, 1999a). There have been general moves from contracts to 'Compacts' and 'concordats'. As Klein (1998) puts it, Etzioni has replaced Enthoven. 'Purchasers' and 'providers' are no longer linked by simple principal–agency relationships. Instead of NHS Trusts simply competing for the contracts of health authorities, they now take an active role in producing a plan (the Health Improvement Plan). Short-term contracts have become longer-term 'agreements'. In short, there have been moves towards relational or soft contracting. At the same time, new hierarchical, command-and-control regulatory mechanisms – 'naming and shaming' of 'failing' organisations, reserve powers, 'hit squads', National Service Frameworks and the new institutions of the National Institute for Clinical Excellence and the Commission for Health Improvement – have also been introduced (Klein, 1998; Paton, 1999; Powell 1999a). In short, how do the rhetoric and practice of partnerships fit with these wider market and hierarchical structures?

It is unrealistic to expect definitive answers to all these questions in this book. However, simply asking them moves the debate forward a little, as this book reveals New Labour 'partnerships' to be complex and sometimes highly problematic phenomena. Drawing on both theoretical and empirical material, the book shows how New Labour partnerships do (and do not) differ from earlier versions and from each other, enabling us to move towards a theory of welfare partnerships.

References

6, P. (1997) *Holistic government*, London: Demos.

Audit Commission (1998) *A fruitful partnership: Effective partnership working*, London: Audit Commission.

Balloch, S. and Taylor, M. (eds) (2001a) *Partnership working: Policy and practice*, Bristol: The Policy Press.

Balloch, S. and Taylor, M. (2001b) 'Introduction', in S. Balloch and M. Taylor (eds) *Partnership working: Policy and practice*, Bristol: The Policy Press.

Beveridge, Sir W. (1942) *Social insurance and allied services*, London: HMSO.

Beveridge, Sir W. (1948) *Voluntary action: A report on methods of social advance*, London: George Allen and Unwin.

Brenton, M. (1985) *The voluntary sector in British social services*, Harlow: Longman.

Cabinet Office (2001) *A new commitment to neighbourhood renewal*, London: Cabinet Office/Social Exclusion Unit.

Challis, L., Fuller, S., Henwood, M., Klein, R., Plowden, W., Webb, A., Whittingham, P. and Wistow, G. (1988) *Joint approaches to social policy*, Cambridge: Cambridge University Press.

Clarence, E. and Painter, C. (1998) 'Public services under New Labour: collaborative discourses and local networking', *Public Policy and Administration*, vol 13, no 1, pp 8-22.

Davies, H., Nutley, S.M. and Smith, P. (2000) *What works?: Evidence-based policy and practice in public services*, Bristol: The Policy Press.

Deacon, B. (1997) *Global social policy*, London: Sage Publications.

DETR (Department of the Environment, Transport and the Regions) (2000) *Joining it up locally. The evidence base*, London: DETR.

Drakeford, M. (2000) *Privatisation and social policy*, Harlow: Longman.

Exworthy, M., Powell, M. and Mohan, J. (1999) 'The NHS: quasi-market, quasi-hierarchy and quasi-network', *Public Money and Management*, vol 19, no 4, pp 15-22.

Fairclough, N. (2000) *New Labour, new language?*, London: Routledge.

Finlayson, G. (1994) *Citizen, state and social welfare in Britain 1830-1990*, Oxford: Clarendon Press.

Giddens, A. (1998) *The third way: The renewal of social democracy*, Cambridge: Polity Press.

Hastings, A. (1996) 'Unravelling the process of "partnership" in urban regeneration policy', *Urban Studies*, vol 33, no 2, pp 253-68.

Haywood, J. and Wright, V. (2000) 'Governing from the centre', in R. Rhodes (ed) *Transforming British government, vol 2: Roles and relationships*, Basingstoke: Macmillan.

Hudson, B. (1999) 'Dismantling the Berlin Wall: developments at the health–social care interface', in H. Dean and R. Woods (eds) *Social Policy Review 11*, Luton: SPA, pp 187-204.

Hudson, B. (2000) 'Conclusion', in B. Hudson (ed) *The changing role of social care*, London: Jessica Kingsley Publishers.

Hudson, B., Hardy, B., Henwood, M. and Wistow, G. (1999) 'In pursuit of inter-agency collaboration in the public sector', *Public Management*, vol 1, no 2, pp 235-60.

Huxham, C. (2000) 'The challenge of collaborative governance', *Public Management*, vol 2, no 3, pp 337-57.

Jessop, B. (2000) 'Governance failure', in G. Stoker (ed) *The new politics of British local governance*, Basingstoke: Macmillan.

Johnson, N. (1999) *Mixed economies of welfare*, Hemel Hempstead: Prentice Hall Europe.

Kirkpatrick, I. (1999) 'The worst of both worlds?', *Public Money and Management*, vol 19, no 4, pp 7-14.

Klein, R. (1998) 'Why Britain is re-organising its National Health Service – yet again', *Health Affairs*, vol 17, no 4, pp 111-25.

Lewis, J. (1999a) 'Reviewing the relationship between the voluntary sector and the state in Britain in the 1990s', *Voluntas*, vol 10, no 3, pp 255-70.

Lewis, J. (1999b) 'Voluntary and informal welfare', in R. Page and R. Silburn (eds) *British social welfare in the twentieth century*, Basingstoke: Palgrave.

Ling, T. (2000) 'Unpacking partnership: the case of health care', in J. Clarke, S. Gewirtz and E. McLaughlin (eds) *New managerialism, new welfare?*, London: Sage Publications.

Macadam, E. (1934) *The new philanthropy*, London: George Allen and Unwin.

Mackintosh, M. (1992) 'Partnerships: issues of policy and negotiation', *Local Economy*, vol 7, no 3, pp 210-24.

Mackintosh, M. (2000) 'Flexible contracting? Economic cultures and implicit contracts in social care', *Journal of Social Policy*, vol 29, no 1, pp 1-19.

McCall, C. and Williamson, A. (2000) 'Fledgling social partnership in the Irish Border Region', *Policy & Politics*, vol 28, no 3, pp 397-411.

Mess, H. (1948) *Voluntary social services since 1918*, London: K.P. Tench, Trubner and Co.

Miles, N. (1948) 'The position of voluntary social services in 1918', in H. Mess *Voluntary social services since 1918*, London: K.P. Tench, Trubner and Co.

Owen, D. (1965) *English philanthropy 1660-1969*, London: Oxford University Press.

Painter, C. (1999) 'Public service reform from Thatcher to Blair: a third way', *Parliamentary Affairs*, vol 52, no 1, pp 94-112.

Paton, C. (1999) 'New Labour's health policy', in M. Powell (ed) *New Labour, new welfare state?: The 'third way' in British social policy*, Bristol: The Policy Press.

Peters, B.G. (1998) 'Managing horizontal government: the politics of coordination', *Public Administration*, vol 76, no 2, pp 295-311.

Powell, M. (1999a) 'New Labour and the third way in the British NHS', *International Journal of Health Services*, vol 29, no 2, pp 353-70.

Powell, M. (ed) (1999b) *New Labour, new welfare state?: The 'third way' in British social policy*, Bristol: The Policy Press.

Powell, M., Exworthy, M. and Berney, L. (2001) 'Playing the game of partnership', in R. Sykes, C. Bochel and N. Ellison (eds) *Social Policy Review 13: Developments and debates 2000-2001*, Bristol: The Policy Press and the SPA, pp 39-62.

Pressman, J. and Wildavsky, A. (1984) *Implementation*, Berkeley, CA: University of California Press.

Rhodes, R. (1997) *Understanding governance*, Buckingham: Open University Press.

Rhodes, R. (2000) 'The governance narrative', *Public Administration*, vol 78, no 2, pp 345-63.

Rooff, M. (1957) *Voluntary societies and social policy*, London: Routledge and Kegan Paul.

Simey, T. (1937) *Principles of social administration*, London: Oxford University Press.

Thomas, N. and Stoten, B. (1974) 'The NHS and local government', in K. Jones (ed) *The yearbook of social policy in Britain 1973*, London: Routledge and Kegan Paul.

Whelan, R. (ed) (1999) *Involuntary action*, London: IEA.

Wilkinson, D. and Appelbee, E. (1999) *Implementing holistic government: Joined-up action on the ground*, Bristol: The Policy Press.

TWO

Partnerships, quasi-networks and social policy

Martin Powell and Mark Exworthy

Introduction

Hierarchies, markets and networks are well-established 'models of coordination' or 'governing structures', with different coordinating mechanisms. "If it is price competition that is the central coordinating mechanism of the market and administrative orders that of hierarchies, then it is trust and cooperation that centrally articulates networks" (Thompson et al, 1991, p 15).

New Labour's main operating code rejects both state hierarchies, or the 'command-and-control' of Old Labour, and the market mechanisms of the last Conservative government, and favours instead a Third Way of 'intermediate' or 'network' forms of organisation (for example, Clarence and Painter, 1998; Exworthy et al, 1999; Kirkpatrick, 1999; Powell, 1999a, 1999b; Rhodes, 2000). However, this is a rather stylised picture of markets, hierarchies and networks. The claim that the original post-war classic, and the Conservative restructured, welfare states can be seen as hierarchies and markets respectively, represents something of an oversimplification; 'pure' forms of hierarchy and market were rare (Exworthy et al, 1999). In a path-breaking account, Le Grand and Bartlett (1993) argued that much of Conservative social policy was more accurately seen in terms of 'quasi-markets' that differed from 'real' markets in a number of important respects. Exworthy et al (1999) followed this line in claiming that it is more accurate to talk in terms of 'quasi-hierarchies' and 'quasi-networks'.

Sako (1992, pp 22-3) claims that networks, strategic alliances and other intermediate forms of organisation have become a fashionable topic, but also that this area of study has recently suffered from excessive neologism. Although New Labour rarely uses the term 'network', there have been many references to the key characteristics of networks (for example, Rhodes, 1997, 2000; Clarence and Painter, 1998). Many terms have been used by New Labour to characterise their 'collaborative discourse' (Clarence and Painter, 1998), such as partnership, inter-agency working, cooperation, coordination, 'joined-up government' and 'seamless services' (for example, DoH, 1997, 1998b, 1998c, 1998d, 1999, 2000; see also Hudson et al, 1999; Huxham, 2000; Ling, 2000; Balloch and Taylor, 2001a, 2001b). Cognate terms appear to include horizontal government (Peters, 1998), multi-organisational partnerships (Lowndes and Skelcher, 1998), collaborative governance (Huxham, 2000), inter-agency collaboration (Hudson et al, 1999), networks (Kirkpatrick, 1999), and inter-organisational relationships and networks (Hage and Alter, 1997). Most writers, therefore, roughly equate a number of terms, including networks, with partnerships.

On the other hand, Lowndes and Skelcher (1998, p 314) argue that partnership is an organisational structure, which is analytically distinct from network as a mode of governance – the means by which social coordination is achieved. The creation of a partnership board, for example, does not imply that relations between actors are conducted on the basis of mutual benefit, trust and reciprocity – the characteristics of a network mode of governance. Rather, partnerships are associated with a variety of forms of social coordination – including networks, hierarchies and markets. However, according to Huxham (2000, p 339), many words are used to describe governance structures that involve cross-organisational working. These include partnership, alliance, collaboration, coordination, cooperation, network, joint working and multi-party working. Although practitioners often claim different meanings for these labels, typically arguing that a particular situation is a 'collaboration' but not a 'partnership' or vice versa, and some writers claim clear definitional distinctions between the terms, there appears to be no consistency between practitioners or authors in this respect. So the terminology remains confusing. For example, Hage and Alter (1997, p 97) point out that the term 'network' is much used and abused, and that there are many cognates such as relationships, joint ventures, linkages and alliances. From the opposite direction, Mitchell and Shortell (2000, p 242) refer to the term 'partnership' as coalitions, alliances, consortia and related forms of inter-organisational relations.

We follow Huxham (2000), as the title of this chapter suggests, and view 'partnership' as a quasi-network or intermediate form of organisation that is distinctive from both hierarchies and markets. Le Grand and Bartlett (1993) use neoclassical economic theory in order to specify the assumptions under which organisations in the quasi-market achieve their objectives. We use a similar approach to establish how quasi-networks achieve their objectives. Our argument is more tentative, as the relevant literature is less developed and is scattered across a number of disciplines and approaches. This preliminary account sacrifices depth for breadth, and takes two different approaches. The deductive approach examines the huge and disparate literature that has some relevance to partnership, and attempts to establish which concepts are viewed as significant. The inductive approach examines accounts of partnership in policy and practice settings, and seeks to distil out concepts. We then compare the two approaches to ascertain the extent to which they are interrelated.

Understanding quasi-networks: a deductive approach

Sako (1992, p 24) notes that there has been much theorising about intermediate (or network) modes of coordinating production in the past decade or so. Sako reviews the theories of transaction-cost economics, relational contract theory, a sociological approach to networks, and networks and management strategy.

Similarly, we examine a number of narratives of network coordination in welfare. We place a little empirical flesh on the abstract bones with some examples drawn largely from healthcare.

Economics

We give a brief overview of two relevant economic perspectives on welfare services (see also Lunt et al, 1996). First, according to principal–agent theory (Milgrom and Roberts, 1992), agents act on behalf of principals to achieve an end. In quasi-markets, contracts have been seen as the mechanism regulating the relations between purchasers (principals) and providers (agents). There is often a problem of information asymmetry, in that agents generally have more information about services than principals. Therefore, principals must devise an incentive structure to ensure that their objectives are achieved. Davies et al (1999) identify two mechanisms for agent control: fostering congruence of objectives, and developing a market whereby agents compete for the contracts of principals. They see trust as the basis of both approaches. With a potential for opportunism and the partiality of monitoring mechanisms, trust becomes a crucial ingredient within network relations. Shared objectives, possibly fostered by an incentive system, facilitate such trust. Davies et al (1999) regard trust as a 'social lubricant' and as an alternative to expensive transaction costs. Goddard and Mannion (1998, p 106) observe that nurturing long-term relationships based on cooperation and trust can be viewed as an explicit attempt to solve the basic principal–agent problem in the purchaser/provider split.

Second, new institutional economics suggests that market failures are often associated with transaction costs, which may play a central role in determining whether markets or hierarchies are the most efficient governance structure in any given situation (Williamson, 1975). The associated factors include bounded rationality, uncertainty, opportunism and 'atmosphere' (Lunt et al, 1996). Similarly, transaction costs may be important in determining whether 'hard'/ 'adversarial' or 'soft'/'relational' contracts are more efficient (Sako, 1992; Bartlett et al, 1998). For example, drawing on Williamson, Sako argues that obligational contractual relations (OCR) are more likely to emerge if suppliers contribute to the product design and development process than if they do not. Mackintosh (2000) differentiates 'partnerships contracts' with non-profit providers, who actively seek risk and responsibility from an arm's length contracting culture with commercial suppliers. New Labour claims that cooperation has replaced competition in the new NHS (DoH, 1997). Thus longer-term agreements are emphasised, and purchasers and providers are no longer seen in a simple principal–agent relationship. However, some commentators argue that the market was never as red in tooth and claw as proposed by advocates or as feared by critics. In short, Labour has reduced and refined, but not abolished, the market in healthcare (Powell, 1999a). It may be more accurate to see moves from 'hard' towards 'soft' contracting as an attempt to reduce transaction costs and to solve principal–agent asymmetries (for example, Goddard and Mannion, 1998; Mackintosh, 2000).

Political science

The search for greater coordination to solve 'wicked' or 'interconnected' problems has been a major feature of 'traditional public administration' (for example, Challis et al, 1988; Perri 6, 1997; Peters, 1998). Networks are sometimes viewed as the least worst mode of coordination. Traditional command-and-control hierarchies suffer from problems of separate vertical lines of authority from centre to periphery. Orders are transmitted down vertical 'silos' and there is little evidence of joined-up thinking, either between the 'policy villages' of the central Whitehall departments or between local agencies (Rhodes, 1997, 2000; Kavanagh and Richards, 2001). Perri 6 (1997, p 37) argues that 'wicked' problems can be solved only by more 'holistic' government – that is, horizontal integration and linkage between fields and function.

According to Rhodes (2000, p 345), the governance narrative (see Chapter Three), with its emphasis on networks, contrasts sharply both with the Westminster model and its story of a strong executive running a unitary state, and with new public management (NPM) and its story of the search for efficiency through markets and contracts. Rhodes defines governance as "self-organizing, inter-organisational networks" that are interdependent and have a significant degree of autonomy from the state. Trust is the central coordinating mechanism of networks, in the same way that commands and price competition are the key mechanisms for hierarchies and markets respectively (Rhodes, 2000, p 353).

Rhodes (2000, p 346) regards New Labour's key objective of joined-up government as a guise for governance. For example, he claims that the White Paper on '*Modernising government*' (Cabinet Office, 1999) aspires to 'joined-up' or 'holistic' government; both phrases are synonyms for steering networks. He describes the challenge as getting different parts of government to work together by "designing policy around shared goals". Specific proposals include organising work around cross-cutting issues, pooled budgets, cross-cutting performance measures and area-based initiatives such as Health Action Zones. Stoker (2000, p 98) focuses on urban partnerships. Steering in the context of governance recognises that government cannot impose its policy, but must rather negotiate both policy and implementation with partners in the public, private and voluntary sectors.

Management

The management literature covers a number of disparate approaches, such as contractual relations; 'new public management'; post-Fordist and post-Taylorist approaches; and organisational and individual influences on the collaborative culture (see Ferlie and Pettigrew, 1996; Hudson et al, 1999). Sako (1992) claims that obligational contractual relations (OCR) are associated with lower transaction costs than adversarial contractual relations (ACR). OCR is often associated with Japanese industry and the microprocessor industry (see also Hage and Alter, 1997; Hudson et al, 1999). It is based on a clear perception of dependence and a sense of fairness and shared norms, particularly between power unequal partners. OCR is characterised by a greater transactional dependence on trading partners; a longer projected length of trading; a greater willingness to offer orders before prices are negotiated and fixed; and a greater degree of uncosted sharing of technological know-how and risks associated with business fluctuations. In short, trust is integral to networks. Similarly, Ferlie and Pettigrew (1996) argue that the NHS is best characterised in terms of relational rather than crude classical models of contracting (see also 'Economics', discussed previously).

New public management (NPM) often eludes easy definition. Ferlie et al (1996) identify four broad approaches: the efficiency drive; downsizing and decentralisation; a search for excellence; and public service orientation. In all but the first approach, quasi-networks form an (often) implicit basis. In particular, elements of the NPM literature, which draw on the 'excellence school' of Peters and Waterman (1982), stress flatter, network-like organisational forms. However, in practice, it has been noted that NPM approaches under both Conservative and New Labour governments tend to emphasise top-down, vertical hierarchical line management, rather than flat, horizontal networks (for example, Clarke and Newman, 1997; Newman, 2000; Rhodes, 2000).

Wilkinson and Appelbee (1999, p 32) claim that post-Fordist and post-Taylorist paradigms have emerged from the manufacturing revolution, led by a number of Japanese car manufacturers. Post-Fordism is associated with the move away from the Weberian/modernist form of organisations, which were marked by rules, procedures and lines of authority within hierarchical relations (Exworthy and Halford, 1999, p 11). Applied to the welfare state, Ferlie and Pettigrew (1996, p 82) state that since the 1970s increasing evidence has been accumulating of a shift towards more flexible post-Fordist modes of organising. Ferlie et al (1996, p 48) regard a post-Fordist model as one in which the organisation is fragmented in a large number of operational units, which are then *loosely coordinated* by a central organisation. The centre no longer retains control through hierarchy, but through a mixture of subcontracting, franchising and partnership arrangements.

Hudson et al (1999) point out that both organisations and individual actors can influence the 'collaborative culture'. Organisational style or culture is important (Ferlie and Pettigrew, 1996; Hudson et al, 1999). Changing the culture of organisations is central to the 'excellence school' of NPM (Peters and Waterman, 1982; Ferlie et al, 1996). However, the links between an organisational lead and wide ownership are not fully clear. Two facets of working towards wide organisational ownership can be identified: recognising and nurturing 'reticulists'; and engaging with front-line staff. Thus the literature recognises the importance of 'champions of change' – committed and charismatic staff who can drive change. In the case of inter-agency working, those individuals with the relevant networking skills have been termed 'reticulists' (Challis et al, 1988) or 'partnership champions' (Audit Commission, 1998). As Hudson et al (1999, p 251) point out, the characteristics of reticulists are likely to include not only technical or competency-based factors, but also social and inter-personal skills. Rhodes (2000, pp 355-6) notes that the attribute of 'diplomacy' or 'management by negotiation' lies at the heart of steering networks. He contrasts this style of 'hands-off management' or keeping an arm's length relationship with the 'macho-manager'. Ferlie and Pettigrew (1996) report the results of their survey of NHS managers, who claimed that the characteristics and skills needed within network-based forms of management included trust, reciprocity, understanding and credibility. The second facet of working towards wide organisational ownership – engaging front-line staff – focuses on the importance of providing incentives and developing multi-professional working (Hudson et al, 1999; see also Chapter Five).

Sociology

Two broad elements of sociological literature will be explored: the importance of social relations; and a renewed emphasis on 'bottom-up', community or civil society initiatives. Commentators associated with economic sociology and socio-legal studies point out that all transactions and contracts are rooted in social relations. Particular attention has been paid to the notions of relational markets, embeddedness and trust (Granovetter, 1985; see also Ferlie at al, 1996; Lunt et al, 1996). In other words, exchanges contain both economic and social components; the focus is thus upon the relationship and not simply the transaction (Exworthy, 1998, p 459). Recurrent social exchanges generate norms and conventions that are replete with expectations and which shape economic behaviour. In complex markets, informal information transmitted through social networks concerning issues such as quality, trust, reputation and status is viewed as possibly more important than price (Flynn et al, 1996; Lunt et al, 1996; Bartlett et al, 1998; Mackintosh, 2000).

The second stream of sociological literature sees various solutions from empowering the community through 'bottom-up perspectives'. Solutions cannot simply be imposed on, or parachuted into, areas. Commentators use various terms including community development, civil society, capacity building, community governance, social and civic entrepreneurs, voluntary and mutual solutions and associational welfare (for example, Wilkinson and Appelbee, 1999; DETR, 2000b; see also Chapters Seven to Nine). To take one example, Putnam (2000) argues that economic and civic success is more likely in societies with more 'social capital'. This elusive concept has been viewed in terms of membership of organisations, voting levels and trust in others. Putnam argues that social capital develops most in societies characterised by horizontal, rather than vertical, social relations. The National Neighbourhood Strategy proposed by the Social Exclusion Unit and, to a lesser extent Health Action Zones, make clear reference to these ideas of social capital. Putnam was invited to explain this thesis to both former President Clinton and Prime Minister Tony Blair (*The Daily Telegraph*, 9 March 2001). It remains unclear whether these initiatives represent a genuine devolution of power and resources resulting in local empowerment, or whether they simply legitimise disengagement by the state.

Overview

This brief tour through disciplinary perspectives shows that approaches to networks are partially common, but complex and contextual. To some extent, the disciplines speak a common language, but with different accents. For example, economists studying quasi-markets in the UK in the 1990s emphasised social as well as economic factors. These factors include trust, collaboration and the institutional environment (Lunt et al, 1996; Bartlett et al, 1998). However, while sociologists have emphasised the embedded nature of trust in social norms and conventions, economists have seen it as instrumental and its benefits calculable (Roberts et al, 1998, p 282). Some commentators (for example, Sako, 1992) draw on concepts from a number of disciplines. Although terms may vary, there appears to be some agreement on the importance of reducing transaction costs through developing trusting, long-term, embedded, obligational relationships (for example, Ferlie and Pettigrew, 1996; Bartlett et al, 1998; Mackintosh, 2000). However, behind a superficial similarity of terms may hide a diversity of complex meanings. For example, there is a huge literature on diverse forms of trust, and discussion of trust often does not get beyond "irritating rhetorical flabbiness" (Gambetta, 1988, p 214). Divided by a common language, it is generally agreed that there are some contexts in which networks are the best (or least worst) mode of coordination, as compared with markets and hierarchies. The success of networks is regarded as contextual. There are therefore circumstances when networks, hierarchies or markets are likely to work best (for example, Thompson et al, 1991; Flynn et al, 1996; Exworthy et al, 1999; Kirkpatrick, 1999; Rhodes, 2000).

Understanding quasi-networks: an inductive approach

There is no shortage of advice on how to 'do partnerships' (Ling, 2000, p 93). However, the validity and reliability of this input into 'evidence-based policy making' is less clear. According to Chartered Institute of Public Finance and Accountancy (CIPFA, 1997, p 102), objective evaluation of the impact of all partnerships is generally lacking. The value added by partners and the associated impacts attributed to them need to be better measured and documented. Similarly, Department for the Environment, Transport and the Regions (DETR, 2000b, p 19) states that simply setting up new partnerships is no recipe for success. There needs to be more rigorous thinking about the nature, form and terms of inter-organisational collaboration. A more optimistic line is taken by the Health Select Committee (2001), which asserts that there is now a respectable body of research identifying the success criteria to ensure effective partnerships. The Health Select Committee therefore urges the government to apply these success criteria to its own proposals to establish new partnerships in the form of Local Strategic Partnerships and its wider 'joined-up' policy agenda across government departments.

In contrast, by enforcing partnerships in many sectors, the government has already decided that partnerships are, by default, better than hierarchies or markets. However, some years ago, Ferlie and Pettigrew (1996, p 95) reported that NHS managers were unclear on the success criteria of networks. Managing networks consumed a lot of time, but did not necessarily lead to tangible outcomes, with the consequent risk that the means of managerial process might drive out the end of delivering better services. A further problem was the uneasy combination of network-based forms of management with a strong performance orientation, with its focus on quantification and short-term target setting (see also Exworthy and Berney, 2000). According to DETR (2000b, p 47), the history of partnership initiatives suggests that failure is often due to lack of clarity on the basic intention and objectives. Many initiatives are marked by uncertainty of purpose: whether the aim is outcome-orientated (doing something that makes a difference); process-orientated (working in new ways to make a difference); or experimental (doing something to see whether it makes a difference).

In this section, we review the evolving academic literature which uses empirical evidence to identify the ingredients of successful partnerships in various different social welfare settings. Hardy et al (1992) examine five categories of barriers to collaboration in the sphere of community care: structural, procedural, financial, professional, and status and legitimacy. Addressing a wider range of partnerships, the Audit Commission (1998) sets out a 'checklist' of 28 questions under five headings: deciding to go into partnership; getting started; operating efficiently and effectively; reviewing the partnership's success; and reviewing what the partnerships can expect to achieve (see also Chapter Four). In a study of partnerships to reduce health inequalities, Evans and Killoran (2000) suggest six categories of enabling factors: shared strategic vision; leadership and management; relations and local ownership; accountability; organisational readiness; and responsiveness to a changing environment. Ling (2000) sets out four dimensions through which partnerships might be compared: membership; links; scale and boundaries; and the context of partnership. Powell et al (2001) suggest a 'ladder of partnership' with the rungs being isolation, encounter, communication, collaboration and integration (after Hudson et al, 1999); these are examined in terms of policy, process and process streams. In the US, Mitchell and Shortell (2000) examine six dimensions of community health partnership: governance of strategic intent and reasons for organising; determining the partnership's domain and setting the strategic direction; partnership composition; resources; coordination and integration issues; and accountability.

The government sees the ingredients of successful partnership working in the health and social care sectors as follows (DoH, 1998a, 1998d):

- a clarification of the purpose of the partnership;
- recognition and resolution of areas of conflict;
- agreement on a shared approach to partnership;
- development of strong leadership;
- continuous adaptation to reflect the lessons learned from the experience;
- incentives to reward effective working across organisational (and geographical) boundaries.

A parallel perspective is provided by the work of Policy Action Team 17 for the National Strategy for Neighbourhood Renewal (DETR, 2000a, 2000b). According to the Team's report (DETR, 2000a), there are several principles for effective joint working in deprived areas:

- Empowerment. Unless the residents of deprived communities are partners in joint working, nothing will change.
- Leadership and commitment. Partnership can be an excuse for everyone to do nothing. The most successful joint working has strong leadership and involves real – rather than token – commitment from all partners.
- Prevention is better than cure. Joint action should be focused on spotting problems.
- A radical change of culture. Public service culture needs to move away from focusing on the inputs and outputs of particular services, towards achieving shared outcome targets.
- All levels of government need to be involved.
- Mainstream services are the key.
- Central government as a facilitator.

A wider framework is provided by Challis et al (1988), who contrast the optimistic with the pessimistic tradition. The optimistic tradition assumes organisational altruism and rationality. In contrast, the pessimistic tradition assumes that individual and group interests are multiple and divergent, and the net result is competition, bargaining and conflict. Challis et al claim that neither the optimistic nor the pessimistic model fully captures the complexity of the world of policy making. They therefore suggest a new model – the planned bargaining model – which takes into account structure and agency; organisational structures and behaviour; costs and benefits; and incentives and sanctions.

It is clear that there is a degree of consensus between academics and policy makers regarding the key ingredients of a successful partnership. (See also Hudson et al, 1999; Ling, 2000; Powell et al, 2001.)

Table 2.1 shows some themes arising from these studies, classified as far as possible by terms used by the original authors. Factors such as the purpose of partnerships or shared vision, organisational arrangements, ownership and trust appear to be common across studies. These are discussed below.

Shared vision

A shared set of values and a broadly based consensus have long been recognised as important factors (Hardy et al, 1992, pp 18-93; DETR, 2000b, p 19; Huxham, 2000). As Hudson et al (1999, p 247) sum up, "Most approaches to collaboration take it for granted that an explicit statement of shared vision is a prerequisite to success". However, while the ends may be commonly agreed, the means to achieve these ends may be disputed. Hence, organisational arrangements are a common feature of many studies promoting effective partnerships.

Table 2.1: Comparison of components of 'effective partnerships'

Authors	Focus of study	Purpose/ aims/ direction	Former problems	Organisation/ structure	Ownership/ trust	Leadership	Monitoring/ evaluation/ adaption	Accountability	Resources/ incentives	Other
Audit Commission (1998)	Checklist for partnership	Deciding to enter partnership		Getting started	Expectations		Review 'success'		Efficiency & effectiveness	
Evans and Killoran (2000)	Partnerships to reduce inequalities	Shared strategic vision		Organisational readiness	Relations & ownership	Leadership & management	Responsiveness to changing environment	Accountability		
Hardy et al (1992)	Barriers to partnership	Procedural barrier	Professional/ status barrier	Structural barriers				Legitimacy barrier	Financial barrier	
Hardy et al (2000)	Principles of partnership	Clarity/ realism		Robust arrangements	Commitment/ ownership; develop/ maintain trust		Monitor/ measure/learn			
Labour Government eg, DoH (1998d, 1999)	Ingredients of success	Clarify purpose	Resolution of conflict		Shared approach	Strong leadership	Continuous adaption		Incentives to reward effective work	
Ling (2000)	Measure/ compare partnerships	Context		Membership; links						Scale & boundaries
Mitchell and Shortell (2000)	Governance of community health partnerships	Partnership domain & strategic direction		Composition; coordination; integration				Accountability	Resources	
Powell et al (2001)	Ladder of partnership & streams	Policy stream		Process stream					Resource stream	Rungs of ladder of partnership

Resources

Resources are sometimes seen as distinct from organisational structure (see Table 2.1); however, we examine them together, as staff resources are clearly related to financial resources. The most obvious resource is money, and many other resources, such as staff time, flow from this and also incur opportunity costs. As most public organisations have multiple priorities, the commitment of financial resources is a good test of whether stated or paper priorities (the shared vision) are backed by hard cash. Similarly, in a crowded policy agenda, the allocation of staff time may be crucial. In particular, the value of individuals with skills to work across boundaries, variously termed 'partnership champions' (Audit Commission, 1998) or 'reticulists' (Challis et al, 1998), is clear. However, their cross-agency role may mean that they lack sufficient (organisational) power to effect change, as they may lack adequate legitimacy within either organisation. Challis et al (1988, p 137) claim that policy coordination can be bought by offering a financial incentive to cross boundaries – 'crocks of gold'. Conflicts over resources and accountability between partners are likely, with the possibility of cost shunting. Costs may be shunted vertically within an organisation or horizontally between organisations. However, cost shunting or blame transfer indicates a lack of shared ownership between partner agencies. These difficulties may undermine partnerships, if resources are spent on areas considered to be beyond the 'normal remit' of either agency.

Although cash is the most obvious resource, other resources, such as trust and power, are no less important. Indeed, for most partnerships, building trust is the most important ingredient for success (CIPFA, 1997; Audit Commission, 1998, p 26; see also Sako, 1992; Flynn et al, 1996; Hardy et al, 2000; Rhodes, 2000). The importance of trust has been recognised in documents such as the NHS Plan (DoH, 2000, pp 56-7). This introduces a new delivery system based on the NHS as a 'high trust' organisation, which is glued together by a bond of trust between staff and patient. However, trust is often a resource in short supply. Many commentators claim that market relations corrode trust, and that mechanisms to build or rebuild trust remain problematic (Davies, 1999; Exworthy, 1998).

Autonomy and power

Networks are flatter organisational forms than hierarchies (Thompson et al, 1991). Hudson et al (1999, p 255) argue that networks achieve coordination through less formal and more egalitarian means than a hierarchy. Balloch and Taylor (2001b) claim that partnership reflects ideals of participatory democracy and equality between partners. Hage and Alter (1997, p 96) claim that networks differ from hierarchical coordination because of the autonomy of each member. While networks do not necessarily remove issues of power and dominance, there are degrees of both independence and interdependence between network members. In the perfectly competitive market, there is no dependence, as no organisation can have an effect on price. In a hierarchy, subordinate organisations are completely dependent on their superior. For Rhodes (1997, 2000), governance refers to self-governing, inter-organisational networks that have a significant degree of autonomy from the state. Hardy et al (2000, p 16) claim that partnerships work best where each partner is perceived to have an equivalent status, even though some may have more of some resources than others. For example, according to the Cabinet Office (2001, pp 43-5), it is crucial that the partnership is one of equal players. On the other hand, Sako (1992, p 45) claims that trust may exist in highly unequal power relationships. Moreover, OCR trading partners may be more willing to accept unequal power relations than ACR partners.

If the majority line is accepted, it follows that power asymmetries set a limit to networks. How much inequality of power is possible before a network becomes a hierarchy? The answer, in part, depends on the definition of power either in the traditional, Weberian sense as an observable commodity, or in the Foucauldian sense as diffuse, localised and invisible. The former sees power as part of a zero sum game in which, if one individual or agency gains power, another *necessarily* loses it. The latter does not necessarily see power as coercive, but a dispersed practice to which all participate and are subjected.

Power relations may be explored in horizontal and vertical dimensions. Resource asymmetry may be at the root of power struggles in local partnerships (Cloke et al, 2000). Indeed, such asymmetry is explicit in relation to 'lead' agencies which are often advocated by government (for example, DoH, 1998d). A 'lead' agency necessarily implies a 'following' partner agency. Moreover, some agencies may be excluded from the partnership in the first place. Community groups or agencies not considered to have a contribution to the shared vision will thus suffer in terms of claims upon resources. Stoker (2000, p 100) argues that an 'iron law' in partnerships which involve locally elected representatives appears to be the unavoidable tendency for them to question the legitimacy and representativeness of all other partners.

Clarence and Painter (1998, p 15) argue that the government's collaborative discourse is countered by another conflicting and contradictory discourse of central performance that drills down separate vertical silos. Rhodes (2000, p 361) argues that New Labour operates a "command operating code in a velvet glove". This stresses the importance of hierarchy, regulation and inspection in the NHS, through organisations such as the National Institute for Clinical Excellence (NICE) and the Commission for Health Improvement (CHI). Similarly, the NHS Plan (DoH, 2000) proposes a 'traffic light' system in which autonomy is 'earned'. In essence, local agencies can do as they like, as long as they comply with government wishes. The Cabinet Office (2001, p 50) states that if a partnership is failing to develop or deliver, Government Offices of the Regions may have to intervene to ensure effective leadership from another source. This seems to have more in common with the authority of a hierarchy than with the trust of a network (see also Chapter Three). Thus, according to most commentators, hierarchies and local resource asymmetries, as well as markets, may corrode trust.

Themes less commonly addressed in inductive approaches include some aspects of resources, leadership and accountability. It is perhaps surprising that resources and, to a lesser extent, accountability, are considered less crucial factors, since they seem to lie at the heart of notions of power, network composition and hence cross-agency partnerships.

The main problem with a 'shopping list' approach to identifying the features of effective partnerships (Table 2.1) is that it is difficult to deal with any tensions or trade-offs between the dimensions. For example, there may be a trade-off between 'strong leadership' and 'widespread ownership'. While 'policy champions' or working parties can galvanise action for a particular partnership, they may also create a sense in which responsibility and ownership is deferred to such leadership. Partnership working can therefore fail to permeate across agencies. This tension is highlighted in the Cabinet Office (2001) report on neighbourhood renewal. Compare:

- "Strange as it may seem, it's been no-one's job at local level to pull together all the different agencies with an impact on deprived neighbourhoods" (p 44); and
- "Local Strategic Partnerships will operate by consensus in order to reflect and retain the buy-in of partners" (p 45).

Conclusions: towards a shared vision of quasi-networks?

Some commentators suggest a remarkably loose definition of partnership. For example, Ling (2000, p 84) writes that they may be based on very trusting relationships and long-term reciprocity, but equally, they may be based on cautious, short-term alliances, which will be broken as soon as narrow sectional interests are compromised. Often there will be a lead agency and relationships may be hierarchical, with some partners obviously exercising more power than others. The purpose of the partnership may be tightly or loosely defined. However, we have suggested a more tightly defined version of partnership as a quasi-network. While it may contain elements of market and hierarchy, any meaningful definition of a partnership must have more in common with a network than a market or a hierarchy (see also Hage and Alter, 1997; Rhodes, 1997, 2000; Lowndes and Skelcher, 1998). The definition is bounded on the one side by the division between ACR and OCR, and on the other side by the degree of autonomy from other stakeholders. In short, a quasi-network cannot be likened to customers purchasing goods from supermarkets, nor to an army, which similarly is not a 'partnership' of colonels and corporals.

Although New Labour rarely uses the term 'network', it has made many references to the key characteristics of networks (for example, Thompson et al, 1991; Rhodes, 1997, 2000; Clarence and Painter, 1998), such as trust, cooperation, collaboration, partnership, alliances and working together. It is possible to argue that 'quasi-networks' are to New Labour what 'quasi-markets' were to the Conservatives. Otherwise, it is premature to specify in detail the conditions under which quasi-networks deliver social policy objectives (Le Grand and Bartlett, 1993). While the analysis of quasi-markets was based on neoclassical economics, material on quasi-networks comes from a variety of disciplines. A comparison of our inductive and deductive approaches shows some common themes. Some issues appear strongly in both approaches – trust is perhaps the clearest example. By contrast, characteristics such as 'shared vision' appear in inductive approaches, but are less prominent in the deductive approaches. Similarly, notions of equal power and status or of accountability are common in inductive approaches, but not so in deductive approaches. While there is some shared vision between the deductive and inductive approaches, differences persist.

This lack of consensus about quasi-networks has profound implications for government and policy. First, our understanding of the ingredients for effective partnerships is not as advanced as the Health Select Committee (2001) suggests. While many lessons can be learned from quasi-markets (Bartlett et al, 1998), the ingredients and, crucially, the tensions between them, are less clear. Government can steer networks only imperfectly (Rhodes 1997, 2000) because the steering mechanisms are poorly understood and because the levers at their disposal are arguably less effective than hierarchies or markets. Even when there is general agreement on an ingredient such as trust, it may be difficult to develop, easy to destroy and hard to replace. Second, building on the markets and hierarchies literature (for example, Williamson, 1975), effective quasi-networks will be contextual. They may work in some situations, but markets or hierarchies may be more effective in others. For example, Rhodes (2000, p 355) claims that networks are seen as preferable:

- when actors need reliable, 'thicker' information;
- when quality cannot be specified or is difficult to define and measure;
- when commodities are difficult to price;
- where professional discretion and expertise are core values;
- where flexibility is required to meet localised needs;
- where cross-sector, multi-agency cooperation and production is required;
- when monitoring and evaluation incur high political and transaction costs;
- when implementation involves bargaining.

These hypotheses need to be refined and examined in a variety of contexts. Our understanding of quasi-networks is clearly rudimentary. Further analysis needs to build on the work of quasi-markets (Le Grand and Bartlett, 1993; Bartlett et al, 1998), to analyse the essence, ingredients and policy levers of quasi-networks. Moreover, multi-disciplinary perspectives will be vital in determining what works best, when and where.

Acknowledgements

We are grateful for the support of the Economic and Social Research Council (ESRC) Health Variations Programme (phase 2) (award ref no L128251039), which funded the research project on which this chapter is based.

References

6, P. (1997) *Holistic government*, London: Demos.

Audit Commission (1998) *A fruitful partnership: Effective partnership working*, London: Audit Commission.

Balloch, S. and Taylor, M. (2001a) *Partnership working: Policy and practice*, Bristol: The Policy Press.

Balloch, S. and Taylor, M. (2001b) 'Introduction', in S. Balloch and M. Taylor (eds) *Partnership working: Policy and practice*, Bristol: The Policy Press.

Bartlett, W., Roberts, J. and Le Grand, J. (eds) (1998) *A revolution in social policy: Quasi-market reforms in the 1990s*, Bristol: The Policy Press.

Cabinet Office (1999) *Modernising government*, London: The Stationery Office.

Cabinet Office (2001) *A new commitment to neighbourhood renewal*, London: Cabinet Office/Social Exclusion Unit.

Challis, L., Fuller, S., Henwood, M., Klein, R., Plowden, W., Webb, A., Whittingham, P. and Wistow, G. (1988) *Joint approaches to social policy*, Cambridge: Cambridge University Press.

CIPFA (Chartered Institute of Public Finance and Accountancy) (1997) *Building effective partnerships*, London: CIPFA.

Clarence, E. and Painter, C. (1998) 'Public services under New Labour: collaborative discourses and local networking', *Public Policy and Administration*, vol 13, no 1, pp 8-22.

Clarke, J. and Newman, J. (1997) *The managerial state: Power, politics and ideology in the remaking of social welfare*, London: Sage Publications.

Cloke, P., Milbourne, P. and Widdowfield, R. (2000) 'Partnership and policy networks in rural local governance', *Public Administration*, vol 78, no 1, pp 111-33.

Davies, H. (1999) 'Falling public trust in health services: implications for accountability', *Journal of Health Services Research and Policy*, vol 4, pp 193-4.

Davies, H., Crombie, I. and Mannion, R. (1999) 'Performance indicators: guiding lights or wreckers' lanterns?', in H.T.O. Davies, M. Malek, A. Neilson and M. Tavakoli (eds) *Managing quality and controlling cost*, Aldershot: Ashgate.

DETR (Department of the Environment, Transport and the Regions) (2000a) *Report of policy action team 17: Joining it up locally*, London: DETR.

DETR (2000b) *Joining it up locally. The evidence base*, London: DETR.

DoH (Department of Health) (1997) *The new NHS: Modern, dependable*, London: The Stationery Office.

DoH (1998a) *Health of the nation: A policy assessed*, London: The Stationery Office.

DoH (1998b) *Modernising social services*, London: The Stationery Office.

DoH (1998c) *Our healthier nation*, London: The Stationery Office.

DoH (1998d) *Partnership in action*, London: DoH.

DoH (1999) *Saving lives: Our healthier nation*, London: The Stationery Office.

DoH (2000) *The NHS plan*, London: The Stationery Office.

Evans, D. and Killoran, A. (2000) 'Tackling health inequalities through partnership working', *Critical Public Health*, vol 10, pp 125-40.

Exworthy, M. (1998) 'Localism in the NHS quasi-market', *Environment and Planning C: Government and Policy*, vol 16, pp 449-62.

Exworthy, M. and Berney, L. (2000) 'What counts and what works? Evaluating policies to tackle health inequalities', *Renewal*, vol 8, no 4, pp 47-55.

Exworthy, M. and Halford, S. (eds) (2000) *Professionals and the new managerialism in the public sector*, Buckingham: Open University Press.

Exworthy, M., Powell, M. and Mohan, J. (1999) 'The NHS: quasi-market, quasi-hierarchy and quasi-network', *Public Money and Management*, vol 19, no 4, pp 15-22.

Ferlie, E. and Pettigrew, A. (1996) 'Managing through networks: some issues and implications for the NHS', *British Journal of Management*, vol 7 (special issue), pp S81-99.

Ferlie, E., Ashburner, L., Fitzgerald, L. and Pettigrew, A. (1996) *The new public management in action*, Oxford: Oxford University Press.

Flynn, R., Williams, G. and Pickard, S. (1996) *Markets and networks: Contracting in community health services*, Buckingham: Open University Press.

Gambetta, D. (1988) *Trust: Making and breaking co-operative relations*, Oxford; Blackwell.

Goddard, M. and Mannion, R. (1998) 'From competition to co-operation', *Health Economics*, vol 7, pp 105-19.

Granovetter, M. (1985) 'Economic action and social structure: the problem of embeddedness', *American Journal of Sociology*, vol 91, pp 481-510.

Hage, J. and Alter, C. (1997) 'A typology of inter-organizational relationships and networks', in J.R. Hollingsworth and R. Boyer (eds) *Contemporary capitalism*, pp 94-126, Cambridge: Cambridge University Press.

Hardy, B., Turrell, A. and Wistow, G. (1992) *Innovations in community care management*, Aldershot: Avebury.

Hardy, B., Hudson, B. and Waddington, E. (2000) *What makes a good partnership?*, Leeds: Nuffield Institute for Health.

Health Select Committee (2001) *Inquiry into public health: Second report*, London: The Stationery Office.

Hudson, B. (1999) 'Dismantling the Berlin Wall: developments at the health–social care interface', in H. Dean and R. Woods (eds) *Social Policy Review 11*, Luton: SPA, pp 187-204.

Hudson, B., Hardy, B., Henwood, M. and Wistow, G. (1999) 'In pursuit of inter-agency collaboration in the public sector', *Public Management*, vol 1, no 2, pp 235-60.

Huxham, C. (2000) 'The challenge of collaborative governance', *Public Management,* vol 2, no 3, pp 337-57.

Kavanagh, D. and Richards, D. (2001) 'Departmentalism and joined-up government: back to the future?', *Public Administration*, vol 54, pp 1-18.

Kirkpatrick, I. (1999) 'The worst of both worlds? Public services without markets or bureaucracy', *Public Money and Management*, vol 19, no 4, pp 7-14.

Le Grand, J. and Bartlett, W. (1993) *Quasi-markets and social policy*, Basingstoke: Macmillan.

Ling, T. (2000) 'Unpacking partnership: the case of health care', in J. Clarke, S. Gewirtz and E. McLaughlin (eds) *New managerialism, new welfare?*, London: Sage Publications.

Lowndes, V. and Skelcher, C. (1998) 'The dynamics of multi-organizational partnerships', *Public Administration*, vol 76, pp 313-33.

Lunt, N., Mannion, R. and Smith, P. (1996) 'Economic discourse and the market: the case of community care', *Public Administration*, vol 74, pp 369-91.

Mackintosh, M. (2000) 'Flexible contracting? Economic cultures and implicit contracts in social care', *Journal of Social Policy*, vol 29, pp 1-19.

Milgrom, P. and Roberts, J. (1992) *Economics, organisation and management*, London: Prentice Hall.

Mitchell, S. and Shortell, S. (2000) 'The governance and management of effective community health partnerships', *The Milbank Quarterly*, vol 78, pp 241-89.

Newman, J. (2000) 'Beyond the new public management?', in J. Clarke, S. Gewirtz and E. McLaughlin (eds) *New managerialism, new welfare?*, London: Sage Publications.

Peters, B.G. (1998) 'Managing horizontal government: the politics of coordination', *Public Administration*, vol 76, pp 295-311.

Peters, T. and Waterman, R. (1982) *In search of excellence*, London: Harper and Row.

Powell, M. (1999a) 'New Labour and the 'third way' in the British NHS', *International Journal of Health Services*, vol 29, pp 353-70.

Powell, M. (ed) (1999b) *New Labour, new welfare state?: The 'third way' in British social policy*, Bristol: The Policy Press.

Powell, M., Exworthy, M. and Berney, L. (2001) 'Playing the game of partnership', in R. Sykes, C. Bochel and N. Ellison (eds) *Social Policy Review 13*, Bristol: The Policy Press and the SPA, pp 39-62.

Putnam, R. (2000) *Bowling alone*, New York, NY: Simon and Schuster.

Rhodes, R. (1997) *Understanding governance*, Buckingham: Open University Press.

Rhodes, R. (2000) 'The governance narrative', *Public Administration*, vol 78, pp 345-63.

Roberts, J., Le Grand, J. and Bartlett, W. (1998) 'Lessons from experience of quasi-markets in 1990s', in W. Bartlett, J. Roberts and J. Le Grand (eds) *A revolution in social policy: Quasi-market reforms in the 1990s*, Bristol: The Policy Press, pp 275-91.

Sako, M. (1992) *Price, quality and trust*, Cambridge: Cambridge University Press.

Stoker, G. (2000) 'Urban political science and the challenge of urban governance', in J. Pierre (ed) *Debating governance: Authority, steering and democracy*, Oxford: Oxford University Press.

Thompson, G., Frances, J., Levacic, R. and Mitchell, J. (1991) *Markets, hierarchies, networks: The coordination of social life*, London: Sage Publications.

Wilkinson, D. and Appelbee, E. (1999) *Implementing holistic government: Joined-up action on the ground*, Bristol: The Policy Press.

Williamson, O.E. (1975) *Markets and hierarchies*, New York, NY: Free Press.

THREE

Partnership and the remaking of welfare governance

John Clarke and Caroline Glendinning

Introduction

Partnership has emerged as a central theme in 'Third Way' politics, rhetoric and policies. It exemplifies the drive to move beyond the old politics of organising public services, in which choices were made between state control and market anarchy. This juxtaposition (Old Left = statism; New Right = market individualism) is a characteristic feature of Third Way analysis and argument (for example, Blair, 1998; Giddens, 1998). Partnership embodies the 'between and beyond' spirit of the Third Way, being neither a state bureaucratic system nor a market place of contending interests. As such, it expresses the non-ideological, non-dogmatic orientation of the Third Way, moving beyond the 'old' ideological commitments to the market or the state. Partnership exemplifies the pursuit of pragmatic solutions to policy problems. It promises to restore a collaborative and integrative orientation to a world of public services battered by the ideological, fiscal and organisational assaults of the New Right.

Partnership has the advantage – in terms of political rhetoric, at least – of being relatively non-specific. While this lack of specificity may be a source of concern to policy analysts, it has some distinctive political benefits. Like 'community', partnership is a word of obvious virtue (what sensible person would choose conflict over collaboration?). It is unspecific about the dimensions, axes or composition of particular 'partnerships'; partnerships can exist between sectors, between organisations, between government departments, between central and local government, between local government and local communities, and between state and citizen (at least). Despite their wide variations in organisational and social relationships, processes and arrangements, partnerships provide a key, overarching and unifying imagery of this Third Way approach to governing.

The proliferation of partnerships in both political rhetoric and policy initiatives gives rise to a number of analytical challenges. Four main lines of inquiry have developed around the place of partnerships in social and public policy. The first concerns the challenge of defining, mapping and conceptualising partnerships in the coordination of public services (see Chapter Two). The second is the problem of evaluating partnership as a form of coordinating or delivering services (see Chapter Four; Glendinning, 2002). A third line of inquiry (to which most of this book is addressed) focuses more specifically on current political discourse and examines whether, and to what extent, there is a distinctive New Labour/Third Way role for partnerships in the reform of public services. Finally, there is the question of whether partnerships are part of a broader, longer-term shift in the governance systems and processes of modern societies. In this context, partnerships can be viewed as one element in a cluster of changing relationships between state and society, in which new forms of governing have emerged. In this chapter, we focus on the intersection of these last two issues – whether there is a distinctive New Labour/Third Way approach to partnership in public services; and whether partnerships form part of a wider shift in governance systems.

We will argue that the current emphasis on partnerships is not an exclusive 'New Labour' preoccupation, but needs to be understood as part of a broader transition to new modes of governing statutory welfare services. We argue that the current drive to encourage (and ultimately to compel) partnerships penetrates much further and deeper than previous attempts. This in turn raises new questions about the role of the state in determining the obligations of public sector services; the activities of professionals; and ultimately the experiences of, and outcomes for, welfare subjects.

'Governance' has become an increasingly significant focus for the study of public services and state–society relationships (for example, Kooiman, 1993; Rhodes, 1997; Stoker, 1997, 2000; Pierre, 2000; Newman, 2001). It has been argued (most explicitly in the work of Rhodes and Stoker) that the changing forms of coordinating public services constitute a systematic shift from bureaucratic hierarchy to the market, and subsequently from markets to networks. Partnerships are intrinsically associated with networked forms of governance. Thus, what Rhodes (2000) terms the 'governance narrative' has a significance over and above the activities of specific governments, political parties or ideological positions. For example, the 'governance narrative' suggests that the shift from centralised state bureaucracies to markets involved more than the choices of Conservative governments or neo-liberal political ideologies. Rather, it also signified the inability of hierarchical command systems to provide effective means of control and coordination; their limitations provoked the search for, and introduction of, alternative forms of governing. The move from markets to networks similarly reflects the limitations and inadequacies of market mechanisms and relationships in meeting the challenges of governing modern societies. Contemporary governments, Rhodes and others have argued, can only achieve their objectives through indirect means, by surrendering the power of direct control and bringing other social actors and organisations into networks of mutual interdependence, which can shape, refashion and deliver policies more effectively. Similarly, Kooiman (1993, 2000) claims that the dynamics and complexities of modern social systems need to be reflected in processes of co-governance, rather than hierarchical direction.

These arguments about changing forms of governance frame our discussion of New Labour's partnerships. They also highlight the limitations of considering partnerships solely as a product of party politics and instead point to the need also to consider broader changes in the relationships between state and society. In this chapter we will examine the contemporary configurations of 'partnerships', and their role in the wider evolution of new forms of governance, by focusing on New Labour's attempts to reform the long and troubled relationship between health and social care. This chapter therefore develops and critically examines the arguments introduced in Chapter Two; that partnerships constitute an integral feature of networked modes of governance.

Encountering the 'Berlin Wall' between health and social services

There are a number of reasons why New Labour's reforms of the relationships between health and social care services provide a useful context for exploring the problematic links between partnerships and new modes of governance. Relationships between the two sectors have been regarded as problematic by a long succession of governments and attempts to improve these relationships have proved remarkably unresponsive to previous reorganisations and initiatives. Indeed it could be argued that, although increasing forms of departmental separation from the mid-1970s onwards may have 'clarified' bureaucratic and departmental structures of responsibility and control, these simultaneously increased the difficulties of collaboration and service coordination.

Successive attempts to counteract these trends have focused on a number of different points of potential coordination. For example, the role of general practitioners (GPs) as key 'gatekeepers' to a range of services has been the focus of several policy documents (for example, DoH, 1989, 1990, 1994). Care management, mandated upon social services departments by the 1990 NHS and Community Care Act, was intended to facilitate the purchase of 'packages' of services tailored to meet individual needs (although in practice care managers have only limited ability to commit resources). Joint consultative committees and joint care planning teams were established during the 1980s to manage the transition from institutional to community care. Some successes were reported in relation to specific, small-scale and marginal activities, but impacts on the strategic roles or mainstream activities of either health or social care organisations were rare (Audit Commission, 1986; Nocon, 1994). Such shortcomings led to a new emphasis during the early 1990s on drawing mainstream service programmes, major contracts and large budgets into joint activities, through the active promotion of joint commissioning (DoH, 1995). In many localities, progress in joint commissioning and other inter-sectoral activities was greatest in relation to services for learning disabled people and people with mental health problems; the growth of the large independent residential and nursing home sector for older people during the 1980s substantially diverted pressures for statutory authorities to develop effective joint commissioning programmes for older people (Poxton, 1999). Moreover, GPs, housing departments and other stakeholders were largely uninvolved in any of these earlier collaborative initiatives, an exclusion whose consequences may take some time to overcome (Glendinning et al, 1998; Rummery and Glendinning, 2000).

The divisions between NHS and local authority social services were problematic for the New Right governments of the 1980s and early 1990s because they were considered to cause duplication and overlap which, according to quasi-market criteria, could only be wasteful and inefficient. The response was the introduction of market-related forms of coordination, predominantly contracts. However, the use of contracts as the basis for delivering welfare services arguably encouraged yet further the sharpening of organisational and service boundaries, by reinforcing conceptions of the 'core business' of organisations (Charlesworth et al, 1996). Contracts enabled service responsibilities to be clarified and legitimated, but these boundaries were often determined by the size of the purchaser's budget and without reference to the activities of other organisations (Richardson and Pearson, 1995).

More recently, the growing mutual interdependence of the two service sectors has heightened the search for new forms of coordination. To meet high-profile policy and political goals, both health and social care organisations increasingly need the cooperation of each other. This is particularly true of New Labour policy goals, which set out clear, ambitious objectives for improving the performance of (or 'modernising') public sector services. Commitments to reducing hospital waiting lists and other waiting times for treatment, for example, depend on the efficient use of acute hospital resources, including preventing the admission of people who could be supported in other ways and discharging quickly people who no longer need acute medical care. But achieving this level of efficiency depends on the availability of social services funding and provision to support people outside acute hospital settings, and collaboration with wider local authority and voluntary sector initiatives to maximise independence and prevent ill health in the first place. For New Labour, the interdependencies between health and social services have especially high political salience and this provides a further rationale for examining the governance implications of partnerships through this particular inter-sectoral 'lens'.

In pursuit of partnership: New Labour's approach to health and social services

Although 'partnerships' are a pervasive feature of New Labour policy, they have been given particular prominence in relation to health and social services. Thus both Labour governments since 1997 have produced a stream of policy guidance, legislation and moral exhortations (some of which are backed by substantial amounts of 'badged', or ring-fenced, funding) to develop partnerships between NHS and local authority organisations (and social services departments in particular). Measures include Health Action Zones (see Chapter Six); Health Improvement Plans, to which both local authorities and NHS organisations are signatories; the mandatory representation of local authority social services departments in the governance of the new Primary Care Groups and Trusts

(Glendinning et al, 2001); a new statutory 'duty of partnership' on all NHS organisations; shared service objectives for health and social services organisations; Joint Investment Plans; and earmarked resources to support new services (particularly in the area of intermediate care) to be developed and provided jointly by NHS and social services organisations (DoH, 2001a, 2001b, 2001c). The 1999 Health Act removed several structural constraints on joint working, thus allowing NHS and local authority organisations to pool budgets; delegate commissioning responsibilities to a single 'lead' commissioning organisation; and/or integrate services within a single managerial structure. Subsequently, the 2001 Health and Social Care Act contained measures allowing the Secretary of State for Health to compel the use of these new 'flexibilities', where health and local authorities are judged not to be working together closely enough. The 2001 Health and Social Care Act also provides the legal framework for the establishment of Care Trusts – new organisations that allow health and local authorities to align governance arrangements, strategic commissioning activities and front-line service provision for particular groups of service users who need high levels of services from both sectors (DoH, 2001a). Overall, these measures pave the way for health and local authority partnerships to progress to the top of the collaborative ladder, from linkage, through coordination, to full integration (Leutz, 1999).

This raft of new measures indicates that some lessons have been learned from the past failures of joint planning and joint commissioning. New attempts are being made to align the statutory obligations of health and social services authorities. Health Improvement Plans and Joint Investment Plans constitute platforms for joint assessments of local needs, investment reviews, service planning and commissioning between health and local authorities. These responsibilities are mirrored in local authorities' responsibilities to lead Local Strategic Partnerships. The drive to develop partnerships has also been supported by significant injections of 'badged' resources. The NHS Plan for England (DoH, 2000, Chapters Five and Twelve) promises an injection of £900 million up to 2003/04 for new intermediate care and related services developed jointly by NHS and local authority organisations. Further financial incentives to 'encourage and reward joint working' include up to £100 million for NHS organisations, ring-fenced through the National Performance Fund; and £50 million a year from April 2002 to reward improvements in social services' joint working arrangements.

The size of these investments suggests that the promotion of partnerships is not motivated simply by the prospect of short-term efficiency gains. However, the timescales within which the benefits and outcomes of closer NHS–local authority partnerships are to be achieved are very demanding. Moreover, these tight timetables have to be negotiated alongside many other major imperatives required of both NHS and local authority organisations (see, for example, Wilkin et al, 2001).

A further source of uncertainty about the likely success of these initiatives is the increasingly clear indication that partnerships are not optional, but mandatory. The emphasis on partnership is thus expressed in new mechanisms for the performance management of these obligations, particularly in relation to Joint Investment Plans; the investments of the Social Services Modernisation Fund; the representation of local authority interests in health commissioning fora; and, ultimately, in the new powers of the Secretary of State to require use of the 1999 Health Act flexibilities in cases of 'partnership failure'. This reflects what Paton (1999, p 69) terms 'statutory voluntarism', in which "partnership and co-operation and collaboration are emphasised and mandated at every turn". The tight, and increasingly aligned, performance management of partnerships may help to reduce some of the conflicting pressures on health and social services agencies, which have hitherto diverted attention away from common, collaborative endeavours back to their separate 'core business' objectives (such as implementing new community care policies or reducing hospital waiting lists). Integrating regulatory and audit processes across service boundaries is an important element of the endeavours to institutionalise partnership working and of the pursuit of 'joined-up government' more generally (Newman, 2001). On the other hand, there is no evidence that partnerships that are mandated, whether through performance management regimes or stronger sanctions, from reluctant partners, rather than developing out of shared objectives and common strategies, are likely to be more successful than the hostile relationships that preceded them (see also Chapter Four).

The 1999 Health Act flexibilities undoubtedly have the potential to facilitate closer collaboration between health and social services. Legal barriers to budget pooling have long been alleged to present major constraints on partnerships. Unlike the 1993 community care reforms, which only covered the range of services funded by local authority social services departments (Lewis and Glennerster, 1996), pooled budgets allow the principles of care management to be extended across the health/social care divide, thus enabling a much wider range of services to be purchased as part of individualised care 'packages'. However, problems may still arise in negotiating the thorny issue of charges for the 'social' but not the 'health' elements of such packages (Rummery and Glendinning, 2000). Leutz (1999) describes this as the 'square peg in a round hole' problem, where service integration may be frustrated by the different bases of entitlement to those services.

Other long-standing barriers to partnerships between health and social services persist, despite the extensive raft of new policy initiatives. One barrier is the continuing lack of common organisational and geographical boundaries – a problem exacerbated by the recent rolling programme of local government reorganisation and the formation of, and subsequent mergers between, Primary Care Groups and Trusts (PCG/Ts). The responsibilities of PCG/Ts cover the populations registered with their member general practitioners, which do not fall within neat cartographical boundaries; almost half of social services departments cover four or more different PCGs (Glendinning et al, 2001).

A further potential barrier is the dominance of general practitioners within New Labour's policies for the NHS and their professional hegemony in the implementation of those policies at local levels. The new PCGs are dominated by GPs – "a group whose professional culture has not been one of collaboration"

(Callaghan et al, 2000, p 25). Indeed, a major gap in the history of joint planning and joint commissioning over the past 30 years is that GPs were largely uninvolved. As fundholders, some GPs did collaborate with social services departments to purchase additional care management services that could alleviate pressures on their own practice-based services (Glendinning et al, 1998; Rummery and Glendinning, 2000). However, their engagement with wider service policy and planning was minimal (Myles et al, 1998).

We now turn to some broader conceptual and theoretical questions about partnerships and the Third Way, before considering the implications for changing forms of welfare governance.

Third Way partnerships – from margin to mainstream?

A key question, reflecting the overarching theme of this book, is whether New Labour's approach to the relationships between health and social services marks a new and distinctive incarnation of partnership. At least rhetorically, the commitment to partnership working exemplifies and embodies Third Way thinking – a way of transcending the limitations of the state and the market (see, for example, Stoker, 2000); partnership "provides a 'Third Way' between stifling top-down command and control on the one hand, and a random and wasteful grass roots free-for-all on the other" (DoH, 1997c, p 27). But do Third Way approaches to partnership have a greater potential than previous initiatives to penetrate and transform the structures and cultures of their 'parent' organisations, rather than remaining peripheral (and often transitory) activities? Are other features of the government's 'modernisation' programme likely to reinforce or undermine the drive to partnership working?

Certainly there are some promising signs. Despite the historical exclusion of GPs from collaborative activities, PCG/Ts have already established wide-ranging networks of relationships with local authority community development, education, leisure, welfare rights and housing departments (Coleman and Glendinning, 2001). These relationships are commonly concerned with initiatives to improve the health of local people, as set out in local Health Improvement Plans. However, the relatively high level of generality at which such common objectives are specified may encourage a formalist approach to partnerships (compliance with the duty, rather than commitment to the practice).

Similarly, the requirement for each sector to be represented on governing bodies of the other may help to reduce professional mistrust and suspicion and embed such links in mainstream corporate governance arrangements. Again, however, the evidence is rather mixed. Social services representatives on PCG Boards do indeed report a continuing improvement in the attitudes of other Board members (GPs, community nurses) towards them. However, opportunities to represent social services interests in Board discussions and to influence PCG decisions remain low. Moreover, social services representatives complain of the undiminishing dominance of medical culture and service models, which continues to marginalise their own organisational and professional concerns (Coleman and Glendinning, 2001). Such patterns raise questions about whether, and under what circumstances, partnerships can develop their own 'core business', rather than being driven by the concerns of one (or more) dominant partners (see also Chapter Four).

More broadly, the extent to which relationships between health and social services are equal or hierarchical (Ling, 2000; see also Chapter Two) is a further important issue. Long-standing professional inequalities between medicine and social work (and accompanying concerns about the medicalisation of the social domain) may remain very considerable barriers. These difficulties may be intensified if, for example, there are suspicions that the priorities of health and social care partnerships are driven by narrow clinical, rather than wider social, priorities; or if pooled budgets are being used disproportionately to fund medical rather than social services. These are very real risks in relation to the new intermediate care services proposed in the NHS Plan for England (DoH, 2000) and the subsequent National Service Framework for older people (DoH, 2001c). Although these services are intended to be developed through cross-agency and inter-professional working, they focus almost exclusively on short-term pre-admission and post-discharge services, which will reduce preventable hospitalisation and delays in discharging patients from hospital (DoH, 2001b).

Health and social services partnerships also pose potential threats to equity, which, paradoxically, also features as a major objective of New Labour's health and social services policies. The 1997 NHS White Paper pledged to reverse wide variations in access to, and quality of, health services, through mechanisms such as National Service Frameworks and the National Institute of Clinical Effectiveness (DoH, 1997c). Similarly, the Joint Audit Commission/Social Services Inspectorate reviews of social services departments are beginning to address major discrepancies in the departments' levels and standards of services. However, health and social services partnerships risk introducing new inequities – in relation to the mechanisms and criteria for accessing services; the levels and standards of those services; and, because social services are involved, the financial contributions users are required to make towards services. These new inequalities are also likely to emerge in relation to the proposed Care Trusts – the apotheosis of New Labour's drive to organisational partnerships in health and social care. The organisational frameworks for Care Trusts assume non-coterminous boundaries between NHS and local authorities and thus allow Care Trusts to be established between an NHS Primary Care Trust and one of possibly several local authorities, which cover the same area. Conversely, a Care Trust may provide health services to patients, some of whom it does not provide local authority services for (DoH, 2001b). This will heighten existing tensions for central government that are inherent in policies of decentralisation, with attendant localising effects (see also Mohan, 1999).

Finally, the capacity of New Labour's partnerships to penetrate and transform the core business of the partner organisations may be impaired by its very heavy emphasis on the management and measurement of performance as a key element of its strategy to modernise the NHS (and, indeed, the wider public sector as a whole). The relationship between 'partnership and performance'

(DoH, 1997c, p 10) is potentially highly problematic, not only for the transformational capacity of Third Way partnerships, but also because of the wider implications for the governance of welfare services (this latter issue is discussed later). Here, we focus on whether partnerships will be effectively supported or undermined by the simultaneous drive to demonstrate 'performance'. If both the construction of partnerships and the common objectives of these partnerships are key performance indicators against which organisational achievement is assessed, then New Labour's performance focus may provide a framework that enhances partnership working. However, there are aspects of the performance approach, and its methodology, that are likely to run counter to partnership working. One aspect concerns the kinds of evidence that are used to measure and evaluate performance; these are currently dominated by simple, accessible and readily measurable indicators. Performance indicators, and regulatory/audit systems in general, tend to be structured around departmental and service boundaries, rather than reflecting the pursuit of cross-cutting or 'joined-up' objectives (Cope and Goodship, 1999; Newman, 2000). Such indicators therefore tend to be mono-organisational (indeed, they are intended to promote comparisons *between* discrete organisations), rather than being system wide or multi-organisational. It is far more difficult to measure, for example, whether partnerships succeed in making organisations, communities and individuals 'more responsible' for health outcomes. Given the centrality of performance systems to New Labour's 'modernisation' agenda, any disjunctures between service delivery processes and scrutiny processes are likely to pull the former towards the mono-organisational objectives and concerns defined in performance evaluation (Clarke et al, 2000; see also Power, 1997).

These unresolved tensions suggest that partnerships are located on a somewhat unsteady footing within New Labour's 'Third Way'. A range of processes, flexibilities, incentives and penalties have been introduced to make partnerships a key feature of a 'modernised' welfare system. At the same time, however, these new partnerships have to deal with the traditional tensions of working across organisational, budgetary, contractual and professional boundaries, and must overcome some of the less helpful dynamics that are also intrinsic to the 'modernisation' of public services.

This discussion also hints at some of the challenges involved in evaluating the success or failure of partnerships in the remaking of health and social care (see Chapter Four; also Glendinning, 2002). The normal tendency is to concentrate on the organisational or inter-organisational level of analysis. However, we cannot assume that 'success' in policy terms (reductions in health inequalities, for example) can be adequately measured by aggregating organisational outcomes. This is partly the problem of what is not included in either the targets for, or the evaluation of, organisational performance; and partly the potentially perverse effects of organisational attention being focused on what is being measured (combined with incentives to demonstrate success). As a result, organisational successes may not add up to policy or public interest successes (Clarke, 1999).

Finally, partnerships currently have very high political salience. They are not only intended to create better-performing organisations, but they also have a significant place in political calculation and in overall assessments of the performance of government. Partnerships are intended to *exemplify* 'Third Way' modernisation and the 'newness' of New Labour. They are expected to deliver symbolic results, for example, in the form of health-related 'success stories' (which have been in short supply for some years). Consequently, evaluating the extent to which New Labour partnerships have succeeded in penetrating and transforming the organisation, culture and activities of health and social care partner organisations is likely to be confounded by a variety of government actions intended to affect popular perceptions of success and failure in partnership working in this politically important area. Thus, substantial extra resources have already been made available to bolster partnership performance during and beyond the government's first five years in office. A second, alternative scenario is that local health and social care partnerships could be popularly castigated, as contemporary incarnations of the 'local management' that is held 'responsible' for policy failures. A third, and very real, possibility is that the model of managing 'poor' performance that has been developed in relation to schools and education authorities will be pursued, with partnerships that are judged (by whatever criteria) to be failing becoming subject to direct intervention by 'hit squads', or 'direct rule' from the Department of Health. Indeed, the NHS Plan for England (DoH, 2000) warns that action will be taken against ineffective local health–social care partnerships, which could be compelled to use the new flexibilities of pooled budgets, lead commissioning and integrated provider organisations. Powers to allow the Secretary of State to intervene in this way were subsequently included in the 2001 Health and Social Care Act. Partnerships, particularly between health and social services, have thus been one of the key settings for what Dunleavy calls political 'hyperactivism'. This, he argues, "occurs when politicians individually and collectively gain 'points' with the media and party colleagues from making new initiatives almost for their own sake" (1995, p 61). In these respects, policy cannot be simply and readily separated from politics. All governments engage in the process of political calculation and the management of public debate. As a result, successes in relation to public services over the past 20 years have tended to be announced, rather than demonstrated. The symbolic significance of partnerships within New Labour's Third Way may well add weight to this tendency.

Partnerships and 'networked governance'

Using the rhetoric and mechanisms of 'partnership' to transform patterns of coordination and control in public services raises a number of questions for the study of governance. As many commentators have suggested, changes in dominant modes of governance bring about new problems and possibilities for public services, particularly questions about how they can be made accountable (for example, Stoker, 1997, 2000; Skelcher, 1998; Pierre, 2000). Here we explore the implications of partnership for questions of accountability; the processes of organisational governance within partnerships; and the significance of partnerships in the wider remaking of state–society governance relationships.

There appears to be a characteristic instability within the New Labour approach to 'modernising' government. The concern to enhance participation, inclusion and citizen participation sits uncomfortably alongside a strengthening of central powers of control and direction (Newman, 2000, 2001). This uncertainty about whether, and how far, to trust locally devised arrangements is also reflected in central government's view of partnerships. For example, the 'statutory voluntarism' that requires partnership as a duty is backed by powers to take over 'failing' partnerships, either directly or by proxy management. Such arrangements – and the tensions around power that they imply – place the policy and practice of partnerships at some distance from the concepts and models of networks within the governance literature (for example, Kooiman, 1993; Rhodes, 1997; Stoker, 1997). Mandatory and imposed partnerships do not fit descriptions of 'self-regulating' or 'co-steering' networked systems. We may therefore need to consider 'Third Way' partnerships rather more as externally managed systems, whose internal dynamics coexist, potentially uncomfortably, with powerful external direction and intervention (Jessop, 2000).

The accountability of local partnerships to local communities, electorates, taxpayers or service users is also potentially problematic. For example, it is increasingly common for local partnerships using the 1999 Health Act flexibilities, and other 'joined-up' initiatives such as Health Action Zones, to be managed by partnership boards. These commonly consist of councillors and non-executive members of the constituent health and local authorities as the accountable investment bodies, with powers to co-opt representatives from other organisations. Their responsibilities are likely to include setting objectives; agreeing budget and expenditure plans; and reviewing performance. The impression is of top-down management, with few opportunities for 'active citizenship' in the setting of priorities or the allocation and expenditure of (very substantial) resources. Nor is it clear whether the local authority membership of partnership boards carries a mandate from, or accountability to, the rest of the authority, which might provide an indirect link with local democracy. A similar lack of clarity is apparent in the public accountability arrangements for the proposed new Care Trusts. Leutz (1999) points out that many service integration initiatives in the US and UK are driven by providers and professionals, rather than publics and payers. This leaves some important questions about the scope, objectives and financing of partnerships unanswered (and in some cases, unasked).

Similarly, although guidance on using the Health Act flexibilities recommends consultation with local communities and user groups (a process which will in any case be far more familiar to the social services than the health partners), this is not a required condition of using the flexibilities. A survey of the first localities to use the Health Act flexibilities revealed little involvement of service users or local communities in planning or implementing the new partnership arrangements. In only a third of the responding sites were any user or patient organisations named as participating partners and the majority of sites had 'consulted' with their 'general publics' only after detailed proposals for the new partnership arrangements had been completed, rather than at earlier stages in the planning process. Overall, local publics and communities were less likely to have been consulted or involved at any stage in planning the new partnership than organisations representing specific groups of patients and other service users (Hudson et al, 2001). The range and types of organisations involved in these new Third Way partnerships may therefore be considerably narrower than under previous arrangements for collaboration, because the mechanisms for securing local democratic participation appear relatively weak. This lack of attention to local involvement and accountability is somewhat at odds with the government's vision for local government: "When we were elected, we pledged to ... bring government back to the people.... Our agenda is the renewal of local democratic government.... We want councils to gain a new democratic legitimacy" (DETR, 1998, preface).

There are also unresolved issues about governance processes *within* partnerships and how partnerships are to be made accountable, whether as autonomous entities or through their constituent organisations. In relation to partnerships using the Health Act flexibilities, for example, it is far from clear how decisions are made within each partner agency about the resources to be committed to a pooled budget or what new services to develop; and what independent inspection, monitoring and complaints procedures will be available. This creates a risk that new partnerships may incur significant opportunity costs, if their start-up costs are not recognised or if resources are diverted from other services in order to secure the success of high-profile new partnership schemes.

These issues suggest that health–social care partnerships, when viewed as a form of 'network' (Stoker, 1997) or 'co-steering' (Kooiman, 1993), have typically complex processes and relationships of coordination. Indeed, some proponents of the 'new governance' argue that such complexity – and underspecification – is precisely what makes governance by networks particularly suited to the demands of adaptation, responsiveness and flexibility created by new social conditions (for example, Rhodes, 1997). However, this flexibility implies the loss of other capacities that have traditionally been valued in the provision of public services. In particular, the complexity and flexibility of new Third Way partnerships make internal processes of decision-making and resource allocation less clear or 'transparent'. Equally, there is a risk that the new partnerships effectively attenuate or even disrupt processes of formal hierarchical accountability, whether these flow upwards or downwards. Instead, partnerships may become sites in which contending interests are negotiated and accommodated; but only some interests may be well enough organised or articulated to be included in this process.

To some extent, new processes of accounting for public services have already begun to displace previous systems – in particular, new audit, inspection and regulation regimes intended to oversee the efficiency and quality of services (Power, 1997). As we have already noted, in contrast to the audit and regulation of services that are funded, planned and delivered on a single departmental basis, partnerships create a new need for 'joined-up' evaluation. Moreover, the agencies carrying out such evaluations, and the processes by which these are conducted, do not fit easily into existing hierarchy, market or networked models of governance. They are certainly a system through which state power is being remade and extended in significant directions – while being, at least nominally, at 'arm's length' from central government. Such issues about the remaking of power are central to understanding the new governance, but are often neglected (see Clarke et al, 2000).

Conclusions

Governance issues arise in the context of specific organisational processes and in relation to changing state forms (Clarke and Newman, 1997). New Labour's approach to partnerships can be interpreted as part of a wider shift from direct rule, through integral systems (government and bureaucracy), to indirect control through 'steering' and networked relationships (Rhodes, 1997). Some of the models deployed in these analyses of the shift from government to governance echo (or even prefigure) the Third Way conception, identifying governance networks as the successors to 'hierarchy' and 'markets' (Rhodes, 1997; Stoker, 1997, 2000).

However, our examination of partnerships leads us to two rather different conclusions. The first concerns the lack of 'fit' between the empirical complexity of Third Way partnerships and the formal, abstract model. If partnerships are indeed part of a move towards 'networked governance', then it is a slow, partial and uneven process, in the course of which strange organisational formations are being created – compound models, with contradictory demands and tendencies embedded in them. New Labour's 'compulsory partnerships' exemplify this compound and contradictory outcome – intense central power that directs and reinforces local 'autonomy' and 'working together'. It might be argued that empirical examples will always be more 'untidy' than abstracted models. We would nevertheless suggest that some of the dimensions of this untidiness are so significant that they need to be at the centre of, rather than peripheral to, the analysis. In particular, studying 'partnership' (especially in its Third Way guise) highlights the need to treat compound organisational forms as the norm (rather than empirical aberrations); to look at the articulation of different levels of governance (in particular the changing forms of central control and power); and to register how different pressures and problems lead to divergent governance solutions. Here the shifting arenas of policy, coordination and political calculation produce different, and sometimes contradictory, responses to questions of governing. We therefore conclude that the formalisation of abstract models of governance – hierarchies, markets and networks – may have diverted attention away from more complex, compound and contradictory processes and systems. Indeed, these contradictory effects of partnerships as a mode of governance may be their most interesting feature – practically, politically and analytically.

Second, much of the discussion of new governance arrangements has tended to divert attention away from the state and state power (or, at least, away from the remaking of the state and state power). Where the state is considered, it is typically described as shrinking; surrendering power (to social partners); or being 'hollowed out' by a combination of globalising and localising tendencies (see Rhodes, 1997). In contrast, we think it is worth considering how the changing processes of governance involve the remaking of state power and its extension through new means (see Clarke and Newman, 1997). This perspective enables us to view New Labour's compulsory partnerships as an attempt to recruit *subordinated* partners into the project of 'modernising' government. Such subordinate roles certainly allow some autonomy and initiative in the processes of working together. However, this autonomy is bounded; is circumscribed by central direction and resource control; is subject to surveillance and evaluation; and is vulnerable to termination or takeover. Jessop argues that these processes reflect the state's capacity for meta-governance – establishing forms and relationships of governance through which it attempts to exercise power and influence. Within the complex of new governance mechanisms, the state "reserves to itself the right to open, close, juggle and re-articulate governance arrangements, not only terms of particular functions, but also from the viewpoint of partisan and overall political advantage" (Jessop, 2000, p 19). Both Conservative and Labour governments have shown themselves not just willing to exercise such rights; but have also expanded the repertoire of powers through which such interventions can be accomplished.

From these perspectives, New Labour's partnerships are indeed part of the new governance – but in a more contingent and unstable way than 'networked governance' might imply. Rather, they are another 'juggle' or 're-articulation' (in Jessop's terms) through which the contradictory demands and pressures of governing might be negotiated. They are the product of contradictory impulses, vulnerable and potentially unstable. The challenge of analysing partnerships as part of the new governance is precisely the question of how to understand them as compound, contingent and potentially contradictory sites of power.

References

Amery, J. (2000) 'Interprofessional working in Health Action Zones: how can this be fostered and sustained?', *Journal of Interprofessional Care*, vol 14, no 1, pp 27-30.

Arora, S., Davies, A. and Thompson, S. (2000) 'Developing health improvement programmes: challenges for a new Millennium', *Journal of Interprofessional Care*, vol 14, no 1, pp 9-18.

Audit Commission (1986) *Making a reality of community care*, London: HMSO.

Berman, P., Hunter, D. and McMahon, L. (1990) 'Keep it integrated', *Health Services Journal*, vol 5, pp 996-7.

Blair, T. (1998) *The third way*, London: Fabian Society.

Booth, T. (1981) 'Collaboration between health and social services: a case study of joint care planning', *Policy & Politics*, vol 19, no 1, pp 23-49.

Callaghan, G., Exworthy, M., Hudson, B. and Peckham, S. (2000) 'Prospects for collaboration in primary care: relationships between social services and the new PCGs', *Journal of Interprofessional Care*, vol 14, no 1, pp 19-26.

Charlesworth, J., Clarke, J. and Cochrane, A. (1996) 'Tangled webs? Managing local mixed economies of care', *Public Administration*, vol 74, pp 67-88.

Clarke, J. (1999) 'Whose business is this? The managerialization of social welfare', in D. Banks and M. Purdy (eds) *Health and social exclusion*, London: Routledge.

Clarke, J. (2002: forthcoming) 'Making a difference? Markets and the reform of public services', in E. Schröder and H. Wollman (eds) *The reform of public services in Britain and Germany*, Basingstoke: Macmillan.

Clarke, J. and Newman, J. (1997) *The managerial state: Power, politics and ideology in the remaking of social welfare*, London: Sage Publications.

Clarke, J., Gewirtz, S., Hughes, G. and Humphrey, J. (2000) 'Guarding the public interest? The rise of audit and evaluation', in J. Clarke, S. Gewirtz and E. McLaughlin (eds) *New managerialism, new welfare?*, London: Sage Publications.

Coleman, A. and Glendinning, C. (2001) 'Partnerships', in D. Wilkin, S. Gillam and A. Coleman (eds) *The national tracker survey of primary care groups and trusts 2000/2001: Modernising the NHS?*, Manchester: NPCRDC and London: King's Fund.

Cope, S. and Goodship, J. (1999) 'Regulating collaborative government: towards joined-up government?', *Public Policy and Administration*, vol 14, no 2, pp 3-16.

DETR (Department of the Environment, Transport and the Regions) (1998) *Modern local government: In touch with the people*, Cm 4014, London: The Stationery Office.

DoH (Department of Health) (1989) *Caring for people: Community care in the next decade and beyond*, Cm 849, London: HMSO.

DoH (1990) *Community care in the next decade and beyond: Policy guidance*, London: HMSO.

DoH (1994) *Implementing caring for people: The role of the GP and primary healthcare team*, London: DoH.

DoH (1995) *Joint commissioning for project leaders*, London: HMSO.

DoH (1997a) *Better services for vulnerable people*, EL(97)62/CI(97)24, London: DoH.

DoH (1997b) *Developing partnerships in mental health*, London: The Stationery Office.

DoH (1997c) *The new NHS: Modern, dependable*, Cm 3897, London: The Stationery Office.

DoH (1998a) *Modernising health and social services: National priorities guidance*, London: DoH.

DoH (1998b) *Partnership in action: A discussion document*, London: DoH.

DoH (1999) *Promoting independence: Partnership, prevention and carers grants – conditions and allocations 1999/2000*, LAC (99)13, London: DoH.

DoH (2000) *The NHS plan. A plan for investment: A plan for reform*, Cm 4818-1, London: The Stationery Office.

DoH (2001a) *Care trusts: Emerging framework* (http://www.doh.gov.uk/caretrusts/index.htm), updated 14 March 2001.

DoH (2001b) *Intermediate care, HSC 2001/01*, LAC (2001)1, London: DoH.

DoH (2001c) *National service frameworks: Older people*, London: DoH.

Dunleavy, P. (1995) 'Policy disasters: explaining the UK's record', *Public Policy and Administration*, vol 10, no 2, pp 52-70.

Giddens, T. (1998) *The third way: The renewal of social democracy*, Cambridge: Polity Press.

Glendinning, C. (1998) 'GPs and contracts: bringing general practice into primary care', *Social Policy and Administration*, vol 33, no 2, pp 115-31.

Glendinning, C. (2002) 'Partnerships between health and social services: developing a framework for evaluation', *Policy & Politics*, vol 30, no 1, pp 115-27.

Glendinning, C., Rummery, K. and Clarke, R. (1998) 'From collaboration to commissioning; developing relationships between primary health and social services', *British Medical Journal*, vol 7151, pp 122-5.

Glendinning, C., Coleman, A., Shipman, C. and Malbon, G. (2001) 'Progress in partnerships', *British Medical Journal*, vol 323, pp 28-31.

Hiscock, J. and Pearson, M. (1999) 'Looking inwards, looking outwards: dismantling the "Berlin Wall" between health and social services?', *Social Policy and Administration*, vol 33, no 2, pp 150-63.

Hudson, B. (1998) 'Circumstances change cases; local government and the NHS', *Social Policy and Administration*, vol 32, no 1, pp 71-86.

Hudson, B., Hardy, B., Henwood, M. and Wistow, G. (1997) *Inter-agency collaboration: Final report*, Leeds: Nuffield Institute for Health.

Hudson, B.,Young, R., Hardy, B. and Glendinning, C. (2001) *National evaluation of notifications for use of the section 31 partnership flexibilities of the Health Act 1999: Interim report*, Leeds: Nuffield Institute for Health and Manchester: NPCRDC.

Jessop, B. (2000) 'Governance failure', in G. Stoker (ed) *The new politics of British local governance*, Basingstoke: Macmillan.

Kooiman, J. (ed) (1993) *Modern governance: New government society interactions*, London: Sage Publications.

Kooiman, J. (2000) 'Societal governance: levels, models and orders of social – political interaction', in J. Pierre (ed) *Debating governance:Authority, steering and democracy*, Oxford: Oxford University Press.

Leutz, W. (1999) 'Five laws for integrating medical and social services: lessons from the United States and United Kingdom', *The Millbank Quarterly*, vol 77, no 1, pp 77-110.

Lewis, J. (1999) 'The concepts of community care and primary care in the UK: the 1960s to the 1990s', *Health and Social Care in the Community*, vol 7, no 5, pp 333-41.

Lewis, J. and Glennerster, H. (1996) *Implementing the new community care*, Buckingham: Open University Press.

Ling, T. (2000) 'Unpacking partnerships: the case of healthcare', in J. Clarke, S. Gewirtz and E. McLaughlin (eds) *New managerialism, new welfare?*, London: Sage Publications.

Mohan, J. (1999) 'So what's new? Some methodological questions in the analysis of change in social policy', Paper presented to ESRC seminar on the Third Way in Public Services, London, 22 April.

Myles, S.,Wyke, S., Popay, J., Scott, J., Campbell, A. and Girling, J. (1998) *Total purchasing and community and continuing care: Lessons for future policy development in the NHS*, London: King's Fund.

Newman, J. (2000) 'Beyond the new public management? Modernising public services', in J. Clarke, S. Gewirtz and E. McLaughlin (eds) *New managerialism, new welfare?*, London: Sage Publications.

Newman, J. (2001) *Modernising governance: New Labour, policy and society*, London: Sage Publications.

Nocon, A. (1994) *Collaboration in community care*, Sunderland: Business Education Publishers.

Paton, C. (1999) 'New Labour's health policy', in M. Powell (ed) *New Labour, new welfare state?:The 'third way' in British social policy*, Bristol:The Policy Press.

Pierre, J. (ed) (2000) *Debating governance:Authority, steering and democracy*, Oxford: Oxford University Press.

Pollitt, C. (1995) 'Justification by works or by faith?', *Evaluation*, vol 1, no 2, pp 133-54.

Power, M. (1997) *The Audit Society*, London: Oxford University Press.

Poxton, R. (1999) *Partnerships in primary and social care*, London: Kings Fund.

Rhodes, R. (1997) *Understanding governance*, Buckingham: Open University Press.

Rhodes, R. (2000) *The governance narrative: Key findings and lessons from the ESRC's Whitehall programme*, London: Public Management and Policy Association.

Richardson, S. and Pearson, M. (1995) 'Dignity and aspirations denied: unmet health and social care needs in an inner city area', *Health and Social Care in the Community*, vol 3, no 5, pp 279-87.

Rummery, K. and Glendinning, C. (2000) *Primary care and social services: Developing new partnerships for older people*, Oxford: Radcliffe Medical Press.

Skelcher, C. (1998) *The appointed state*, Buckingham: Open University Press.

Stewart, J. (1993) *Accountability to the public*, London: European Policy Forum.

Stoker, G. (ed) (1997) *The new management of British local governance*, Basingstoke: Macmillan.

Stoker, G. (ed) (2000) *The new politics of British local governance*, Basingstoke: Macmillan.

Titmuss, R.M. (1968) *Commitment to welfare*, London: Allen and Unwin.

Walker, A. (ed) (1982) *Community care: The family, the state and social policy*, Oxford: Blackwell and Robertson.

Wilkin, D., Gillam, S. and Smith, K. (2001) 'Tackling organisational change in the NHS', *British Medical Journal*, vol 322, 16 June, pp 1464-7.

Wistow, G. and Brookes, T. (eds) (1998) *Joint planning and joint management*, London: Royal Institute of Public Affairs.

Wistow, G. and Hardy, B. (1996) 'Competition, collaboration and markets', *Journal of Interprofessional Care*, vol 10, no 1, pp 5-10.

FOUR

What is a 'successful' partnership and how can it be measured?

Bob Hudson and Brian Hardy

Introduction

'Partnership' and 'modernisation' were the leitmotifs running throughout the policy pronouncements of the first Blair government – across all service areas and sectors of the economy. 'Partnership' was acknowledged by one government minister as "one of those nice feely words beloved by politicians" (Boateng, 1999). In an effort to give a harder edge to what might otherwise be regarded as a rather woolly concept (together with its close cousin 'joined-up government'), complexity theory was invoked to underline the need to see public services, in particular, as dealing with systemic 'wicked' issues; that is, problems spanning, rather than coinciding with, organisational and professional boundaries (Cabinet Office, 2001). This acknowledgement of problem and policy interdependence, together with the rejection of the competition inherent in markets, spawned the attendant New Labour lexicon of partnership, collaboration, coordination, joined-up government and – in the case of health and social care – integrated ('seamless') service planning, management and delivery. Moreover, the rhetoric was of promoting vertical partnerships (between centre and periphery or between local agencies and communities and publics), as well as horizontal partnerships across local organisations responsible for service commissioning and delivery.

In the latter context, the 1997 White Paper, *The new NHS: Modern, dependable* (DoH, 1997), set out what was described as the newly elected government's 'Third Way' of running the NHS. Adopting this Third Way of partnership constituted an explicit rejection of the "old centralised command and control systems of the 1970s" and the "divisive internal market system of the 1990s" (para 2.1). The new government was withering in its criticism of the latter:

> A misconceived attempt to tackle the pressures facing the NHS. It has been an obstacle to the necessary modernisation of the health service. It created more problems than it solved. That is why the government is abolishing it. (DoH, 1997, para 2.9)

In his foreword to the White Paper, the Prime Minister described it as "a turning point for the NHS. It replaces the internal market with integrated care". Much of the early debate in pursuit of this goal was around the 'Berlin Wall' between the NHS and social services; in response to this specific interface, the 1999 Health Act (Section 31) sought to sweep away legal obstacles to closer joint working by permitting three new 'flexibilities' – lead commissioning, pooled (unified) budgets and integrated provision. Within a short period of time, then, the emphasis had shifted from a debate on the *desirability* of partnership working to a more specific focus upon *how* this might be achieved.

In its more recent NHS Plan for England (DoH, 2000b), the government said it was anxious to foster local partnerships widely within, but also widely beyond, the statutory sector. It spoke of rectifying long-standing 'fault lines' – introduced at the inception of the NHS in 1948 – between healthcare and social care and between public sector healthcare (in the NHS) and private and voluntary sector healthcare:

> For decades there has been a stand-off between the NHS and private sector
> providers of health care. This has to end. Ideological boundaries or institutional
> boundaries should not stand in the way of better care for NHS patients. (DoH,
> 2000b, para 11.2)

The Plan referred to the intention to formalise an agreement with the independent sector (private, for-profit, and voluntary not-for-profit providers). This was published three months later in the form of a *concordat* between the government (in respect of patients in England) and the Independent Healthcare Association (DoH, 2000a).

Interestingly, the Welsh equivalent of the NHS Plan, *Improving health in Wales: A plan for the NHS with its partners* (Welsh Assembly, 2001), in some respects – notably its stress on partnership, joined-up planning and service delivery via integrated, seamless care – mirrors those in England and Scotland. The expressed need is for a culture of partnership and openness to working across boundaries; for collaboration; and for the development of multi-disciplinary, cross-agency and cross-sectoral networks. What is different, however, is the extent and nature of this partnership. In neither Scotland or Wales is there the same espousal of partnership with the private sector – or any formal concordats expressing such partnership.

In a recent report on strengthening public health policies and practice, the government's Chief Medical Officer (in England) referred to the development of partnership working as "a mainstream activity for local government and the NHS" (DoH, 2001, para 1.5). He also stated, bluntly, that: "There is a sufficiently robust body of research to enable the success criteria for effective partnerships to be identified" (DoH, 2001, para 5.2).

This chapter sets out success (and failure) criteria based on extensive empirical research carried out over two decades, principally in the fields of health and social care. We have distilled these criteria into six so-called partnership principles. Although developed – and, it is important to stress, field-tested and validated – in one particular context, these are generic principles that are applicable across a range of contexts and not confined to public sector partnerships. A working tool – the Partnership Assessment Tool (Hardy et al, 2000) – was developed and field-tested in five pilot studies; these encompassed partnerships at different stages of development, with differing levels of seniority and pursuing a range of purposes. They included a shadow Primary Care Group Board; a Health Community Executive Group; a Mental Health Commissioning Group; and two Drug Action Teams.

Principle 1: Acknowledgement of the need for partnership

This principle is concerned with two main factors: the extent to which there is a partnership history; and the extent to which there is recognition of the need to work in partnership. These factors are obviously related, in that a strong local history of partnership working should reflect an understanding of the need to work in this manner; while a weak history of partnership working may reflect an insufficient appreciation of the extent to which agencies depend upon one another to achieve organisational goals. Without such an appreciation, genuine partnership working will be unlikely to develop (Hudson, 1987; Huxham and Macdonald, 1992).

The extent to which local agencies have a prior record of successful partnership working has been identified as a crucial determinant of the scale and pace of their future achievements – in short, 'success breeds success' (Callaghan et al, 2000). This does not mean that organisations with limited histories of working together cannot reach the levels attained by more mature partnership networks. However, to begin to do so, there needs to be a mutual awareness of what has been achieved jointly. Those organisations with more substantial joint achievements will also need to be confident that these have been of demonstrable benefit and worthy of further development.

However, partnership working is rarely straightforward. Sometimes the barriers to working together effectively turn out to be too formidable and, even where some measure of success *is* achieved, some barriers to partnership are more difficult to overcome than others. To develop more sustainable relationships, it is important that the nature and extent of any such barrier is identified and steps are taken to minimise their influence. As with the principal factors associated with success, these barriers might be both external to the locality and/or internal to it. Several categories of barrier can be distinguished (see Figure 4.1; also Hardy et al, 1992).

A prerequisite of partnership working is that potential partners have an appreciation of their interdependencies; without this appreciation, collaborative problem-solving makes no sense. If there is objectively no such interdependence, then there is no need to work together. If there *is* some perceived interdependence, but this is insufficiently acknowledged or inadequately understood, then further understanding needs to be acquired before any further partnership development can take place (Gray, 1985; Alter and Hage, 1993). However, not all of an organisation's activities will necessarily require a

Figure 4.1: Five categories of barriers to coordination

Structural
* fragmentation of service responsibilities across agency boundaries, both within and between sectors;
* inter-organisational complexity;
* non-coterminosity of boundaries;
* competition-based systems of governance.

Procedural
* differences in planning horizons and cycles;
* differences in accountability arrangements;
* differences in information systems and protocols regarding access and confidentiality.

Financial
* differences in budgetary cycles and accounting procedures;
* differences in funding mechanisms and bases;
* differences in the stocks and flows of financial resources.

Professional/cultural
* differences in ideologies and values;
* professional self-interest and autonomy;
* inter-professional domain dissensus;
* threats to job security;
* conflicting views about user interests and roles.

Status and legitimacy
* organisational self-interest and autonomy;
* inter-organisational domain dissensus;
* differences in legitimacy between elected and appointed agencies.

---

contribution from a partner in order to be effectively undertaken. The notions of 'domain dissensus and consensus' (Thompson, 1967; Braito et al, 1972) are reminders that organisations will normally have some 'core business' which they would expect to undertake with little or no reference to other partners. This claim to a special 'domain' can be accepted by other agencies and carries with it an acknowledged legitimacy to operate in a certain field of activity and define proper practices within this field. It is important that these parameters are understood and accepted in partnership working, otherwise there is the danger of one agency stepping into the domain of another in a manner that is perceived as threatening or offensive (Braito et al, 1972).

Principle 2: Clarity and realism of purpose

Most approaches to partnership working take it for granted that an explicit statement of shared vision, based on jointly held values, is a prerequisite for success (Mattesich and Monsey, 1992). There may be some scope for deciding whether these conditions need to be in place at the outset of a partnership, or whether they can be developed and refined as work proceeds. It has been normal practice for some years for agencies to attempt to identify the values and principles upon which their service developments are based. Even though these are often expressed in high levels of generality, they give some initial indication of the extent to which separate agencies have sufficient in common to sustain a long-term relationship (Cropper, 1995). At this point, the values and principles may not need to be too explicit and detailed. Indeed, it may be that, as a starting point, a broad vision is more likely to generate movement than a detailed blueprint (Nocon, 1989; Pettigrew et al, 1992). Where there are clear differences of values, principles or perspectives, these will need to be addressed as a precursor to partnership development.

Once values and principles are agreed, parties need to define more specific aims and objectives. Although some ambiguity may initially help to generate commitment where greater clarity would be too threatening, these aims nevertheless need to be clear enough for all partners to be confident of their meaning; goals that lack such clarity will diminish enthusiasm and commitment. Collaboration at this point serves several purposes: providing a source of identity around which agencies can cohere; helping to clarify boundaries and commitments; defining more clearly the scale and scope of joint work; and providing a framework for the regulation of joint arrangements (Cropper, 1995). However, in human services partnerships, there is an additional task. Traditionally, aims and objectives have been expressed in terms of service inputs or service outputs, rather than being articulated as outcomes for service users. The central issue to establish now is in what ways it is anticipated partnership working will lead to an enhanced quality of life for users of services and their carers.

Aims and objectives that are not realistically capable of attainment will soon diminish commitments to partnership. The notion of collaborative capacity is relevant here; it refers to the level and degree of activity a partnership arrangement is able to sustain without any partner losing commitment. Collaborative capacity is related not only to the tangible resources (such as funding), which are central to collaboration, but also to less tangible resources, such as status or autonomy. Demands can both exceed and fall short of thresholds of capacity. An underestimate of collaborative capacity can mean that a committed collaborative effort is confined to marginal tasks, while an overestimate can lead to unrealistic expectations of what can be achieved and within what timescale. Making an accurate judgement on where to strike the balance may be difficult, especially in new partnerships. In such circumstances there will be a degree of 'learning by doing', as relationships and approaches develop (Hudson et al, 1999).

Partnership is likely to be particularly fragile in the early stages, if only because it may imply a threat to existing boundaries and practices – whether organisational, professional or individual. Embryonic partnerships, therefore, need to be alert to threats to their progress and to acknowledge that change will not be accomplished quickly or simply (Hardy et al, 1992; Lowndes, 1997). In the face of this long-term task, it is beneficial to identify 'quick' or 'small' wins. The issues most conducive to a 'quick win' will be those areas of interdependence that have already been identified. However, it is also important to relate any such 'small wins' to potential 'big wins'. A 'big win' is a major gain that may reflect the scale of the task or the scope of planning activity, but may also be one that is accomplished in the face of substantial opposition. A 'small win', on the other hand, rarely involves substantial risk. Nevertheless, it still needs to be informed by a sense of strategic direction and, through a series of small wins, can add up to a 'big win' over time. This is the notion of think big and act small (Bryson, 1988).

Principle 3: Commitment and ownership

Partnership working cannot be guaranteed to be characterised by either spontaneous growth or self-perpetuation; therefore the understandings and agreements developed through the first two principles will need to be supported and reinforced. This third principle is concerned with the ways in which this can be done. It is concerned with issues of leadership, ownership, entrepreneurship and institutionalisation. The research evidence suggests that an organisational commitment to partnership working is more likely to be sustained where there is individual commitment to the venture from the most senior levels of the respective organisations. Without this, it is possible that the efforts of partnership enthusiasts holding middle and lower-level positions will become marginalised and perceived as unrelated to the 'real' core business of each separate agency. Ideally, this senior inter-agency commitment will reflect, or develop into, personal connections between key decision makers, thereby helping to cement a culture of trust (Rhodes, 1988; Marsh and Rhodes, 1992).

Commitment, at whatever level in an organisation, also needs to be consistent – and visibly so. This is part of the process of building a sustainable relationship that will have an enduring presence. Where there are inconsistent attitudes towards partnership working – for example, involving unilateral action to change or withdraw from joint agreements – short- and long-term consequences can be considerable. In the short term, the specific partnership venture will be at risk; but more significantly, a longer-term view may develop that partnership working must be of marginal concern if it is at risk from peremptory actions and behaviour that threaten to undermine rather than foster joint commitment.

The need for seniority of commitment does not imply that wider ownership is any less significant. A well-developed strategy on partnership will count for little unless links are made between the macro and micro levels of organisational activities. In particular, operational staff often possess the capacity to 'make or break' shared arrangements, in that they have considerable contact with outside bodies and often enjoy discretionary powers and considerable day-to-day autonomy from their managers (Lipsky, 1980). Inter-professional work implies a willingness to share, and even cede, exclusive claims to specialised knowledge and authority and a willingness to integrate procedures (see Chapter Five). Since this may often be seen as a professional threat, there need to be incentives for operational staff to work with each other across traditional boundaries (Goodman and Dean, 1982; Carrier and Kendall, 1995).

There are many references to the importance in collaborative working of individuals who are skilled at mapping and developing inter-personal policy networks across agencies – sometimes described as 'reticulists' (Friend et al, 1974; Challis et al, 1988). The characteristics that best underpin the skills and legitimacy of such 'networkers' have not been widely researched, but they include both technical or competency-based factors, as well as social and inter-personal skills. The characteristics of successful 'networkers' include: being perceived as having sufficient legitimacy to assume the role; being perceived as unbiased and able to manage multiple points of view; having a sense of the critical issues and first steps that need to be taken; and having political skills that can encourage others to take risks (McCann and Gray, 1986; Wistow and Whittingham, 1988).

A key feature of networks is that they address the way cooperation and trust are formed and maintained (Frances et al, 1991; Powell, 1991). In contrast to other modes of governance, such as markets or hierarchies, coordination in networks is achieved through less formal and more egalitarian means. Such a description may apply to the activities of 'reticulists', but may also characterise wider ways of working between organisations. The problem with such networks is that they can become heavily dependent upon the continued presence of a small number of key individuals, whose departure can threaten the network's continued existence. The link between the unplanned movement of key personnel and the draining of energy, purpose, commitment and action from major change processes has been established from a range of studies. It is accordingly important that the means are developed to embed the achievements of individual entrepreneurs into more formalised inter-agency networks.

Not all organisations willingly engage in partnership working on a voluntary basis. As noted earlier, collaboration may have few or no qualities of spontaneous growth. In such situations, it may be necessary to devise ways of encouraging reluctant agencies into partnership, through the use of either sanctions or rewards. Although this approach is normally associated with central government – what Paton (1998) refers to as 'statutory voluntarism' – it may also be adapted to a local setting (Benson, 1975).

Principle 4: Development and maintenance of trust

This is simultaneously the most self-evident and the most elusive of the principles that underpin successful partnership working (Luhmann, 1979; Gambetta, 1988). Although joint working is possible with little trust between those involved, the development and maintenance of trust is the basis for the closest, most enduring and most successful partnerships. At whatever level – organisational, professional or individual – the more trust there is, the better will be the chances for a successful partnership. Needless to say, the history of joint working in many policy areas is often characterised by territorial disputes about roles and remits, by claims to exclusive professional competence, or by defensiveness about resources – all of which preclude the development of trust. Trust is, of course, hard won and easily lost, which means that the maintenance of trust is an endless and reciprocal task (Barber, 1983).

The evidence (Hudson et al, 1997) shows that partnerships work best where each partner is perceived – collectively and individually – to have an equivalent status, irrespective of some having more of some resources than others. The resources that each brings may be different and not always readily quantifiable. For example, voluntary organisations may bring information (about service need or successful service provision); experience and expertise; or legitimacy, through their representation of particular user groups. Ensuring equivalent status means ensuring that the partnership avoids having 'senior' and 'junior' partners or 'core' and 'peripheral' groups; if some partners feel marginalised from the partnership's core business, suspicion, erosion of trust and lessening of commitment will result. Ensuring equivalent status also means ensuring fairness in the conduct of a partnership. This entails creating the opportunity for each partner to contribute as much as they wish and in a manner that is appropriate. It means avoiding allowing one or two partners always to set the agenda or define the language for partnership working (Cropper, 1995). Historically, much partnership working has faltered because, for example, one of the principal statutory authorities has, without discussion, hosted and chaired meetings at times and places of its convenience; it has also sought to dictate agendas, priorities and timescales. Clearly much of this is inevitable where one partner has been given a statutory duty to be the 'lead' in some particular area. It is not a question of ignoring such lead responsibilities but merely of being sensitive to the needs and expectations of all partners and, where appropriate and possible, sharing lead responsibilities.

Fairness in the conduct of a partnership also, importantly, encompasses the behaviour of the partners. For example, in northern England, Barnsley Partnership in Action group – a group comprising statutory agencies, service users, carers and independent sector providers – has produced an agreed set of 'Rules of Behaviour'. The stated purpose is to ensure that all meetings and processes are conducted according to a set of values and ways of behaving. There are five values: openness and honesty; participation and equality; open to challenge; fairness; and accountability. Openness and honesty refers to the 'shared responsibility to ensure that all are able to express opinions in safety' (Barnsley MBC, 2001). Fairness means that "all must ensure that everyone involved has an equal voice by whatever means are appropriate". The rules for behaviour are couched, not as a hope, but as an expectation against which all meetings and processes "will be routinely measured". They comprise the following:

> ... respect and accept other people's contribution, even if you disagree; listen, you may learn something; be patient, recognise and accept differences in people's ability to communicate; use clear, simple English; make sure that everyone has the support they need in order to contribute fully: explain processes clearly; recognise and record minority views. (Barnsley MBC, 2001, p 1)

These explicit rules are designed – and prominently displayed – as a means of holding all partners to account for the ways in which they conduct partnership working. For service users and carers in particular, they are seen as an important means of building and maintaining trust.

Although each partner 'signs up' to collective aims and objectives, partners may also aim to secure some benefits of their own. The latter should be transparent, as should the benefits that accrue to individual partners from their collective efforts. Fairness here also means some sharing of such benefits; those accruing to one partner should neither be disproportionate nor unduly at the expense of another (Levine and White, 1961; Benson, 1975). However, partnerships cannot uniformly bring about 'win–win' solutions for all. On the contrary, the health of any partnership could be measured in terms of the 'sacrifice' that one partner is prepared to make for the collective good; that is, the willingness to subsume self-interest to general interest. The mutual acknowledgement and acceptance of such 'altruism' helps to build trust and cement partnership. In practice, altruistic (public-interested) and selfish (self-interested) behaviour coexists in most partnership working.

Although an apparent platitude, the importance of having the right person in the right place at the right time is one of the consistent messages from all studies of inter-agency and inter-professional working (Hardy et al, 1992). Equally, the obverse is to be avoided – having the wrong people in the wrong place at the wrong time. The research evidence confirms the destructive capacity of the 'wrong' people (those committed solely to the pursuit of organisational or professional self-interest) or being in the wrong place; and the importance to joint working of partnership 'champions' who can work in the broader public interest. Having the right people involved in this way is a question of careful selection, the exercise of peer pressure and strong performance management. It is also, of course, partly a question of luck.

While those involved in a particular partnership may develop effectively as a team in pursuit of collective aims and objectives, areas of tension and mistrust can remain elsewhere within their parent organisations. Partnerships need to recognise and address such tensions by being open and honest about their existence. One approach is for the partnership to publicise its success and demonstrate that wider difficulties, whatever their size and significance, need not defeat or adversely affect all local collaboration.

Principle 5: Establishment of clear and robust partnership arrangements

This principle refers to the need to ensure that partnership working is not hindered by unduly cumbersome, elaborate and time-consuming working arrangements. Overly complex structures and processes merely reflect partners' defensiveness about their own interests and uncertainty about degrees of mutual trust. The result of such excessive bureaucracy is frustration among the partners and a sapping of their enthusiasm for, and commitment to, the partnership (Huxham and Vangen, 1994). This is doubly so where, as has often been the case, partnership working is seen as peripheral rather than core business. Partnership working arrangements should therefore be as unambiguous and straightforward as possible. This means ensuring that, in the light of what each partner is bringing to the partnership, it is clear what they are responsible for doing and how they are accountable. The other essential requirement is that the partnership's main focus is on processes and outcomes, rather than structure and inputs; whatever structures are created should therefore be time-limited and task-oriented rather than unfocused.

Partnerships often founder because partners labour under some misapprehension about the financial resources – both capital and revenue – each is bringing to the table. These resources need to be spelt out for a number of reasons. First, there may be uncertainty about how much is devoted by each partner to a specific field of activity – a typical example is the difficulty in the NHS of identifying expenditure on older people. Second, there may be restrictions imposed upon partners by their 'parent' organisations about the use of resources. Finally, there needs to be an understanding of the stability associated with each other's resources and an appreciation that partnerships may have to cope with reductions in previously agreed resource levels. In some respects, this mirrors the principles of clarity of purpose and expectation – not just what people or organisations expect to get from the partnership, but also what they are financially able to contribute to it.

Resources also include other potential partnership assets. Some of these will be tangible, for instance human resources, facilities or services such as information technology. Others are less tangible, such as knowledge, experience, power and legitimacy. Community groups, for example, are likely to have few tangible resources, but their involvement can confer a local legitimacy that would otherwise be lacking. Conversely, the involvement in a partnership of a directly elected body can serve to counterbalance concerns about a 'democratic deficit'.

Significant difficulties can arise when partnerships begin to implement jointly agreed plans, if there has been insufficient clarity about the respective responsibilities of individual partners. First, each partner needs to be clear about – and accept – such divisions of responsibility, whether for areas of funding, staffing or service delivery. Second, each partner needs to recognise any potential conflicts arising from dual accountability. A good example currently is social services representation on English Primary Care Groups and Trusts (PCG/Ts). As employees of the local authority, these representatives are individually accountable for their actions to their employers; but as members of the PCG/T, they are collectively accountable to the health authority. Without clear delineations of responsibility and accountability, there is potential for confusion and mistrust. Partners need to be able, on the one hand, to show each other that they are doing their fair share; on the other hand, they also need to be able to show those within their parent organisation that they haven't 'given away' too much, or 'sold out' and 'gone native'.

There is also a clear need to ensure that the size and complexity of partnership arrangements are commensurate with the identified partnership remit. Many partnership schemes in the fields of health and social care have been overly bureaucratic. This reflects partly relatively low levels of trust between agencies and partly the caution with which partnership has been approached, as it represents some sort of defence against 'giving too much away'. Such caution or pessimism has frequently manifested itself in joint arrangements that are unduly complex, cumbersome or restrictive.

Similarly, it is important to develop structures that are time-limited and task-oriented. The history of joint working in health and social care has been of joint structures that often took a long time to produce very little and, in the process, served only to sap partners' enthusiasm (Hardy et al, 1989). Where joint arrangements worked best, they were typified by joint committees or teams that had a clearly defined task to be completed within a clearly defined period of time. Such concentration of effort is a maxim that can be applied to single-agency working; however, it is even more important in the case of partnership working because the scope for lack of focus is inherently greater when several partners are involved and also because partnership working is often peripheral to individuals' day-to-day working within their parent organisations.

Principle 6: Monitoring, review and organisational learning

This principle refers to the reflective and reflexive elements of partnership working. This review function is, of course, an integral part of any single-agency planning and management process. However, again it is even more important in partnership working, where there may be doubts about levels of commitment or about the costs and benefits to individual partners. The latter is especially the case if the partnership is seen by some as non-core business. Monitoring, reviewing and learning is, therefore, an essential part not just of assessing performance but also of the process to help cement commitment and trust.

Success criteria need to be agreed and made explicit, both for the service aims and objectives and for the partnership itself. As indicated above, service aims and objectives may be successfully achieved, but perhaps ultimately at the cost of a fractured partnership. Conversely, service aims and objectives may have yet to be achieved, despite significant benefits in terms of joint working between the partners; the latter might include improved understanding of a partner agency's resource constraints, better knowledge of constitutional/legal obstacles, or greater levels of trust.

The history of partnership working in the health and social care field is a fairly melancholy one. Examples of successful joint working can be found, but they are not commonplace. 'Success' therefore tends to denote the overcoming of historic barriers and a breaking down of the traditional mistrust surrounding inter-organisational and inter-professional relations. All too often there is some scepticism – among partnership members and parent organisations – about the extent to which the benefits of collaborative working exceed the costs to individual partners. It is, therefore, important to monitor the extent to which collectively agreed aims and objectives are being met and, where necessary, to revise these aims. It is not just a straightforward closing of the management and planning cycle; it is an important element of continuous feedback and, thereby, of organisational learning.

Just as important as examining whether the service aims and objectives of the partnership are being achieved is reviewing how well the partnership itself is working. Even if jointly agreed service aims and objectives are being successfully met, it is important to reflect on how far this is due to the partnership; whether (counterfactually) they would have been achieved irrespective of the partnership; or, indeed, whether they have been achieved only at some cost to individual partnership members, which in the longer term may be disproportionate and unsustainable.

The research evidence shows that partnership schemes have often existed on the periphery of organisations – as atypical initiatives at their respective boundaries (Hardy et al, 1992). One consequence is that the learning from such joint working – whether of success or failure – is seldom systematically fed back to the organisational heartland, or disseminated among other services or across other functions and geographical areas. Without such evaluation taking place, these same lessons are seldom used to inform other partnerships working elsewhere. Moreover, publicising local success can remove the 'fig leaf' from those who would argue that partnership working is inherently problematic and often impossible. It is a way of demonstrating that the barriers can be overcome.

A reconsideration and revision of partnership aims, objectives and arrangements could be described as the logical 'last step' in this audit/assessment cycle, but this element could equally be seen as its starting point. Reconsideration need not lead to revision or refinement of aims, objectives or arrangements, but it does provide an opportunity for recognising, for example, previous overambition or lack of ambition, lack of commitment, or structures and processes that marginalise rather than involve partners appropriately.

Conclusions

Such was the plethora of partnership initiatives by the 1997-2001 Labour administration that the government itself instituted a review to rationalise their formation and development (HM Treasury, 2000). The scope and range of partnerships (both vertical and horizontal) provides a fertile environment for examining the effects of such working in terms of what, in effect, are second-order outcomes (perceived changes to inter-sectoral, inter-organisational, inter-governmental, inter-professional working) and what are, by contrast, first-order outcomes – that is, better-coordinated, better-integrated (more 'joined-up') services delivered to end users with some optimum ratio between quality and cost.

The success criteria outlined here derive from an extensive and extensively validated research base. Although developed in one service and policy context, they are generic partnership principles, which provide an analytical framework for examining partnership working in other contexts. The danger is that, in the process of distillation, they are reduced to the platitudinous and self-evident;

and that, like 'partnership' itself, they comprise warm words with which it is hard to disagree. The research evidence, however, is that even if adherence to such principles does not itself guarantee successful partnership, ignoring them is likely to hinder or undermine partnership working.

References

Alter, C. and Hage, J. (1993) *Organisations working together*, Thousand Oaks, CA: Sage Publications.

Barber, B. (1983) *The logic and limits of trust*, New Brunswick, NJ: Rutgers University Press.

Barnsley MBC (Barnsley Metropolitan Borough Council) (2001) *Barnsley partnership in action rules of behaviour*, Barnsley: Barnsley MBC.

Benson, J.K. (1975) 'The inter-organisational network as a political economy', *Administrative Science Quarterly*, vol 20, June, pp 229-49.

Boateng, P. (1999) *Speech to National Association of Councils for Voluntary Service*, September 1999, London: Home Office.

Braito, R., Paulson, C. and Klongon, G. (1972) 'Domain consensus: a key variable in inter-organisational analysis', in M. Brinkerhoff and P. Kunz (eds) *Complex organisations and their environment*, Dubuque: Wm.C. Brown.

Bryson, J. (1988) 'Strategic planning: big wins and small wins', *Public Money and Management*, autumn, pp 11-15.

Cabinet Office (2001) *Strengthening leadership in the public sector*, A research study by the Performance and Innovation Unit, London: Cabinet Office.

Callaghan, G., Exworthy, M., Hudson, B. and Peckham, S. (2000) 'Prospects for collaboration in primary care: relationships between social services and the new PCGs', *Journal of Interprofessional Care*, vol 14, no 1, pp 19-26.

Carrier, J. and Kendall, I. (1995) 'Professionalism and inter-professionalism in health and community care: some theoretical issues', in P. Owens, J. Carrier and J. Horder (eds) *Interprofessional issues in community and primary health care*, Basingstoke: Macmillan.

Challis, L., Fuller, S., Henwood, M., Klein, R., Plowden, W., Webb, A., Whittingham, P. and Wistow, G. (1988) *Joint approaches to social policy: Rationality and practice*, Cambridge: Cambridge University Press.

Cropper, S. (1995) 'Collaborative working and the issue of sustainability', in C. Huxham (ed) *Creating collaborative advantage*, London: Sage Publications.

DoH (Department of Health) (1997) *The new NHS: Modern, dependable*, London: The Stationery Office.

DoH (2000a) *For the benefit of patients: A concordat between the Department of Health and the Independent Healthcare Association*, London: The Stationery Office.

DoH (2000b) *The NHS plan: A plan for investment, a plan for reform*, Cm 4818-1, London: The Stationery Office.

DoH (2001) *The report of the Chief Medical Officer's project to strengthen the public health function*, London: DoH.

Frances, J., Levacic, R., Mitchell, J. and Thompson, G. (1991) 'Introduction', in G. Thompson, J. Frances, R. Levacic and J. Mitchell *Markets, hierarchies and networks: The coordination of social life*, London: Sage Publications.

Friend, J., Power, J. and Yewlett, C. (1974) *Public planning: The inter-corporate dimension*, London: Tavistock.

Gambetta, D. (1988) 'Can we trust?', in D. Gambetta (ed) *Trust*, Oxford: Blackwell.

Goodman, P.S. and Dean, J.W. (1982) 'Creating long-term organisational change', in P.S. Goodman (ed) *Change in organisations*, San Francisco, CA: Jossey Bass.

Gray, B. (1985) 'Conditions facilitating inter-organisational collaboration', *Human Relations*, vol 38, no 10, pp 911-36.

Hardy, B., Webb, A., Turrel, A. and Wistow, G. (1989) *Collaboration and cost-effectiveness: Final report to Department of Health*, Loughborough: Centre for Research in Social Policy.

Hardy, B., Turrell, A. and Wistow, G. (1992) *Innovations in community care management*, Aldershot: Avebury.

Hardy, B., Hudson, B. and Waddington, E. (2000) *What makes a good partnership? A partnership assessment tool*, Leeds: Nuffield Institute for Health/NHS Executive Trent Region.

HM Treasury (2000) *Prudent for a purpose: Building opportunity for all. 2000 spending review: New public spending plans 2001-2004*, Cm 4807, London: The Stationery Office.

Hudson, B. (1987) 'Collaboration in social welfare: a framework for analysis', *Policy & Politics*, vol 15, no 3, pp 175-82.

Hudson, B., Hardy, B., Henwood, M. and Wistow, G. (1997) *Inter-agency collaboration: Final report*, Leeds: Nuffield Institute for Health.

Hudson, B., Hardy, B., Henwood, M. and Wistow, G. (1999) 'In pursuit of inter-agency collaboration in the public sector: what is the contribution of theory and research?', *Public Management*, vol 1, no 2, pp 235-60.

Huxham, C. and Macdonald, D. (1992) 'Introducing collaborative advantage', *Management Decision*, vol 30, no 3, pp 50-6.

Huxham, C. and Vangen, S. (1994) *Naivety and maturity, inertia and fatigue: Are working relationships between public organisations doomed to fail?*, Strathclyde: Department of Management Science, University of Strathclyde.

Levine, S. and White, P. (1961) 'Exchange as a conceptual framework for the study of inter-organisational relationships', *Administrative Science Quarterly*, vol 5, December, pp 583-601.

Lipsky, M. (1980) *Street-level bureaucracy*, New York, NY: Russell Sage Foundation.

Lowndes, V. (1997) 'We are learning to accommodate mess: four propositions about management change in local governance', *Public Policy and Administration*, vol 12, no 2, pp 80-94.

Luhmann, C. (1979) *Trust and power*, Chichester: Wiley.

Marsh, D. and Rhodes, R.A.W. (eds) (1992) *Policy networks in British government*, Oxford: Clarendon Press.

Mattesich, P. and Monsey, B. (1992) *Collaboration: What makes it work?*, St Paul, Minnesota: Amherst H. Wilder Foundation.

McCann, J. and Gray, B. (1986) 'Power and collaboration in human service domains', *International Journal of Sociology and Social Policy*, vol 6, pp 58-67.

Nocon, A. (1989) 'Forms of ignorance and their role in the joint planning process', *Social Policy and Administration*, vol 23, no 1, pp 31-47.

Paton, C. (1999) 'New Labour's health policy: the new healthcare state', in M. Powell (ed) *New Labour, new welfare state?: The 'third way' in British social policy*, Bristol: The Policy Press, pp 51-75.

Pettigrew, A., Ferlie, E. and McKee, L. (1992) *Shaping strategic change*, London: Sage Publications.

Powell, W. (1991) 'Neither market nor hierarchy: network forms of organisation', in G. Thompson, J. Frances, R. Levacic and J. Mitchell, *Markets, hierarchies and networks: The coordination of social life*, London: Sage Publications.

Rhodes, R.A.W. (1988) *Beyond Westminster and Whitehall: The sub-central governments of Britain*, London: Unwin Hyman.

Thompson, J.D. (1967) *Organisations in action*, New York, NY: McGraw-Hill.

Welsh Assembly (2001) *Improving health in Wales: A plan for the NHS with its partners*, Cardiff: National Assembly for Wales.

Wistow, G. and Whittingham, P. (1988) 'Policy and research into practice', in D. Stockford (ed) *Integrating care provision: Practical perspectives*, London: Longman.

FIVE

Partnership at the front-line: the WellFamily service and primary care

Karen Clarke and Kirstein Rummery

Introduction

Most of the partnerships discussed in this book are relationships between organisations. One aim of such partnerships is to move towards the integration of the different services provided by each organisation in order to achieve more holistic and coordinated services for users. Achieving this integration often involves new, closer ways of working between different professionals, for example, through the creation of multi-professional teams. Different interpretations of teamworking and membership have important implications for the kinds of services that are delivered and the degree of service integration that can be achieved. The way in which partnership between organisations is played out in inter-professional relationships can therefore be of critical importance to the nature of the service integration that is achieved.

This chapter explores inter-professional partnerships between primary healthcare and social care in front-line service delivery, through an analysis of the WellFamily service. This service involves a partnership between NHS primary healthcare services and a voluntary organisation, the Family Welfare Association (FWA), with the aim of responding adequately and in a more integrated way to health and social care needs than traditional statutory services. For the WellFamily workers, the practice of partnership required their membership of the primary health care team (PHCT), in order to provide an integrated service that could meet users' combined health and social needs. We examine the different meanings given to the concept of the 'team' by the various professionals involved in the partnership and the conditions for achieving team integration, in order to identify some of the implications for the future of health–social care partnerships.

The problem of the separation of health services and social services dates back to the inception of the NHS and has resulted in repeated calls for 'integration', with attempts to bring this about through, for example, projects attaching social workers to GP surgeries (Lymbery and Millward, 2000). Such initiatives were given renewed impetus in the early 1990s in relation to services for older people by the implementation of community care legislation (Lymbery,

1998). Most of these initiatives involved partnership between two statutory organisations; GP services and social services. The aim of such partnerships could be characterised as bringing about closer *collaboration* between two distinct services, with individual professionals retaining separate organisational, as well as professional, identities, while working together more closely both in terms of location and communication. Because these partnerships involved two statutory services, each constrained by their statutory basis and by financial limitations, the extent to which *integration* of services was able to occur was limited, as was the ability of these partnerships qualitatively to transform the services provided. On the whole, they seem to have resulted in a closer *parallel* provision of services, with relatively little change to either the healthcare or the social care provided. It is not clear to what extent social workers in this context were expected or able to become integrated into the primary health care teams to which they were attached; or whether this affected the nature of the joint working relationship that developed or the quality of the services provided. It remains to be seen whether pooled budgets and joint commissioning of services will bring about greater integration, or what the consequences at the level of service delivery will be (Hudson et al, 2001).

The concept of a team has so far been treated as relatively unproblematic. However, it is clear from other studies of multi-professional practice that different professionals may operate different philosophies of teamwork. Freeman et al (2000) identified three such philosophics. A *directive* philosophy is based on an assumption of hierarchy, where one professional occupies a position of leadership and is responsible for directing the other team members. Here there is a clear division of labour between different professionals, each of whom has distinctive tasks to perform, but is not expected to contribute to the strategic planning of care for the patient. In Freeman et al's study, this view of teamwork was most frequently held by the medical profession. An *integrative* philosophy of teamworking places much greater importance on collaborative activities and on team membership, with the contributions of each professional to both patient care and other professionals' role development being equally valued. Finally, an *elective* philosophy was adopted by professionals who preferred to work autonomously and only involved other professionals when they saw this as necessary; they essentially saw teamworking as a system of liaison. There was no commitment to developing a shared understanding and the approach to teamworking was essentially instrumental, with participation in the team on the basis of pragmatism, rather than a commitment to the importance of teamworking per se.

In this chapter we review the findings of previous evaluations of projects attaching statutory social workers to GP surgeries, before examining the experience of partnership working between the WellFamily service and primary healthcare. We discuss the significance of team membership, partnership working and the factors that contributed to the integration of the WellFamily workers into the primary health care team. Finally, we consider the relationship between partnership and team membership, and the implications of different types of team 'membership' for transforming the quality of health and social care services.

Front-line health and social care partnerships: problems and benefits

Evaluations of projects in which social workers are 'attached' to a GP practice have identified a number of inter-organisational and inter-professional problems (Lymbery, 1998). The first inter-organisational problem arises from the different funding streams and accountability arrangements for primary health and local authority services. Where these differences are not taken into account, attachment projects may fail.

Insufficient planning of projects that locate social workers in primary care settings, resulting in inadequate managerial and professional support, has also been responsible for many projects failing or not being 'rolled out' across a wider area (Lymbery, 1998; Rummery and Glendinning, 2000). Arrangements need to be made for the continuing professional supervision of social workers (who rely on regular supervision sessions to maintain professional standards) when they are working at a distance from their employing department.

One of the biggest barriers to the success of such schemes lies within the primary health care 'team' itself. Until the integration of primary and community services in Primary Care Trusts (which began to come into operation in 2000), GPs and community nurses were effectively working for separate organisations, with very different systems of accountability and remuneration. There were therefore problems of partnership *within* primary healthcare services themselves, health visitors, district nurses, practice nurses and GPs having very different status and terms and conditions of employment. As independent self-employed contractors, GPs employ some of their fellow 'team' members; this creates a strongly hierarchical set of relationships, which may be antithetical to the very concept of a team. GPs have historically worked in a highly individualistic and non-collaborative culture (North et al, 1999; Callaghan et al, 2000). Until recently, there have been no incentives to encourage GPs to work cooperatively with other GPs or community health professionals, let alone with non-health workers (West and Poulton, 1997). The success of some attachment projects has therefore been limited because social workers were unable to forge effective links with key members of the primary health care team who were not 'signed up' to the project (Hodgson, 1997).

At the inter-professional level, the historical mistrust that characterises relationships between primary health and social care workers has constituted an important barrier to such projects, particularly in their initial stages (Dalley, 1989). Primary healthcare workers are often perceived by social workers as being bound by medical models, which are not compatible with objectives such as enhancing independence, anti-discriminatory practice and combating social exclusion. Conversely, social workers are also often perceived by NHS workers as being too slow in responding, unnecessarily bureaucratic and overly concerned with 'irrelevant' issues.

However, evaluations of collaborative projects have shown that actually working together, with shared priorities and achievable goals, can help the participants to overcome historical mistrust and inter-professional difficulties

(Hudson, 1999). This is an important part of building the trust that Powell and Exworthy refer to in Chapter Two as an integral part of quasi-networks, and Hudson and Hardy argue in Chapter Four is essential for successful partnerships. Quicker referral times, a reduction in delays in accessing services, better information sharing and reduced bureaucracy have been reported as significant benefits, and have also led to improved inter-professional relationships (Pithouse and Butler, 1994; McNally and Mercer, 1996; Stannard, 1996; Ross and Tissier, 1997). These benefits have been achieved under a variety of organisational arrangements; for example, attaching social workers, aligning teams or appointing 'linkworkers' (Tucker and Brown, 1997).

Although both the front-line health and social care workers in these projects experienced significant benefits and improvements in their job satisfaction, GPs and community nurses appeared to experience more benefits, while social workers bore most of the 'costs' of the schemes. Such 'costs' included making substantial changes to their working practices to accommodate the practices of the primary health care team (such as changing their working hours and referral methods) and coping with increased workloads. The increase in social care workloads occurred both because of increased referrals compared to colleagues in traditional social services teams, and because social workers in primary care settings took on work that was not 'core' care management work, such as welfare rights advice or liaising with a wider range of statutory and independent sector services than would normally be the case. They also reported having to ensure that all members of the primary health care team (particularly community nurses, who tended to be left out of the planning stages of such schemes) were involved (Claridge and Rivers, 1997; Cumella and Le Mesurier, 1997; Hodgson, 1997). Conversely, the 'host' service (primary care) did not have to adapt itself to the culture or working practices of its partner (social services).

Benefits to patients of such initiatives included easier access to services, fewer delays and duplicated assessments as a result of improved inter-professional working, and less stigma as a result of accessing services via primary care rather than social services. These schemes did not result in any changes or improvements in the actual services that patients were able to access, since these remained constrained by the resource and statutory frameworks within which NHS and local authority social services departments operated. Nevertheless, the way in which patients gain access to services is often a significant concern to them (Rummery et al, 1999) and accessing services at the appropriate time with minimal delay can reduce the need for more costly and intensive services such as residential care (Clark et al, 1998).

The Family Welfare Association's WellFamily service

The above review provides relatively little insight into the nature of the relationships that developed between the primary health care team and the social workers working with them. We now move on to consider this through the evaluation of a primary care-based family support service, the WellFamily service, established by a national voluntary organisation, the Family Welfare Association (Clarke et al, 2001).

The WellFamily service arose from a small research project carried out at a GP practice in Hackney, East London, to investigate how individuals and families in an inner-city community 'kept well'. The study found that, for most patients, social support networks and an absence of economic hardship played an important part in helping individuals and families through short-term crises; however, there were a number of groups within the practice population who lacked both the material resources and the social support necessary to maintain reasonable health (Family Welfare Association, nd). The study proposed setting up a service based in the practice, with an 'omnicompetent', generalist social worker – a Family Support Coordinator – who would offer a range of help and support to individuals and families. Primary care was seen as providing "an opportunity to reach a range of individuals and families in a non-stigmatising and preventive way" (Baginsky 1997, p 2).

The first WellFamily service was set up in 1996 in the Hackney practice where the initial research study was carried out, with three years' funding from the Department of Health (DoH). The service was subsequently extended for a further two years with additional DoH and charitable funding. In 1998 a further four services were set up in Croydon, Luton, Newham and Swaffham (Norfolk) with funding from the National Lottery Charities Board. Unlike the first WellFamily service, which was the result of a joint initiative between FWA and the Hackney practice, the four Lottery-funded sites were identified through approaches by FWA to senior managers in the health authority and social services departments in each area. These managers suggested GP practices that they thought would be receptive to such a service, but otherwise had relatively little involvement in the service and its development. These different origins have had important consequences for the nature of the relationship that has developed between the health professionals, particularly the GPs, and the Family Support Coordinators (FSCs) (Clarke et al, 2001). Figure 5.1 summarises the differences between the projects.

Figure 5.1: The five WellFamily projects

Location	Description
Croydon	• FSC based in health centre, regular sessions in GP practice.
	• Project instigated by FWA and health and social care managers.
Hackney	• Two years older than other pilots.
	• GPs helped instigate pilot.
	• FSC based in GP surgery.
Newham	• Project instigated by FWA and health and social care managers.
	• FSC worked with several practices.
	• FSC based in social services with regular sessions in GP practices.
Swaffham	• Project instigated by FWA and health and social care managers.
	• FSC worked with several practices.
	• FSC based in local community hospital, no sessions in GP practices.
Luton	• Project instigated by FWA and health and social care managers.
	• FSC based in healthcentre.
	• Worked with several practices; some sessions held in practice.

The Lottery application summarised the brief of the FSCs as follows:

> ... to support families and individuals within them by providing a holistic and strategic view of family health, linking health and social need to local community resources ... to complement and enhance the work of the whole health team whilst at the same time encouraging collaborative working across all sectors. (Family Welfare Association, 1996)

The remit of the service was essentially to offer early intervention and prevent more serious problems developing by providing support, advice and information for individuals and families. The FSCs had a variety of professional backgrounds, including social work qualifications, and most had experience of working in both health and social services settings. Users were either referred to the WellFamily service by their GP or another health professional linked to the practice (such as a health visitor, practice nurse or district nurse), or were able to refer themselves. The primary health care team was initially given very general guidance on the criteria for referral to the service. As the service developed in each area, these referral criteria evolved, with GPs and others increasingly referring cases which the FSCs described as more interesting and complex.

Unlike services provided by GP-attached local authority social workers in many of the demonstration projects reviewed above, which were mainly for older people, the WellFamily service was generic. Users were of all ages and had practical and material problems related to housing, welfare benefits and debt; parenting problems; minor mental health problems (primarily depression and anxiety); and intra-family and relationship difficulties. Because it was provided by a voluntary organisation, the service was able to determine its own eligibility criteria and was able to complement the generic, early intervention ethos of general practice. The service aimed to take a holistic approach by addressing the multiple problems that users experienced; and by working with different family members, either individually or together, as the FSC deemed appropriate.

The service also sought to be holistic in another sense. The FSCs attempted to work in a collaborative way with healthcare professionals, so that the latter acquired a clearer understanding of what users required in terms of social support, with the FSCs either providing this themselves or directing users to more specialist services. The intention was that health professionals would become better informed about the other services in the locality and their understanding of the help and support different agencies could provide would be increased. The FWA hoped that this would promote a more holistic understanding of the complex relationships between health and social needs. There was, therefore, an intention that partnership should result in a qualitative transformation of the services provided by both health and social care professionals, as a result of better inter-professional understanding. This distinguishes it from the statutory partnership initiatives reviewed earlier in the chapter, which did not aim to transform the primary health care team.

Factors affecting team integration: the relationship between the FSCs and the PHCT

Team membership

The FSCs all believed that it was a mark of a successful partnership that they were integrated into the primary health care team, as this was essential for an integrated understanding of, and approach to, health and social care problems.

Almost all the primary health care team members said that they regarded the FSC as part of the team, although there were some very different understandings within and between primary health care teams of what constituted a 'team'. There was a shared belief among primary health care team members that team membership involved regular communication and clear mutual understanding of roles. One GP who dissented from the view that the FSC was a member of the primary health care team believed that membership of the primary health care team required being based in the same premises (which was not the case for this site) and being directly employed by the practice. Other members of the primary health care team not based in this practice were similarly not regarded by her as team members. The idea that team membership meant being an employee of the practice suggests that, for this GP, the 'team' was hierarchically organised and under her control. Other GPs did not take this view.

Communication

Communication was critical, both in helping the primary health care team to understand the role of the FSC and in the development of trust between health professionals and the FSCs. Where the service was fully based in the surgery, as in Hackney, the opportunities for informal communication were greatest. Other FSCs who held sessions in the practice, even if they did not have their office based there, also had opportunities to discuss referrals with GPs and to give feedback on the work undertaken. Where the FSCs did not see users at the surgery or where their sessions did not coincide with the GPs' presence in the surgery, communication had to be done more formally, by letter, which was more time-consuming. Given the other pressures on the time of both the FSCs and GPs, it is not surprising that this was not always done. One FSC also observed that GPs, who tend to work in isolation, found it alien, difficult and time-consuming to do much liaison, which put the onus on the FSC to take the initiative for maintaining communication.

Access to patient notes

Another way in which communication could take place was through patient records. Not all GPs allowed the FSCs access to patients' notes. In cases where access was not allowed, this also applied to other members of the primary health care team and so did not differentiate the FSCs from other team members[1].

In Croydon medical records were computerised and accessible to the FSC. This FSC felt that having a common information base facilitated a more coherent approach and prevented duplication and confusion. Another FSC, who did not have access to medical records, thought that common computerised records of this kind would help to improve communication between herself and other team members. She provided records of her contact with patients, which were filed in patients' notes, but thought that these were not referred to by primary health care team members. Her lack of access to patient records meant that she was also not always aware of referrals made to other services and this sometimes meant that there was duplication of effort. Those GPs who did not allow access to patients' notes did not see this issue as a marker of team membership and it ceased to be a significant issue for those FSCs who were not given access. However, the absence of shared access to information on patients does seem indicative of a less integrated approach to teamworking than that which existed in practices where there was a much greater sharing of information between health professionals and the FSCs.

Co-location

There appeared to be a direct association between physical presence in the surgery and the extent of integration into the primary health care team. The degree of contact with GP surgeries ranged from close daily contact to no regular contact at all. The Hackney service, which was co-located, was also the service where there was the closest working relationship between the FSC and the GPs. In Swaffham, where the FSC had no sessions in the surgeries of the referring GPs and little or no informal contact with them, relationships with the GPs remained relatively distant and the number of referrals was low throughout the period of the evaluation. However, the Swaffham FSC developed close working relationships with district nurses and midwives, who, like her, were based in the nearby community hospital. Elsewhere, a presence in the surgery reminded primary health care team members about the service, allowed them opportunities to explore what it offered, helped to develop trust between the FSCs and other team members, and allowed rapid feedback on cases referred.

Even if the WellFamily service was not actually based in the surgery, where it was attached to a single GP practice, as was the case in Croydon, the FSC was able to spend more time at the practice and develop closer relationships with the health professionals than where she was working across several practices. The Croydon service had the largest number of referrals during the period of the evaluation, and this reflected, at least in part, the very clear understanding of what the service could offer. This practice was an innovative one, receptive to new ideas and operating in an area of high need. All these factors taken together may explain why the service took off so quickly here. In other areas, where the service was spread between several different practices, the FSCs had to spend a great deal of time 'selling' the service to each of the practices and their somewhat dispersed effort may have contributed to a slower start to referrals.

Team ethos

An important factor in team integration was the extent to which a team ethos already existed among the primary health care professionals. Integration of the FSC was easiest and developed best where an integrative approach (Freeman et al, 2000) to teamworking was already well developed within the practice. This was most likely in larger group practices where a number of other health professionals were based in the surgery. Group practices where there were fewer other health professionals on the premises tended to take a directive approach to teamworking and had a relatively remote relationship with the FSC. Single-handed practices were generally less likely to have many other health professionals based in the practice and their approach to teamworking was more likely to be elective.

Different views of the GP role

There were considerable differences between individual GPs in their enthusiasm for, and understanding of, the service and their interest in the relationship between social support and health. Some GPs took a fairly narrow view of their responsibilities. One FSC commented that the GPs in her area "often don't see their role as anything other than dealing with the presenting medical problem". Other GPs had a broader view of the social as well as the physical factors involved in ill health and were therefore already likely to be looking for social care services to complement the medical care that they provided. Such GPs were more receptive to the WellFamily service and more likely to include the FSC in the team. Community nurses, because they saw patients at home rather than in the surgery, had a much clearer sense of how the service might complement their own work.

Team integration, service integration and shared professional understanding

While all the FSCs developed good relationships with primary health professionals who referred patients to the service, the aim of bringing about a more integrated response to people's health and social needs was only achieved in Hackney, which operated in the conditions most conducive to team integration. Here, a system of monthly meetings was instituted by the FSC to discuss particular families and plan a joint approach to their problems. These meetings involved the entire primary health care team and the FSC. The FSC and the GPs also sometimes undertook joint consultations with patients. The WellFamily service therefore appeared to have brought about a real qualitative change in the working practices and approach of health professionals, which involved incorporating a social care perspective into their approach as health practitioners.

In the other areas, joint working essentially involved an improved division of labour between health professionals (mainly GPs) and the FSC, rather than the development of shared understanding, discussion and responsibility. Some steps towards joint working with health visitors were taken in at least two areas, where the FSCs and health visitors sometimes undertook home visits together. However, this was usually a preliminary step to deciding who would work on different problems with the service user, as a means of achieving a more appropriate and efficient division of labour.

The discussion so far has concentrated on the concept of team integration and the factors that contribute to this, in order to understand the development of partnerships at the level of service delivery. But why is it so important to be integrated into a team and in what ways does it contribute to the quality of the services delivered?

The FSCs saw their social and professional integration into the primary health care team as important, not only for their own morale and effectiveness, but also for the quality of service provided to users. Both the FSCs and the health professionals believed that acceptance of the FSC as a member of the team communicated itself to users, so that their trust in the GP practice was extended to the WellFamily service. The FSCs also believed that an integrated approach by health professionals and themselves reflected back to users a sense of being seen as a whole, rather than as a cluster of distinct problems. This, in turn, was an important way of addressing the social exclusion suffered by many of the users of the service.

Primary health professionals identified a number of practical benefits resulting from the inclusion of the FSC in the team, including better information about local services and about the family context of patients. The service also filled a gap in local provision created by the high threshold for statutory social services. Alongside these practical benefits, the WellFamily service, provided as part of the primary health care team's work, enabled problems to be identified and acknowledged that hitherto had been neglected because doctors lacked any means of addressing them. As one of the Hackney GPs described:

> "It changes how you work.... It changes your view, you are much more ready to acknowledge the [psycho-social] problems that you know are there anyway and ready to deal with – because the other thing that we do as GPs is, you know, we see the vast chasm and I am afraid that we can't cope with that.... A lot of the time doctors get very frustrated because what we are dragged into appears to be nothing to do with medicine.... I mean you either block it out or you think ... we will tackle it. And to tackle it you need to have team members [who] see that as their prime job."

Her comments suggest that without access to appropriate services, GPs may find it difficult even to acknowledge the existence of problems that they do not have the skills to address, but which, nevertheless, profoundly affect their patients' health. The lack of early-intervention social support services may itself contribute therefore to the failure to recognise the need for such services. It is only when health professionals have ready access to a service in which they feel confident, and when that service is provided through the team of which they are a part, that these problems can be fully acknowledged. This, in turn, is a necessary first step to addressing them effectively. This illustrates how the involvement and commitment of front-line, operational staff, who are willing to share or even cede exclusive claims to specialised knowledge, can make a real difference to the success of a partnership, as Hudson and Hardy argue in Chapter Four.

Conclusions

The WellFamily service differed from previous schemes designed to bring about closer working between primary and social care services because of its voluntary sector basis. This freed the service from some of the inter-organisational problems that earlier evaluations have identified and allowed inter-professional partnerships and team membership to develop in a context relatively free of the organisational constraints involved in statutory-statutory partnerships. This had important consequences for the inter-professional relationships that were able to emerge and ultimately, it is argued, for the quality of the services provided to users. As a voluntary organisation with grant aid for a pilot service, FWA was not constrained by a statutory role or a tightly specified contract for services to be provided. It was therefore possible for the WellFamily service to be flexible and responsive to local circumstances. This meant it was easily integrated into the general practices with which it was working, albeit very much on the terms of the local health partner. The partnership involved was not one between two large organisations, such as a local authority social services department and a health authority. It was a partnership developed at the level of service delivery with scope for GPs, as independent contractors, and FSCs, as relatively autonomous local representatives of their employing organisation, to shape relationships as they felt appropriate. As with the experience of local authority social workers attached to GP practices, this flexibility was largely one way, with the FSCs adapting their practice to fit the existing culture of the primary health care team and become accepted as members of the team. We have identified some important differences, both within and between different healthcare professionals, in what they mean by a team. These differences affected the way in which the WellFamily service was able to work with different professionals and the nature of the service that developed in each of the five areas.

In four of the five services, the FSC had been absorbed into a hierarchically organised team to varying degrees, without in any way altering its basic structure. In the fifth service, Hackney, the WellFamily service had brought about changes in the way the primary health care team operated and a more integrated style of working had been developed. Although the structure of the team remained hierarchical in terms of the employment conditions and power of those involved, the practice had become much more egalitarian. This change involved developing real reciprocity between team members, with health and social care professionals coming to a shared view of what constitutes well being and how to achieve it – the shared vision which Hudson and Hardy (Chapter Four) identify as a prerequisite for successful partnerships. This, in turn, required mutual trust and respect based on a clear understanding of the different skills that different professions had to offer. A precondition for this would seem to be a reasonable degree of equality within the team and a willingness on the part of GPs to give up some of their status and power. In Hackney this was indicated by GPs' willingness to undertake joint consultations with the FSC, an experience that they admitted was difficult and exposing for them. Obstacles to developments of this kind elsewhere stemmed from the FSCs preconceptions of their status relative to GPs, as well as from GPs' own attitudes. There was evidence towards the end of the evaluation that, as the FSCs' confidence in the value of the service they provided grew, they felt more able to make demands on GPs to develop different ways of joint working. This had begun to lead to a more integrated style of working within these teams, again illustrating a reduction in perceived professional 'threats' (Chapter Four), which can inhibit closer collaboration.

GPs' professional status, both within the hierarchy of primary healthcare professions and relative to social care professionals, remained an obstacle to developing an integrative approach to teamworking, rather than simply improving the division of labour between professionals. Overcoming these difficulties required the FSCs to develop confidence in what they had to offer the PHCT. This, in turn, required positive feedback from the provision of the service over a period of time, so that there was scope for exploration and experimentation.

It seems clear that in front-line service delivery there is a link between effective teamworking and a partnership approach to delivering primary health and social care. In the case of the WellFamily service, it was the statutory partner who seemed to be able to dictate whether the comparatively weaker voluntary sector partner could become part of the team, but the statutory partner nevertheless also accepted the need for the voluntary sector's expertise – a recognition of interdependency, which Hudson and Hardy argue (Chapter Four) is the first principle of successful partnership working. In other words, the barriers to successful teamworking experienced by similar projects could be surmounted by a recognition of the interdependence of both partners in achieving effective 'well being' for patients. Where recognition of, and commitment to, this interdependence was weaker, the ability of the voluntary sector to form effective teams and therefore effective partnerships with the statutory sector was also correspondingly compromised.

Note

[1] In none of the services were PHCT members given access to the FSCs' notes, and information divulged to the FSC was only passed on with patients' permission.

References

Baginsky, M. (1997) *The WellFamily project: An initial evaluation*, London: Family Welfare Association.

Callaghan, G., Exworthy, M., Hudson, B. and Peckham, S. (2000) 'Prospects for collaboration in primary care: relationships between social services and the new PCGs', *Journal of Interprofessional Care*, vol 14, no 1, pp 19-26.

Claridge, B. and Rivers, P. (1997) *Evaluation of social workers attached to GP practices: Report to Southern Derbyshire Health Authority*, Derby: University of Derby School of Health and Community Studies.

Clark, H., Dyer, S. and Horwood, J. (1998) *That bit of help: The high value of low level preventative services for older people*, Bristol: The Policy Press.

Clarke, K., Sarre, S., Glendinning, C. and Datta, J. (2001) *FWA's WellFamily service: Evaluation report*, London: Family Welfare Association.

Cumella, S. and Le Mesurier, N. (1997) *Social work in practice: An evaluation of social work in GP practices in South Worcestershire*, Worcester: The Martley Press.

Dalley, G. (1989) 'Professional ideology or organisational tribalism?', in R. Taylor and J. Ford (eds) *Social work and health care*, *Research highlights* 19, London: Jessica Kingsley.

Family Welfare Association (nd) 'WellFamily project: family support within primary care', unpublished paper, London: Family Welfare Association.

Family Welfare Association (1996) *National Lottery Charities Board grant application*, unpublished.

Freeman, M., Miller, C. and Ross, N. (2000) 'The impact of individual philosophies of teamwork on multi-professional practice and the implications for education', *Journal of Interprofessional Care*, vol 14, pp 237-47.

Hodgson, C.R. (1997) *It's all good practice: Evaluating practice-based care management in Greenwich*, London: South East Institute of Public Health.

Hudson, B. (1999) 'Joint commissioning across the primary health–social care boundary: can it work?', *Health and Social Care in the Community*, vol 7, no 5, pp 358-66.

Hudson, B., Young, R., Hardy, B. and Glendinning, C. (2001) *National evaluation of notifications for use of the s31 partnership flexibilities of the Health Act 1999*, Leeds: Nuffield Institute for Health and Manchester: NPCRDC.

Lymbery, M. (1998) 'Social work in general practice: dilemmas and solutions', *Journal of Interprofessional Care,* vol 12, no 2, pp 199-208.

Lymbery, M. and Millward, A. (2000) 'The primary health care interface', in G. Bradley and J. Manthorpe (eds) *Working on the fault line*, Birmingham: British Association of Social Workers/ Venture Press.

McNally, D. and Mercer, N. (1996) *Social workers attached to practices: Project report*, Knowsley: Knowsley Metropolitan Borough and Knowsley Health.

North, N., Lupton, C. and Kahn, P. (1999) 'General practitioners and the new NHS', *Health and Social Care in the Community*, vol 7, no 6, pp 408-16.

Pithouse, A. and Butler, I. (1994) 'Social work attachments in a group practice: a case study in success?', *Research, Policy and Planning*, vol 12, no 1, pp 16-20.

Ross, F. and Tissier, J. (1997) 'The care management interface with general practice: a case study', *Health and Social Care in the Community*, vol 5, no 3, pp 153-61.

Rummery, K., Ellis, K. and Davis, A. (1999) 'Negotiating access to assessments: perspectives of front-line workers, people with disabilities and carers', *Health and Social Care in the Community*, vol 7, no 4, pp 296-300.

Rummery, K. and Glendinning, C. (2000) *Primary care and social services: Developing new partnerships for older people*, Oxford: Radcliffe Medical Press.

Stannard, J. (1996) *City attached care manager pilot: Final report*, Winchester: Hampshire Social Services.

Tucker, C. and Brown, L. (1997) *Evaluating different models for jointly commissioning community care*, Bath: Wiltshire Social Services and University of Bath Research and Development Partnership Report 4.

West, M.A. and Poulton, B.C. (1997) 'A failure of function: teamwork in primary healthcare', *Journal of Interprofessional Care*, vol 11, no 2, pp 205-16.

SIX

Building capacity for collaboration in English Health Action Zones

Marian Barnes and Helen Sullivan

Introduction

The Health Action Zone (HAZ) was the first of a number of 'zonal' initiatives established by the Labour government between 1997 and 2001 (see also Chapter Twelve on Education Action Zones). The purpose of HAZs was to "bring together all those contributing to the health of the local population to develop and implement a locally agreed strategy for improving the health of local people" (DoH, 1997a). The government was explicit that HAZ strategies would need to be wide-ranging and ambitious; address the causes of ill health, including poor housing, unemployment, inadequate diet and smoking; and improve service interventions both in the NHS and by other relevant providers. According to the then Secretary of State:

> The NHS will have a major role – in identifying the things that make people
> ill – promoting public health and reducing the present gross inequalities in
> health. But we have got to use the whole machinery of Government to
> tackle things that make people ill. (DoH, 1997b)

Partnership was understood to be the key vehicle that would enable the resources of government to be brought to bear on improving health, reducing inequalities and improving services in a coordinated and coherent manner. HAZ partnerships would enable joint working between key service providers, including the NHS and local authorities, and would also facilitate the involvement of other interested stakeholders, such as community health councils, community organisations and the private sector. In order to achieve HAZ status, local areas would have to demonstrate their commitment to working in partnership to develop a local health strategy, in addition to justifying their bid with reference to prevailing health inequalities.

The invitation to bid for HAZ status was sent to health authorities, since they were generally perceived to be the lead partners in the bidding process. However, health authorities worked quickly to engage relevant local authorities. Local government representatives also saw themselves as senior partners in the

HAZ initiative, because of their public health and social care responsibilities and also because of their past experience of working in partnership. According to one spokesperson:

> Local authorities are unique in the diversity of partnerships they have developed and have great experience in working with the voluntary and private sectors. Although social service departments have an important role in providing personal social care, local government must make a further corporate response to this initiative across all of its functions – including housing, anti-poverty and community safety. (Rita Stringfellow, quoted in DoH, 1997a)

Bids for HAZ status cited various other partners, including hospital Trusts, emerging Primary Care Groups, public sector bodies such as training and enterprise councils, the police, housing associations, local universities and representatives of the private and voluntary sectors such as chambers of commerce and voluntary service councils. A key obligation upon HAZs was engagement with, and involvement from, 'the public' in the shape of service user groups and community groups (whether based on communities of interest, identity and/ or geography).

In order to provide some overarching framework for this potentially large and wide-ranging pool of partners and stakeholders, government determined that each HAZ would need to be managed through a formal partnership mechanism. The invitation to bid stated:"… it is envisaged that HAZs will set up partnership boards with representation from local stakeholders" (DoH, 1997c, para 12).

The boards would have responsibility for managing the HAZ programmes and projects; monitoring performance and reporting on it to the regional NHS Executive; and linking HAZ activity into the relevant local organisations. In practice, where boards were established they tended to assume a strategic role and their composition followed this function, with members consisting of strategic-level representatives of key service providers and stakeholder interests.

However, another important and distinctive feature of HAZs was the emphasis on them being dynamic forces for change within localities. By bringing professionals, communities and organisations together, it was envisaged that HAZs would create a capacity for change throughout the health system, reducing red tape, transforming service design and delivery, fostering innovation, disseminating good practice and 'joining-up' other existing initiatives. In this respect, HAZs were unusual as area-based initiatives, primarily constituting agents of change rather than deliverers of regeneration programmes. Partnership in this context meant creating conditions for change through developing sustainable cross-sector relationships. The partnership boards and HAZ programmes were important but, nevertheless, partial contributors to this process. Equally important were the range and nature of the relationships that could be developed across the public policy system, which would contribute to a system transformation.

There were two rounds of bidding for HAZ status, resulting in the designation of 26 English HAZs in 1998/99. HAZs vary enormously; some comprise single, coterminous health and local authority areas, such as Sheffield, while others involve multiple health and local authorities, for example Merseyside. The majority are urban, but several cover large rural areas, such as Cornwall and the Isles of Scilly. In total, HAZs cover 34 health authorities and 73 local authorities.

HAZ funding takes a number of forms. As well as dedicated resources, HAZs were allowed access to special funds and opportunities, such as joint finance. In addition, a new approach to working with the Department of Health was promised: "The centre will expect to work in partnership with the zone, delivering support and 'investment' against agreed milestones" (DoH, 1997c, para 2).

In this way, access to specific resources such as the Innovations Fund and HAZ Fellowships would be determined as part of a joint approach. This approach was intended to emphasise the significance of HAZs as 'trailblazers' for change in the NHS and the development and delivery of health policy. To realise this opportunity, HAZs were established as long-term programmes (spanning from five to seven years), with developmental and learning support offered from within the National Health Service Executive and from local and national evaluations.

At the time of writing, it was uncertain whether HAZs would continue after 2002. However, it would be incorrect to assume that the premature ending of the HAZ initiative signifies failure. The very nature of HAZ as a change agent means that its success may be gauged by the mainstreaming of the HAZ approach, with HAZ objectives being accepted as mainstream objectives that do not require a special initiative to champion them. This chapter considers the strategies developed within English HAZs to develop partnerships across organisations within the public sector and between the statutory and voluntary and community sectors, in pursuit of HAZ goals. It examines emerging evidence concerning the capacity of these bodies to work together and to operationalise the HAZ approach – with the important proviso that the story being charted is, as yet, incomplete.

The emergence of HAZ

The invitation to bid for HAZ status was distinguished by an apparent acceptance of the role of the state as an instrument for creating the conditions in which citizens can achieve good health and well being. This was a role that had been denied under previous Conservative administrations, during which a much greater emphasis had been placed on individual responsibility for health, through mechanisms such as health promotion and the encouragement of private health insurance.

The HAZ antecedents lay in the evidence about health inequalities contained within the Black Report (Townsend and Davidson, 1982) and reinforced by subsequent evidence of an increasing health gap between rich and poor and the realisation that inequality per se is bad for health (Wilkinson, 1996). The optimistic mood at the start of Labour's first term was ripe for a policy initiative that did not try to disguise such evidence by reference to 'variations' in health, but both acknowledged this evidence and accepted the responsibility of government to address this dimension of the overarching problem of 'social exclusion'.

Other developments that also informed the HAZ programme lay in the 'Alliances for Health' movement, typified by the 'Healthy Cities' and 'Health for All' initiatives. These national and international initiatives emphasised the essential role of cross-sector collaboration in promoting health among local communities (WHO, 2000), reinforcing earlier messages about the multifaceted nature of health:

> ... health services are important, but they are not the only sector influencing people's well being: other sectors also have a contribution to make to health and intersectorality must therefore be an essential feature of such reform. (WHO, 1996, p 1)

This appeal to a collective commitment to a common end is an important characteristic of the New Labour approach to welfare. It recognises that the state can play an important role in creating the conditions for such collective commitments to be expressed and also extends beyond public services to embrace expectations about the conditions of 'communities' and individual citizens to achieving policy objectives (Barnes and Prior, 2000; see also Chapter Six). This focus on communities as actors in the process reflects another influence on the development of HAZ.

This combination of influences helped define the three overarching strategic objectives associated with the HAZ. These were:

- to identify and address the public health needs of the local area;
- to increase the effectiveness, efficiency and responsiveness of services;
- to develop partnerships for improving people's health and relevant services, adding value through creating synergy between the work of different agencies. (DoH, 1997c).

Realising these objectives presented particular challenges to potential HAZ partnerships. The nature of these is outlined below.

The HAZ challenge

The transformational aspirations of New Labour, which envisaged HAZs 'harnessing the dynamism of local people', 'releasing local energy and innovation', 'developing bespoke approaches to local problems and challenges' and working with other strategic initiatives to create a local synergy to tackle social exclusion (Richards et al, 1999), require more than simply a commitment to partnership working. In this transformative context, partnership is associated with other characteristics that denote the emergence of a new working environment. A vision of this new environment is set out clearly in the Tyne and Wear HAZ implementation plan:

> Our HAZ vision is of all the separate parts of the system achieving a shared and common purpose, converting the current partial networks and partnerships into a self-organising and sustaining system. The governance of this will be rooted in creating conditions in which accountability is not simply to a superior, professional group or organisation, but for contribution to the achievement of health improvement. Accountability for shared purpose cannot be imposed. The system of governance is about new and diverse ways of working together, more than new structure. This form of governance assumes a whole system will only work with clear principles of behaviour, not by controls alone. (Tyne and Wear HAZ, 1997, p 1)

In theory at least, HAZs were therefore intended to characterise the kind of governance that Clarke and Glendinning maintain in Chapter Three to have been largely illusory in health and social care policies under New Labour to date.

However, the emergence of this new environment was by no means certain without support from a superordinate body. Central government sought to provide this support by establishing a series of principles that HAZ partnerships were expected to reflect in their strategies and programmes of work. These were:

- Achieving equity – reducing health inequalities, promoting equality of access to services and improving equity in resource allocation.
- Engaging communities – involving the public in planning services and empowering service users and patients to take responsibility for their own health and decisions about care.
- Working in partnership – recognising that people receive services from a range of different agencies and that these services need to be coordinated to achieve maximum benefit.
- Engaging front-line staff – involving staff in developing and implementing strategy, developing flexible and responsive organisations and encouraging and supporting innovation in service delivery.
- Taking an evidence-based approach – developing a more structured, evidence-based approach to service planning and delivery, as well as clinically effective procedures and interventions.
- Developing a person-centred approach to service delivery – developing services around the needs of people and delivering them as close to people as appropriate.
- Taking a whole-systems approach – recognising that health, social and other services are interdependent and need to be planned and organised on a whole-systems basis, in order to deliver seamless care and tackle the wider determinants of health. (DoH, 1997d)

While these principles go some way to providing a framework for the development of sustainable transformation through partnership, in practice HAZs face problems familiar from previous examples of collaboration or joint working across health and local government (for example, Challis et al, 1988; Goss and Kent, 1995; Lewis et al, 1995). These problems include cultural differences; practical and systemic differences; competing philosophies and models of health; and professional defensiveness. While working with service users and communities might have a shorter history, there is also past evidence of the problems as well as the potential, particularly the issues of inequalities of power (see also Chapters Eight and Nine); the danger of co-option; and the cynicism that can result from raised expectations being dashed (for example, Craig and Mayo, 1995; Barnes et al, 1999). But in HAZs there are other challenges to partnership that have not always been present in previous examples of collaboration in health, such as Joint Consultative Committees and joint finance initiatives. These are:

- Complexity – the sheer range of problems that HAZs were invited to address and the numbers of partners they were encouraged to involve make the task of developing programmes and processes hugely complex. Initial evaluation reveals that few of those involved on the ground have a sense of 'the HAZ' as a whole, because of the wide variety of stakeholders and activities associated with it. (Barnes et al, 2001)
- Temporality – HAZs were originally assumed to be long-term initiatives. This creates the problem of how to develop ways of working that will sustain partnerships over time in order to pursue preventative policies. This is particularly problematic in a dynamic environment, where both the context and the nature of the problems to be addressed can change suddenly.
- Verticality – the original HAZ vision was of 'bottom-up' solutions to address locally defined problems. The local diversity implicit within this vision has been hard to sustain in the face of centrally driven priorities and targets. The potential for central–local partnerships, which were part of the original vision, may therefore only be realised if local partners are afforded greater discretion and flexibility in their actions – again a tension discussed in Chapter Three.

Given the nature of the challenges faced by putative HAZ partnerships, an overarching question in evaluating them concerns how and whether partnerships can secure the necessary collaborative capacity.

Building capacity for collaboration

Whether, and how, HAZs can build and sustain partnerships are important for several reasons. Government envisaged collaboration through partnership as central to the achievement of HAZ goals. However, the development of partnerships did not occur uniformly across HAZ localities. The interaction of national policies with local contexts acted to shape how HAZ partnerships evolved. For example, in areas such as Sandwell, the HAZ has built on an existing health partnership, bringing together coterminous health and local authorities with other public sector and voluntary agencies. By contrast, in other areas, such as Manchester, Salford and Trafford, the HAZ needed to build collaboration across multiple health and local authorities with little previous experience of working together, very different political and cultural histories and a vast number of stakeholders. As Hudson and Hardy point out in Chapter Four, such major differences in collaborative histories are likely to have implications for the future success of new partnerships.

In addition, beyond the HAZ context, are examples of other partnerships that interconnect or interface with HAZ: other 'action zones' such as Education Action Zones (see Chapter Twelve); regeneration initiatives (see Chapter Eleven); and strategic initiatives such as community safety partnerships (see Chapter Ten). These partnerships often cut across conventional mechanisms for securing accountability and probity – key values in the public sector. As they increase in number and significance in localities, their operation will begin to influence the way in which localities are governed (see Chapter Three). The contribution made by HAZ partnerships to this process in different localities is important to delineate, particularly in view of the emerging preference for an overarching locality partnership, as evidenced in the development of Local Strategic Partnerships (LSPs).

A key element of the capacity of HAZ partnerships to achieve their goals relates to the breadth and depth of community involvement within them. Here, too, context is significant because of the nature of the 'communities' within different HAZ areas. By definition, HAZs cover populations experiencing poor health as well as other dimensions of deprivation, such as unemployment (for example, Wakefield and District) and rural poverty (for example, Cornwall and the Isles of Scilly). Many of those areas also include diverse ethnic populations and in some there is a substantial transient population of asylum seekers or homeless people. These varying contexts alert us to the fact that community groups, service users and local citizens may have different reasons for taking part in an HAZ and, more significantly, may define their objectives differently from statutory agencies. (This issue, of the potentially divergent objectives of statutory and community 'partners', is discussed in Chapter Nine.) This diversity is important when the HAZ task is both to build the capacity of communities and the capacity of partner organisations to work with those communities.

The hugely varied contexts within which HAZs are seeking to develop collaboration mean that they face very different capacity challenges. In the national evaluation of HAZs, four key questions provide a common focus on building capacity, while allowing investigation of the particular challenges presented in different HAZs:

- What contribution does community involvement make to achieving HAZ objectives?
- What contribution do inter-agency partnerships make to achieving HAZ objectives?

- Can HAZs create the conditions in which community involvement meets the objectives of community participants as well as those of statutory agencies?
- What is the contribution made by HAZ to the development of inter-agency partnerships as a mode of governance?

These questions acknowledge the need to understand whether, and how, collaborative mechanisms can achieve the intended changes; and whether HAZ itself is an effective mechanism for building collaborative capacity. Initial investigation reveals five types of capacity development that require examination:

- Strategic capacity – developing and refining the HAZ vision and key themes.
- Governance capacity – accountability upwards to the DoH and downwards to communities.
- Operational capacity – the organisational structures and processes to deliver new activities.
- Practice capacity – skills and abilities among workers.
- Community and citizen capacity – the cultural, material and personal resources to take part in change processes.

It was also necessary to secure an evaluation framework both flexible enough to embrace this complexity and robust enough to provide answers to questions. One approach that purports to facilitate the evaluation of collaborative ventures like HAZs is 'theories of change'; this is defined as "a systematic and cumulative study of the links between activities, outcomes and contexts of the initiative" (Connell and Kubisch, 1998, p 16).

This approach seeks to engage all stakeholders in elaborating the 'theory' of an initiative; that is, what long-term outcomes of the initiative are expected, and how and why the activities of the initiative will contribute to achieving those outcomes. In this way, a theory of change can aid evaluation by specifying prospectively how collaborative endeavour will contribute to desired change, thus reducing problems associated with causal attribution. The measurement and data collection elements of the evaluation process should also be facilitated, as the targets to be achieved will be clearly established (Judge, 2000).

Practical application of the framework has revealed its limitations (Barnes, 2000). Nonetheless, in relation to building capacity for collaboration, the 'theories of change' approach facilitates evaluation by requiring a focus on the following (discussed in more detail in Sullivan et al, 2000):

- HAZ partnerships need to articulate the collaborative nature of 'process outcome' relationships within a 'whole-systems' approach to health.
- HAZ partners need to specify the type and level of collaborative capacity necessary to deliver HAZ objectives.
- HAZ partnerships need to identify the key components necessary to build collaborative capacity.
- HAZ partners need to examine the contribution of the HAZ to wider community goals.

The remainder of this chapter draws on those elements of the national HAZ evaluation that are concerned with building capacity for collaboration, and applies the 'theories of change' framework to a core sample of five HAZ case studies and an investigation of community involvement in 19 HAZs. This is supplemented by documentary analysis of all 26 HAZ partnership arrangements.

Understanding local strategies

The initial stages of the HAZ evaluation have focused on unpacking HAZ strategies to identify the rationales informing the development of partnerships between organisations and communities. This required an examination of the different contexts within which HAZs operate; the purposes attached to partnership working; and the forms and activities developed to deliver those purposes.

Context

The 'logic of partnership', that is the acknowledgement that the achievement of HAZ goals depends upon the successful development and operation of collaborative arrangements, is accepted by most stakeholders. (This also constitutes the first principle of successful partnership working outlined by Hudson and Hardy in Chapter Four.) This acknowledgement was informed by a number of key local contextual factors, including past experience, perception of the prevailing policy context and assessment of the contribution made by partnerships to previous policy goals. Acknowledging the need for partnership also informed subsequent decisions about building HAZ partnerships. Key factors determining different approaches to HAZ partnerships included:

- Nature of HAZ boundaries – where the HAZ boundaries were simple, covering a single health and local authority, there was increased likelihood of partners having worked together previously, so the HAZ could build upon that base and extend its coverage to a wider range of stakeholders. In HAZ areas with multiple health and local authorities and less experience of working together, more attention had to be paid to developing a modus operandi between core partners, particularly at strategic levels.
- Legitimacy of the HAZ – where HAZ partnerships were perceived to have a contribution to make beyond the life of the HAZ, there was a stronger sense of commitment to developing sustainable structures and processes. However, in some of the HAZs, especially the more complex ones where the HAZ represented the only instance of that particular group of partners coming together, partnerships were less likely to be considered as legitimate beyond the lifetime of the HAZ.
- Nature and dynamics of local communities – the perceived stability of communities was a significant factor in determining the strategies adopted by HAZs. Although HAZs contained diverse populations, and some were experiencing fundamental changes in the composition of their local

populations, the local infrastructure of community and voluntary organisations meant that it was usually possible to develop strategies to engage communities of geography, identity and interest. However, in some HAZs the local populations were unstable, as a result of the arrival of asylum seekers or refugees, or because of high mobility due to the age profile of the population (for example, Lambeth, Southwark and Lewisham). Here, very different strategies were needed.

Purposes

Analysis of the 26 HAZs reveals a number of common purposes for partnerships associated both with process and outcomes. These are:

- improving health and reducing health inequalities;
- the joint provision of improved services;
- establishing efficient and accountable systems of governance;
- achieving successful and embedded cross-agency and cross-sector working.

Common outcomes concern the creation and release of synergy via collaborative action and the transformation of the 'whole system' of the health economy. Most HAZs find it difficult to describe what the release of synergy amounts to, although at the very least it includes maximising the application of available resources. There is rather more detail on system transformation, with HAZs commonly emphasising the creation of more responsive and flexible delivery of health services characterised by greater interaction between health and social care professionals, enhanced influence for users and communities and delivery of shared outcomes. What is striking is the emphasis on using the HAZ as an opportunity to do things differently, rather than perceiving it as a vehicle for acquiring additional central government funds.

While these objectives were apparent across all HAZs, most attention was devoted to the development of new forms of collaborative activity that would improve health and service delivery. Least attention was given to the development of governance systems, although some HAZs requested flexibilities from government so they could establish new governance arrangements (for example, Camden and Islington). Concerns over local governance arrangements may have been diluted by the emphasis on performance management that came to dominate HAZs in their early stages (see also Chapter Three).

Securing and/or enhancing community involvement was a key government objective for HAZs. Local interpretations of this objective include:

- contributing to improving health and reducing inequalities;
- supporting improvements to service delivery;
- creating an informed public with an understanding of HAZ;
- generating evidence and accessing lay knowledge;
- enhancing the accountability of key service providers.

In practice, the emphasis in HAZs has been on building community involvement to improve health and service delivery, with clear programmes of work identified to support these objectives. Some HAZs (for example, Northumberland) decided early on to develop a public information strategy, while others devoted considerable energy to accessing community knowledge (for example, Tyne and Wear). However, these initiatives were also primarily geared towards outcomes for health improvement and service delivery.

The interaction of context and purposes gave rise to a range of local HAZ strategies; these can be categorised in the following way:

- Working within the mainstream – this approach requires a clear focus on building organisational capacity, so as to operate more effectively across service and sector boundaries. Innovative projects were funded in priority areas in order to provide models of good practice that could be adopted within the mainstream. Organisational support was complemented with community capacity building to enhance public and user involvement and influence.
- Targeting activity to model transformation elsewhere – this approach involves selecting a key priority, such as children, and focusing HAZ activity on tackling inequalities and improving services around that priority. The system transformation that is achieved can then form a model for wider application.
- A combined approach – the most typical of HAZ strategies, this approach attempts to combine targeted activity with zone-wide initiatives, linking HAZ programmes with mainstream services and area-based initiatives, and supporting community capacity building via interventions with individuals.

However, strategies have not remained static over time but have changed in response to particular circumstances. In some HAZs, these changes represent nothing more than marginal adjustments, while in others, HAZ strategies have themselves been transformed following the initial experiences of implementation and/or the intervention of central government. For example, Lambeth, Southwark and Lewisham's initial strategy focused on working together to address the root causes of ill health among children and young people. In their local context, it made sense to define the HAZ partnership's mission as:"To use the opportunities presented by the HAZ to improve the future of children and young people in South East London by promoting health, improving services and building on strong local partnerships" (Lambeth, Southwark and Lewisham HAZ, 1998). Yet within the first year, both Lambeth, Southwark and Lewisham, and Manchester, Salford and Trafford, which had also decided to focus on young people, were informed by the government that their focus was too narrow. They, and the other 24 HAZs, were now required to respond to three national priorities – cancer, coronary heart disease and mental health.

Forms of collaboration

All HAZs are required to set up and operate partnership mechanisms to deliver the HAZ programme. While board arrangements dominate, there is still variety in how they manifest themselves. Partnership arrangements include:

- HAZ Partnership Board (for example, Cumbria) – a single board comprising all key partners, including the health authority, NHS Trusts, local authority and voluntary sector, with decision-making powers and responsibility for programme oversight.
- Steering Group/Executive split (for example, Brent) – two bodies that exist in parallel. The steering group includes wider representation and is concerned with strategic direction, while the executive focuses on operational activity. These bodies can be composed either entirely of officers or of a mixture of officers, local authority-elected members and non-executive directors of NHS organisations.
- Health Partnership (for example, Sandwell) – this partnership has broad responsibility for health in the locality. HAZ activities may be contained within it and/or as the subject of a HAZ sub-committee. Again membership can include officers and elected or appointed members, although it is more usual for day-to-day management to be undertaken by a sub-committee of officers.
- Health Stakeholder Groups with Joint Management Team (for example, Walsall) – deliberation and discussion is conducted in stakeholder groups, which may be narrowly focused and/or organised to represent particular user interests. Delivery and accountability for the HAZ is to a joint management team of officers from the partner organisation.

Each of these options may be augmented by links to a community/voluntary sector forum for the purposes of consultation; and/or to a wider strategic partnership charged with overseeing regeneration. Meetings of partnership groups were more frequent in the 'setting up' phase of the HAZ. Once established, however, certain patterns emerged; groups with a 'steering' role tend to meet once or twice a year, while those with executive responsibilities meet monthly or bi-monthly.

Below the strategic level a variety of arrangements pertain. Most HAZs have some form of organisational support, such as a coordinator and key staff to resource the work of the HAZ. Operational or geographically based partnerships may also be established for particular streams of HAZ work. The degree of formality attached to these lower-level partnerships varies greatly, in some cases mirroring almost exactly the constitution of the strategic partnership, but in others forming more of a network.

Ways of working with communities are equally varied, depending on the definitions of 'community' and 'users' applied in individual HAZs. Local implementation plans reflect an awareness of both conceptual and empirical diversity here. In some HAZs it was intended that bodies such as community health councils, councils of voluntary service and other voluntary sector groups would play a representative role; in others the direct participation of people in their roles as service users, citizens or community members was sought or encouraged.

Partnership mechanisms employed

HAZs have adopted a number of different mechanisms to deliver their programmes. While high-profile mechanisms such as 'pooled budgets' and joint commissioning have been widely used in some areas of health and social care, most HAZs have tended to make wider use of other, less eye-catching mechanisms. The national HAZ evaluation shows that local strategies are being delivered through:

- Formal agreements, such as contracts between organisations. For example, Manchester, Salford and Trafford HAZ made arrangements with voluntary sector bodies to develop a particular element of the HAZ programme. Other formal agreements cover new ways of working; for example, in Bradford the development of the district Health Improvement Programme was led from within the local authority, not the health authority.
- Informal agreements between organisations, where people simply agree to take on new tasks or do things in a different way.
- Secondments/Fellowships – the introduction of specific resources to help create links between partners and deliver a particular aspect of the HAZ programme.

Action to involve communities has absorbed a great deal of the HAZ budget. Again, while local contexts determine the exact nature of community programmes within HAZs, common patterns include:

- 'Bespoke' community programmes that attempt to build community involvement into the HAZ programme via a range of engagement, involvement and capacity-building activities.
- Community development funding that focuses exclusively on building capacity in particular communities within the HAZ. These may be communities of geography, interest or identity.
- Public information strategies that seek to inform and educate the whole HAZ population about health and their role in their own health.

Most HAZs have elements of all three, though generally with a particular emphasis.

Conclusions

The evaluation of HAZs is by no means complete, so it is inappropriate to offer any firm conclusions about the success of HAZ partnerships. However, some emerging issues about 'building capacity for collaboration' in HAZs are discernable.

Collaborative capacity, in all its forms, appears key to successful partnership development, although it is most difficult to develop in relation to governance. Partnership development takes considerable time and those HAZs that have experienced most difficulty are those that have least collective collaborative memory to draw upon – again, an experience consistent with the principles outlined in Chapter Four. Similarly, developing partnerships with particular sectors requires tailored effort. For example, private sector organisations have to be engaged in something tangible and communities need to be involved at the point at which collaboration makes most sense to them. In the case of both the voluntary and the community sectors, participation in collaborative activity requires significant resources; even when these have been made available, much more remains to be done.

The experience of HAZs to date confirms previous evaluations in suggesting that a commitment to partnership cannot of itself equalise power imbalances between stakeholders. The biggest gaps are between the statutory and non-statutory sectors, with communities having the least leverage. The disproportionate command over resources of organisations such as health and local authorities is central to this imbalance, as is the relative commonality of interest between health and social services based on past experiences of working together. For one voluntary sector respondent, this relationship was "like being Luxembourg in the EC up against Germany and France. You know you have a veto but you're not sure what difference it actually makes in practice". (These themes are developed further in Chapters Eight and Nine.)

However, there is also evidence to suggest that 'newer' health providers – NHS Trusts and non-health bodies such as housing, education and the police – have also found it difficult to break into established partnership arrangements between health authorities and social services. Strategies for addressing these imbalances may lie in developing partnership arrangements that are as robust at neighbourhood or service levels as they are at strategic level.

This chapter demonstrates that the 'logic of partnership' is firmly established at local level. However, while HAZ partnerships could demonstrate broad rationales for why partnership was important and what it could achieve, they were less confident about how to 'do' partnership. This led to tensions in some partnerships, where mechanisms for decision making and oversight were perceived to be too cumbersome by partners who were used to more efficient mechanisms and too exclusive by those partners used to extensive systems of accountability. These performance/conformance tensions are likely to remain a key issue in a governance environment that prioritises efficiency and involvement equally.

An overriding message from HAZs to date is that it is not possible to understand local partnerships divorced from their national context, nor expect them to deliver if national policy is not moving in the same direction. There is no doubt that the national policy environment is more conducive to collaborative working now than at the time of the 1997 general election and

HAZ leaders recognise the progress made in redesigning central/local relationships through HAZs.

What remains fragile is central government's capacity to support the consequences of its agenda for local collaborative action. The initial expectation that HAZs would be implemented rather differently in each locality suggested that the government recognised that diverse contexts would lead to the identification of diverse priorities and ways of addressing these. Subsequent requirements for HAZs to contribute to the achievement of national targets, coupled with significant cuts in HAZ budgets, have resulted in local priorities being squeezed or deleted from HAZ programmes. In addition, the performance management regime of the Department of Health has reinforced the primacy of vertical relationships over horizontal arrangements. This replicates past experience of other regeneration programmes, for example, the Single Regeneration Budget (see Chapter Eleven), and also features in the management and operation of proposed Local Strategic Partnerships.

There is, nevertheless, evidence of progress. For example, a unique feature of HAZs was the offer of 'freedoms and flexibilities' to aid efficiency and effectiveness. The success of this initiative is evident in the subsequent mainstreaming of joint commissioning, pooled budgets and integrated provision, and the prospect of Care Trusts. Whether central government can sustain this approach across its relationships with local bodies will be significant in determining the success of HAZs and other future partnership initiatives.

Acknowledgements

The work reported in this chapter was undertaken by Marian Barnes and Helen Sullivan, with funding from the Department of Health. However, the views expressed are those of the authors, not necessarily those of the Department of Health.

References

Barnes, M. (2000) 'Health action zones and community empowerment. Whose theories?', Paper given at *Partnerships for health seminar* at the Kings Fund, May.

Barnes, M. and Prior, D. (2000) *Private lives as public policy*, Birmingham: Venture Press.

Barnes, M., Harrison, S., Mort, M. and Shardlow, P. (1999) *Unequal partners: User groups and community care*, Bristol: The Policy Press.

Barnes, M., Sullivan, H. and Matka, E. (2001) *National HAZ evaluation: Findings from strategic level analysis of case studies*, Birmingham: University of Birmingham.

Challis, L., Fuller, S., Henwood, M., Klein, R., Plowden, W., Webb, A., Whittingham, P. and Wistow, G. (1988) *Joint approaches to social policy, rationality and practice*, Cambridge: Cambridge University Press.

Connell, J.P. and Kubisch, A.C. (1998) 'Applying a theory of change approach to the evaluation of comprehensive community initiatives: progress, prospects and problems', in K. Fullbright-Anderson, A.C. Kubisch and J.P. Connell (eds) *New approaches to evaluating community Initiatives. Volume 2 theory, measurement and analysis*, Washington DC: The Aspen Institute, pp 15-44.

Craig, G. and Mayo, M. (eds) (1995) *Community empowerment. A reader in participation and development*, London: Zed Books.

DoH (Department of Health) (1997a) '£30 million for new partnerships to target health inequalities', Press release no 312, October.

DoH (1997b) 'Health Action Zones envisaged as cooperative NHS partnerships', Press release no 145, June.

DoH (1997c) 'Health Action Zones – invitation to bid', EL(97)65, Leeds: NHS Executive.

DoH (1997d) 'What are Health Action Zones?' (www.haznet.org.uk).

Goss, S. and Kent, C. (1995) *Health and housing: Working together*, Bristol: The Policy Press/JRF.

Judge, K. (2000) 'Testing evaluation to the limits: the case of English Health Action Zones', *Journal of Health Services Research and Policy*, vol 5, no 1, pp 3-5.

Lambeth, Southwark and Lewisham HAZ (1998) *Children first*, London: Lambeth, Southwark and Lewisham Health Authorities.

Lewis, J., Bernstock, P. and Bovell, V. (1995) 'The community care changes: unresolved tensions and policy issues in implementation', *Journal of Social Policy*, vol 24, no 1, pp 73-94.

Newman, J. (1994) 'Beyond the vision: cultural change in the public sector', *Public Money and Management*, April/June, pp 59-64.

Richards, S., Barnes, M., Coulson, A., Gaster, L., Leach, B. and Sullivan, H. (1999) *Cross-cutting issues in public policy and public services*, London: DETR.

Sullivan, H., Barnes, M. and Matka, E. (2000) 'Building collaborative capacity through "theories of change": lessons from health action zones', Paper presented to Evaluation Society Conference, December.

Townsend, P. and Davidson, N. (eds) (1982) *Inequalities in health: The Black Report*, Harmondsworth: Penguin.

Tyne and Wear HAZ (1997) *HAZ implementation plan*, Newcastle/Sunderland: Gateshead, South Tyneside, Newcastle, North Tyneside and Sunderland Health Authorities.

Wilkinson, R. (1996) *Unhealthy societies: The afflictions of inequality*, London: Routledge.

WHO (World Health Organisation) (1996) *Ljubljana charter on reforming health care (European region)*, Geneva: WHO.

WHO (2000) *Health for all*, Geneva: WHO.

SEVEN

Partnerships for local governance: citizens, communities and accountability

Guy Daly and Howard Davis

Introduction

'New Labour', as part of its democratic renewal and modernisation agendas, has championed new and different forms of decision making in public services. In local government this change can be construed as a shift in emphasis away from representative democracy towards partnership and participatory decision making. New Labour has encouraged the active involvement of citizens in their communities. For their part, local authorities are developing new approaches and structures to facilitate such engagement.

Local government, as in other areas of public policy, is also undergoing a new phase of reshaping and redefinition. There has been a shift in emphasis from hierarchies, to markets and now to partnership. This current emphasis on local authority partnerships has a number of strands – with other parts of the public sector, with the private and voluntary sectors, and with citizens and communities. This chapter is concerned with partnerships between local authorities and their citizens and communities.

The chapter explores New Labour's democratic renewal agenda and its application to local government, before moving on to consider partnership and participation. It then examines examples of partnership being developed by a local authority, Birmingham City Council, particularly emphasising governance partnerships at the ward level. In analysing Birmingham's approach, the way in which this authority is utilising its version of partnership is questioned. In particular, it identifies and analyses concerns that relate to the representativeness, social inclusion, accountability and utility of these governance partnerships. The chapter's conclusions seek to draw out implications for the wider local government community.

Democratic renewal

Recent years have seen a loss of confidence in democratic structures and ideals. "Even the most democratic countries are not democratic enough" (Giddens, 2001, p 6). As Giddens (1998, p 2) had stated earlier, "Political ideas today seem to have lost their capacity to inspire and political leaders their ability to lead". In particular, representative democracy is seen as insufficiently responsive and representative. Criticism has pointed to, among other things, low electoral turnout, particularly at local elections (Blair, 1998, p 14). Much of local government is viewed as unresponsive and living in the past, with a feeling that many 'rotten boroughs' in which 'one-party states' operate still persist. The quality of local services is often seen as leaving something to be desired and a further sign of the democratic state's malaise. Lying behind this is the perceived loss of confidence in democratic structures and ideals in recent years. Giddens (1999, p 72) states that "in the mature democracies ... there is widespread disillusionment with democratic processes".

In his introduction to Labour's 1997 manifesto Tony Blair declared, "The vision is one of national renewal, a country with drive, purpose and energy" (Labour Party, 1997, p 2). Democratic renewal has therefore been a central plank of the government's agenda of reforms to the structures of government and public services. New Labour wanted:

> ... to make Britain's democracy work better: to bring politics closer to the people, to strengthen the rights of every citizen, and to make government more open, responsive and accountable. [We want] to build a more dynamic Britain by modernising the constitution so that people have greater control over their own lives. (The Government's Annual Report, 1998, p 84)

Labour's manifesto for the 2001 general election reaffirmed this agenda:

> Our purpose is simple: to create a Britain that is democratic, decentralised and diverse, with decisions always taken as close to the people as is consistent with efficiency and equity. (Labour Party, 2001, p 31)

The Third Way and local government

Specifically in relation to local government, the Prime Minister has made it clear that:

> We need a new – a different – local government to continue the task of modernising Britain. A new role for the new millennium. A role that challenges the sense of inevitable decline that has hung over local government for the past 20 years and provides local people and their representatives with new opportunities.

> At the heart of local government's new role is leadership – leadership that
> gives vision, *partnership* and quality of life to cities, towns and villages all over
> Britain.... *It is in partnership with others ... that local government's future lies.*
> (Blair, 1998, p 13; emphasis added)

Some may question whether leadership and partnership are compatible concepts.
The government's argument was later developed in the local government White
Paper *Modern local government: In touch with the people*, which stated that:

> Too often within a council the members and officers take the paternalistic
> view that it is for them to decide what services are to be provided, on the basis
> of what suits the council as a service provider. The interests of the public
> come a poor second best.... Too often local people are indifferent about local
> democracy, paralleling, and probably reflecting, this culture of inwardness.
> (DETR, 1998, paras 1.10 and 1.11)

New Labour's strategy has therefore been "to build councils which are in
touch with their local people and get the best for them" (DETR, 1998, p 6).
Partnerships are seen to be key to achieving this, reflecting a shift of emphasis
from the more inward-looking focus of the past. The government is providing
"a new framework which will give councils the opportunities to modernise
and the incentives to do so" (DETR, 1998, p 6).

Participatory local governance

This chapter examines the example of one local authority's citizen partnership
initiatives. It could be argued that we are witnessing a shift from politics and
governance legitimised through representative democratic structures to local
governance that is now increasingly seeking to be legitimised via participatory
democratic techniques (Davis and Daly, 1998, 1999; Cowen and Daly, 1999;
Daly and Cowen, 2000).

   This shift can be explained by Gyford et al's (1989) model of the 'three pulls'
on representative democracy, in which market democracy, delegate democracy
and participative democracy are regarded as competing democratic forms.
Gyford et al's analysis reflects a period when policy and politics were in the
midst of attacks by 'New Right' Conservative administrations on representative
democracy, and assertions about the supremacy of 'market democracy' in
particular (Waldegrave, 1993), as illustrated by the privatisation of public services,
the introduction of quasi-markets and the introduction of service charters (Prior
et al, 1993; Hill, 1994; Barnes, 1997; Rouse and Smith, 1999).

   New Labour's Third Way is neither a straightforward continuation of 'New
Right' market democracy approaches nor a return to 'Old Labour' reliance on
local representative structures. Rather, for New Labour, "what counts is what
works" (Labour Party, 1997, p 4). Although Powell (1999) argues that "the
elusive nature of the Third Way makes it difficult to be sure about where Labour's
social policy resides on [the political] spectrum", in terms of democratic

approaches we believe that the direction is clear. In local government, authorities are being required to pay greater attention to the needs and wishes of their communities. This will lead to greater opportunities for public participation, for example, through greater use of citizens' panels, citizens' juries, user groups, housing tenants' management boards, information and communications technology (ICT), and so forth (Rouse and Smith, 1999, p 249). However, as Leach and Wingfield (1999, p 47) have said, with reference to Arnstein (1971), "there is some ambiguity about how far up the ladder of citizen participation the government is advocating local authorities should go".

These ambiguities notwithstanding, the government has set local authorities the challenge of 're-engaging' with the communities they serve and embracing the 'community governance' agenda. In the event that councils are "unwilling or unable to work to the modern agenda, then the government will have to look to other partners to take on [their] role" (Blair, 1998, p 22). Therefore, local government must 'modernise' or perish.

Partnership and participation

Partnership has been part and parcel of local government for many years. In the past this usually operated around service delivery issues, but recently partnership for governance has also become an important priority. There are many imperatives for this, including the fragmentation of service delivery among a variety of agencies during the Conservative years; the perceived poor performance of many local authority services; and the lack of citizen engagement referred to above.

The Best Value duties now placed on local authorities and a range of other local government-related bodies (1999 Local Government Act) bring together a number of these strands (Martin et al, 1999, 2001). Given the government's desire to ensure that "above all ... local people and local communities are put first" (Blair, 1999), it seems reasonable to expect that "Best Value may give a new impetus to types of partnership which involve the direct participation of local communities" (Geddes, 1998, p 18).

The growth of these new governance partnerships may have significant implications for accountability and social inclusion. First, there is a potential slippery slope from collaboration to cosiness to collusion to corruption (at least in the sense of corruption of purpose). It is important therefore not to lose sight of the question, 'whose interests are being served by a particular partnership?'. Second, partnerships are as likely to be exclusive as inclusive, and indeed some may be specifically designed to be so.

Partnerships in Birmingham

The focus of this next section is an analysis of Birmingham City Council's attempts to develop partnerships for governance rather than partnerships for service delivery. The City Council is placing much emphasis on "a new partnership approach to the governance of the city" (BCC, 2001a, p 8), which goes further than current government requirements. In choosing to focus on Birmingham, our intention is to focus on one authority's approach to partnership with its citizens; analyse the nature of its approach; and draw out issues that are of significance to the wider world of local government and public policy more generally.

Partnership working in local government has expanded massively and rapidly in the years since 1997. Therefore, getting to grips with partnership issues is a major challenge for all in local government and indeed other parts of the public sector (Audit Commission, 1998). In presenting this example, we recognise the limitations of the case study approach. Nor are we intending simply to criticise the authority. Innovation requires experimentation. The point here is to illustrate the practical implications of some of the issues stemming from an increased emphasis on partnership approaches.

Birmingham has been the focus of a number of historical, political and academic studies over the years (Tiptaft, 1945; Briggs, 1963; Newton, 1976; Hattersley, 2001), although none has directly addressed the issues that are the concern of this chapter. The city has been Labour-controlled since 1984. It has a diverse, multi-ethnic population of around one million, around 30% of whom are from minority ethnic groups (BCC, 2001b, para 31). It has 39 wards, each with three councillors, and therefore a total council membership of 117.

The authority has invested a great deal of energy and resources since the mid-1980s in redefining the city. Birmingham traditionally relied heavily on manufacturing industries, but since the recession of the 1980s the council has concentrated on attracting inward investment to promote a more diversified city economy. It sees this as the way "to provide the range of job opportunities needed within Birmingham" (BCC, 2000a, p 11). As a consequence, a number of service industries have relocated to the city. At the same time, the City Council has been successful in capturing European funding, which has been used to fund various large civic enterprises, including a convention centre, exhibition centre and indoor sports arena. The city has, therefore, had some success in reinventing itself, so that it no longer sees itself solely as a manufacturing heartland but increasingly as an international business and conference city with a wide range of employment sectors.

Much of this renaissance has involved partnership working and the authority is continuing to use partnership as a means of 'adding value' to the lives of the city's citizens. The council's cabinet has stated that:

> Progress can only be made through a modern Council, in touch with the way people live their lives today, more suited to *building partnerships* with local communities, businesses and other agencies, and more capable of joined-up working across boundaries. (BCC, 2000a, p 2; emphasis added)

The council envisages two key strands to its partnership working: partnership with communities for local governance; and partnership with providers to deliver the best possible services:

> A successful city relies on strong community networks.... The essence of
> partnership government is the joining together in mutually supportive
> networks of ... various resources and interests, based on a commitment to a
> common interest in making Birmingham a more successful city for all. (BCC,
> 2001a, p 8)

This is very much in line with the government's Third Way thinking, emphasising
citizen engagement and delivering the best possible services.

City-wide partnerships

The 'overall vision for Birmingham' is 'held in custodianship' by the 'City
Pride Partnership' made up of public, private and voluntary sector agencies.
This was set up in the mid-1990s. This partnership is neither a partnership for
governance nor a partnership for service delivery. Rather, the City Pride
Partnership produces 'a set of strategic objectives' to underpin the vision for
Birmingham and uses 'a set of quality of life indicators to assess how the agreed
vision for Birmingham is being realised':

> In doing this, all partners, including the City Council, will be held to account
> for their actions. (BCC, 2000a, p 13)

The mechanisms for delivering this accountability are not entirely clear. There
also exist a number of other mechanisms concerned with developing a vision
for the city. These include the so-called Highbury events, whereby "key players
from the world of business, commerce, politics, the arts and the public sector"
(*The Birmingham Voice*, 17 January 2001) from Birmingham and beyond receive
personal invitations to the city. At the most recent event, in February 2001, the
100 or so participants were asked "to plan the transformation of the city over
the next decade" (*The Birmingham Voice*, 17 January 2001). This is notwithstanding
that the City Council had in 1999 established a 'Futures Panel', many of whose
members could be described as belonging to the 'local elite', which set out "to
create a vision for the future of the city and then work to make it happen" (*The
Birmingham Voice*, 24 May 2000). The council's majority political group also, of
course, regularly discusses its own priorities for the city. Neither the relationship
between these varying mechanisms nor the criteria by which their success is to
be measured are always clear.

   The council is currently considering what arrangements it needs to put in
place at the strategic level in order to respond to the 2000 Local Government
Act, in particular the requirement for a Community Plan for promoting the
economic, social and environmental well being of the city, its citizens and its
communities. Alongside this, the council is considering how to respond to the
government's National Strategy for Neighbourhood Renewal, through which
the city is to receive £49.5m over the period 2001/02 to 2003/04. As set out
in *A new partnership for governance* (BCC, 2001a), which was published for
consultation during the summer 2001, the City Council is proposing to set up

a Local Strategic Partnership (LSP) at the city-wide level, in order to oversee the delivery of Community Planning and the Neighbourhood Renewal Strategy.

Partnerships with local agencies

The council has also been nurturing partnerships with other local agencies in all sectors (public, private and voluntary). The council itself is central to a number of partnerships in health and social care, in housing, in transportation and in education, lifelong learning and work. In health and social care, for example, the City Council is working with the health authority, Primary Care Groups and agencies in the voluntary sector to:

> ... develop programmes which help the people of Birmingham to lead healthier lives, thereby reducing health inequalities across the city. (BCC, 2000a, p 8)

In social care, the council intends "to secure partnerships to deliver the integrated services people need ... [working] closer with partners in the voluntary, community and private sectors, in a respectful and equal way, to provide social care and support" (BCC, 2000a, p 8).

In relation to housing provision, the council is exploring a controversial transfer of its own stock, as well as enhancing partnership with the private sector. Lack of finance for essential maintenance and development of the housing stock is a key motivating factor.

Partnerships with citizens and communities

Birmingham has decentralised its service provision and devolved its political decision making in an incremental manner. Decentralisation of services from the mid-1980s involved the establishment of a number of neighbourhood offices, later developing into a city-wide network. These offices provide a range of local services (housing management and benefits advice in the main). However, there was no accompanying devolution of political decision-making and lines of control remained centralised.

Area sub-committees, based on the city's then 12 parliamentary constituencies, were established by the late 1980s, with a membership comprised of the councillors for the wards within the constituency and the local MP. The powers of the area sub-committees were insubstantial and did not include the control of the already established neighbourhood offices. In 1991 the 12 area sub-committees were replaced by ward sub-committees in each of the 39 wards. At the same time the council agreed that it would encourage the setting up of 'neighbourhood forums' where requested by the public. These forums would encourage the public to take an interest in the issues affecting the areas where they lived. In practice, promoting the development of neighbourhood forums, which are seen by the authority as a mechanism for local consultation, has received little priority. Although there are now between 50 and 60 forums across the city, their coverage is patchy.

In October 1997 the authority launched the Local Involvement, Local Action (LILA) initiative, where for the first time some political decision making was devolved to the ward councillors through the ward sub-committees.

> We established Local Involvement, Local Action to give a new perspective to the partnership between the Council and the citizens, enabling residents to become involved in proposing local projects, influencing the spend of local budgets and identifying longer term needs and priorities through Ward Development Plans. (BCC, 2000a, p 15)

Ward committees and ward advisory boards

The 39 ward sub-committees are now known as 'ward committees', and are still made up of the three councillors for the ward. Until recently the ward committees were largely consultative forums, which met in public in their ward areas, typically debating a range of issues concerned with the quality of the local environment (for example, planning applications, traffic issues and local leisure facilities). However, in more recent times, firstly under the 'Meeting Needs Across the City' initiative and subsequently under LILA, they have been given limited budgets to spend locally.

More recently, Ward Advisory Boards (WABs), consisting of the ward councillors and local community organisations, have been established in line with a local political manifesto commitment "to give much more opportunity and responsibility to local residents and local communities" and a promise to "create a new vision of popular, open and democratic local government in the city" (Labour Party, 1999, p 6). As well as working with the ward councillors on the production of Ward Development Plans, the WABs also have a role in expressing views and providing recommendations on local spending priorities and services.

The model constitution for WABs outlines a 'core membership' of the three ward councillors, the local Member of Parliament, two representatives from each neighbourhood forum within the ward, one representative from each Residents Association and one representative from each Housing Liaison Board (these boards exist to represent the views of the council's housing tenants). Ward committees (that is, the three ward councillors) can also invite representation from other interest groups (BCC, 2000b); therefore, these are far from a partnership of equals.

Each WAB has helped to guide and determine the production of a Ward Development Plan. The 'plans' vary widely in size (from four pages to 40) and arguably in comprehensiveness, in some instances possibly representing little more than unprioritised local 'wish lists'. Nevertheless, the council's cabinet has indicated its intention to "make sure that Ward Development Plans have increasing influence over Council services" (BCC, 2000a, p 15).

From WABs to WaSPs

The City Council is currently proposing to develop further the arrangements at ward level for local involvement and decision making. This is a response in part to the government's agenda for LSPs to implement community planning and the National Strategy for Neighbourhood Renewal. It is also partly a response to the City Council's recognition of a number of shortcomings in its existing arrangements for local involvement and decision making (BCC, 2000c, 2001a). The City Council's Green Paper '*A new partnership for governance*' suggests bringing together the role of the existing ward committees and WABs into new Ward Strategic Partnerships (WaSPs), and giving them a much greater range of responsibilities. The composition and role of the WaSPs, as set out below, would be different from the WABs in that, among other changes, they would be:

> ... bringing third-party organisations into these governance arrangements consistently across the city.... Those participating in [the WaSPs] would be equal members of the partnership, with something to contribute to the improvement of the local area and something to gain from working alongside others. (BCC, 2001a, p 32)

It is expected that each WaSP would include the three ward councillors, the local MP (who de facto would be a member of three or four WaSPs), two representatives from each of the neighbourhood forums in the ward (where they exist) and representatives from any parish council in the ward (currently there is only one parish council within the city of Birmingham). It is also suggested that there could be possible representation of the police, Primary Care Groups, Probation Service, Fire Service, schools in the ward, any higher and further education establishment, the 'Working Age Agency', the Learning and Skills Council, representatives from key local authority services, one or two local business people, representatives of other local voluntary and community organisations, representatives of young people, minority ethnic groups, people with disabilities and older people (BCC, 2001a, pp 32-3).

The WaSPs, which would become 'accountable bodies' under the 2000 Local Government Act, would not only be responsible for the Ward Development Plan, but in addition could become responsible for approving all expenditure delegated to the ward, including appointments to local bodies; consideration of all local planning applications; appointments of school governors; managing certain funding streams such as regeneration funds or the Neighbourhood Renewal fund; coordinating grant aid to the voluntary and community sectors; managing, in consultation with other wards, certain local council services such as street lighting, reactive road maintenance, street cleansing, refuse collection and holiday play schemes; and determining service delivery arrangements for those services controlled at ward level, including management of local tenants' halls and community centres, local regeneration and neighbourhood offices (BCC, 2001a, pp 33-4).

Learning the lessons

Partnership for governance is not unproblematic. The City Council has itself recognised that its initiatives have a number of shortcomings (BCC, 2001a, p 13). The main areas of concern arising from the ward-based devolved structures (and which are also likely to be pertinent to other local authorities wishing to create governance partnerships) are in relation to representativeness, social inclusion, manageability and utility, and accountability.

In terms of *representativeness*, research has identified concerns from community activists, councillors and council officers. One community activist commented:

> "... it's a trick isn't it and it's well used in the city.... In the end, when you do a bit of analysis, they don't represent anyone at all, they're representing themselves ... and they put their own case forward rather than the collective case. And I get very annoyed at that ... the danger always is that the local elite, the man with the loudest voice, will get what he wants and not what the community want."

Another complained that "Everyone seems to be on first name terms with everyone". A majority party inner city councillor noted that "As far as I can see from [my ward] it seems to be the same people who are always having the voice on other forums. So we really need to open the whole process out so it includes everybody". Similarly, the Labour Party nationally has recognised that "There can be a danger that [community empowerment] initiatives ... end up involving the same people in different guises" (Labour Party, 2000, p 14). Thus while the avowed intention is that the ward-based structures should be fully inclusive, the recurring reality is that this is not achieved.

A majority party councillor representing an outer-city ward commented:

> "You see, what bothers me about this devolution of decision-making is that I've got 20,000 electors in my ward and the biggest meeting I've ever had is 100. So even if those people had all put their hands up for something, you can't ever say that that is [the view of] my constituents, my ward."

These issues extend into questions of *social inclusion*. When one inspects WABs city wide, one observes that the pattern and structure of WAB membership vary significantly from one ward to another. Although a systematic promotion of different partnership arrangements to reflect the diversity of the city's wards would be logical, it appears that the different arrangements tend, in practice, to be due to pragmatic, rather than more considered, reasons.

Both the City Council's Equalities Scrutiny Committee report on the *Involvement of under-represented groups in the LILA initiative* (BCC, 2000b) and *Challenges for the future*, the report of the Birmingham Stephen Lawrence Inquiry Commission (BCC, 2001b), have raised concerns about the exclusion of certain voices:

... two wards do not have advisory boards [at all].... Only 12 wards had representation from older people's organisations ... 22 of the 39 wards ... had no members from black and minority ethnic groups ... 30 ... of Ward Advisory Boards had no disabled member ... 23 ... had no youth representation. (BCC, 2000b, p 70)

LILA's focus on wards as the basic building block of community fails to value the richness of the minority ethnic communities that are based on communities of interest and not just communities of place. (BCC, 2001b, para 8.7)

The current membership proposals for the WaSPs (BCC, 2001a, pp 32-3) do not address these criticisms, although the City Council is taking steps to address these issues.

As Geddes has said (1998, p 18), and acknowledged by the City Council itself (BCC, 2001a, p 7), communities need to be thought of in terms "of place, of interest and of identity". Arguably, the membership structures of the WABs or WaSPs do not adequately take account of this. Taking account of the various types of communities will be important for any local authority seeking to establish effective partnerships (see also Chapter Nine).

Turning to the *manageability and utility* of devolved structures, the 2000 Local Government Act requires councils to adopt new political management arrangements in place of committee structures. The preceding local government White Paper commented that: "Traditional committee structures ... lead to inefficient and opaque decision making.... Equally there is little clear political leadership.... People often do not know who is really taking the decisions" (DETR, 1998, paras 3.4-3.7).

The government view is that separating out the executive role will lead to greater efficiency (quicker, more responsive and more accurate decisions); greater transparency (it will be clear who is responsible for decisions); and greater accountability (enabling the measurement of actions against policies) (DETR, 1998, para 3.14). The government has been rather more flexible about desired area and neighbourhood structures, expecting "a wide variety of different arrangements" to be put in place (DETR, 1999, para 3.26).

It is difficult to see, however, how Birmingham's devolved structures properly meet any of the above 'tests'. In the present ward committee/WAB structure, although formal accountability is arguably clear, the role of the WAB can, in practice, lead to some confusion. Transparency is far from complete – WABs still seem to operate 'behind closed doors'. Efficiency is a more difficult concept, but, if measured as suggested above, there is little evidence that ward committees/WABs lead to quicker decision making. They may well be more responsive to certain local individuals and interest groups, though whether this leads to more accurate decisions may well be open to question. If one applies the wider, but nevertheless still appropriate, 'principles of public life' (selflessness – decisions taken solely in terms of the public interest; integrity; objectivity; accountability; openness; honesty and leadership – promoting the principles by leadership and example), which were set out by Lord Nolan (Committee on Standards in Public Life, 1995, p 14), it is difficult to discern any improvement.

If the proposals to replace ward committees and WABs with WaSPs go ahead, it is hard to see how any of these matters will improve. On the basis of the outline membership proposals, the Moseley WaSP, for example, could have around 30 members. This does not have the appearance of a small, streamlined body of the kind that the government seems to believe is necessary for efficient decision making. Members would come with diverse mandates. Just four would be subject to direct, universal, public election. The others would, at best, be 'delegates' from various organisations in the ward but, at worst, may not even be that. This could place local councillors and MPs in the invidious position of being the only members who can be held to account by the wider public, yet very much in the minority on the WaSP. There would be some questionable potential conflicts of interest. For example, schools would be represented on the WaSP, while the WaSP would make appointments to school governing bodies. Indeed, the WaSPs risk being dominated by special interests, leading to a whole range of potential questions about their ability to comply with, and be seen to comply with, Nolan's eminently reasonable 'principles of public life'.

We have noted elsewhere that public service *accountability* presents particular problems. In our view, there are two distinctive elements of accountability, namely: a means for the giving of an account; and a means of holding to account (Stewart and Davis, 1994, p 32). The first of these is, in principle, unproblematic. There is no real reason why Birmingham's devolved partnership or political management structures, current or proposed, cannot find effective means to report regularly on their decisions and activities to the public and others. Indeed, in some cases appropriate mechanisms may already exist.

However, as is so often the case with non-elected bodies, it is the second element (a means of holding to account) that presents difficulties. In practice, there is a lack of effective sanctions that can be utilised by the wider public in the event of dissatisfaction with the decisions and actions of individual partnership participants. Unless they are councillors or MPs, the wider public certainly cannot remove them. Yet the wider public is still expected to pay, through central and local taxation, for the public services about which decisions may be being made. 'No taxation without representation' was a rallying cry of the American Revolution. It is still an appropriate maxim today.

It would not be completely honest to argue that effective accountability for the decisions of devolved structures (such as the ward committees or WaSPs) can be assured through the centralised structures of the authority, such as its cabinet and full council. It is neither reasonable nor realistic to expect the city's leading councillors to have adequate knowledge and control of every activity and decision in every locality. If devolved structures are to be properly accountable, there need to be adequate mechanisms in place at that level.

Those with decision-making responsibilities must have a clear and universal mandate. While this is the principle behind Birmingham's current devolved arrangements of ward committees and WABs, in practice roles are blurred. The ward councillors sit on both the decision-making body (the ward committee) and the body that advises them (the WAB) – they thus advise themselves. This blurring is then compounded by the way in which ward councillors are able to determine WAB membership. Furthermore, the process of discussion and recommendation emerging from the WABs may lead to the local councillors, in their ward committee role, having little alternative but to endorse WAB recommendations, thereby making it far from clear where the 'real' decision has been made.

Alternative arrangements would be to subject the decisions of these devolved partnership bodies to direct democracy, such as referenda, or to exempt from relevant taxation those who are not given adequate means of representation. Neither of these options is unproblematic.

Conclusions

These observations should not be interpreted as indicating that partnerships are of no value or are too problematic to be worthwhile. Neither are there grounds for complacency about the current state of our representative democracy – although it should be recognised that this is by no means simply a problem of this age. The Labour Party nationally states that it "is committed to an open, responsive democracy held to account by the people" (Labour Party, 2000, p 24). With this in mind, the initiatives that are being developed to promote greater partnership and participation in Birmingham and elsewhere are to be welcomed. However, in many instances, much remains to be done to ensure greater inclusion, increased representativeness and clearer lines of accountability. A greater clarity over the purpose of such initiatives would help in achieving these aims.

There is frequently confusion about the relationship between partnership for governance and representative democracy. Both have strengths, both have weaknesses. The imperative is to achieve an effective, workable balance that harnesses interest and energies. What is required, therefore, is a renewed democracy, in which citizens are able to participate as partners *and* be properly represented.

This implies arrangements that are truly representative and that take care to ensure that they do not just involve 'the usual suspects'. Such arrangements should also be fully inclusive. The comprehensibility and manageability of many developing partnership arrangements is complicated beyond belief. These partnerships should be kept simple and straightforward. So far as accountability is concerned, the mixing of mandates is arguably highly problematic. Councillors are being placed in an invidious position and there should be a clear separation between decision-making and advisory roles. Those making decisions must be able to be *held to account* by universal suffrage.

Learning from the lessons outlined above suggests a number of key issues for those wishing to construct effective local governance partnerships:

- partnerships should be based on a thorough, considered, strategic approach with clear aims, rather than on ad hoc and incremental initiatives (Hudson and Hardy refer to this as 'clarity of purpose' in Chapter Four);
- partnerships should be genuine pluralities, reaching out beyond the 'usual suspects' and the 'local elite';
- partnerships should recognise diversity and be inclusive of different types of community, including communities of interest and identity as well as place (a point also noted by Craig and Taylor in Chapter Nine);
- those who participate in partnerships as representatives of communities, of whatever type, should be able to demonstrate their legitimacy;
- the structures and workings of partnerships should be open and transparent;
- partnerships should be 'fit for purpose', with considerations about size of membership, the frequency and timing of meetings, the remit and the 'shelf life' of the partnership fully thought through;
- partnerships should have adequate mechanisms for regularly evaluating their effectiveness and progress in achieving their intended purpose;
- partnerships should observe and honour the Nolan Committee's 'principles of public life';
- partnership and participation should inform conventional representative democratic structures and should only replace them if they can be fully accountable in respect of both of the two elements of accountability, namely the giving of an account and a means of being held to account; and should ensure real and effective means for the operation of both kinds of accountability. Otherwise there is a danger, as Davies points out in Chapter Eleven, of partnerships delivering negative outcomes to communities.

Through such means, clear and effective partnership arrangements can make an important contribution to the goal of democratic renewal.

References

Arnstein, S. (1971) 'A ladder of citizen participation', in R.T. Le Gates and F. Stout (eds) (2000) *The city reader*, 2nd edn, London: Routledge.

Audit Commission (1998) *A fruitful partnership: Effective partnership working*, London: Audit Commission.

Barnes, M. (1997) *Care, communities and citizens*, London: Longman.

BCC (Birmingham City Council) (2000a) *Cabinet statement*, Birmingham: BCC, 1 February.

BCC (2000b) *Involvement of under-represented groups in the LILA initiative: Report of the chair, Equalities Scrutiny Committee*, Birmingham: BCC.

BCC (2000c) *Local voices, local democracy: The report of the Birmingham Democracy Commission*, Birmingham: BCC.

BCC (2001a) *A new partnership for governance: The Birmingham consultation paper on the local level, devolution and citizenship*, Birmingham: BCC.

BCC (2001b) *Challenges for the future: Race equality in Birmingham: Report of the Birmingham Stephen Lawrence Inquiry Commission*, Birmingham: BCC.

Blair, T. (1998) *Leading the way: A new vision for local government*, London: IPPR.

Blair, T. (1999) *Message of support sent to the national best value conference*, 22 November.

Briggs, A. (1963) *Victorian cities*, Harmondsworth: Penguin Books.

Committee on Standards in Public Life (1995) *First report: Volume 1*, Cm 2850-1, HMSO.

Cowen, H. and Daly, G. (1999) 'Democracy and citizenship in the new millennium', Paper presented to The British Sociological Association Annual Conference, University of Glasgow, 6-9 April.

Daly, G. and Cowen, H. (2000) 'Redefining the local citizen', in L. McKie and N. Watson (eds) *Organising bodies: Policy, institutions, and work*, Basingstoke: Macmillan.

Davis, H. and Daly, G. (1998) 'New opportunities for the Health Service: Achieving its democratic potential', Paper presented to The National Health Service: Past, Present and Future Conference, University of Brighton, 3 July.

Davis, H. and Daly, G. (1999) 'Achieving democratic potential in the NHS', *Public Money and Management*, vol 25, no 2, pp 59-62.

DETR (Department of the Environment, Transport and the Regions) (1998) *Modern local government: In touch with the people*, Cm 4014, London: The Stationery Office.

DETR (1999) *Local leadership, local choice*, London: The Stationery Office.

Geddes, M. (1998) *Achieving best value through partnership*, Warwick/DETR Best Value Series Paper no 7, The University of Warwick.

Giddens, A. (1998) *The third way: The renewal of social democracy*, Cambridge: Polity Press.

Giddens, A. (1999) *Runaway world*, London: Profile Books.

Giddens, A. (2001) *The global third way debate*, Cambridge: Polity Press.

The Government's Annual Report 97/98 (1998), Cm 3969, London: The Stationery Office.

Gyford, J., Leach, S. and Game, C. (1989) *The changing politics of local government*, London: Unwin Hyman.

Hattersley, R. (2001) 'Does loss of power mean the death of the town hall?', *The Guardian*, 22 March.

Hill, D. (1994) *Citizens and cities*, Hemel Hempstead: Harvester Wheatsheaf.

HMSO (1999) *Local government act 1999*, London: The Stationery Office.

Labour Party (1997) *New Labour: Because Britain deserves better*, London: Labour Party.

Labour Party (1999) *Delivering a better Birmingham: Labour – putting people first: Labour's election manifesto for 1999*, London: Labour Party.

Labour Party (2000) *Democracy and citizenship: Second year consultation document*, London: Labour Party.

Labour Party (2001) *Ambitions for Britain*, London: Labour Party.

Leach, S. and Wingfield, M. (1999) 'Public participation and the democratic renewal agenda: prioritisation or marginalisation?', *Local Government Studies*, vol 25, no 4, pp 46-59.

Martin, S., Davis, H., Bovaird, T., Geddes, M., Hartley, J., Lewis, M., Sanderson, I. and Sapwel, P. (1999) *Improving local public services: Interim evaluation of the best value pilot programme*, London: DETR.

Martin, S., Davis, H., Bovaird, T., Downe, J., Geddes, M., Hartley, J., Lewis, M., Sanderson, I. and Sapwell, P. (2001) *Improving local public services: Final evaluation of the best value pilot programme*, London: DETR.

Newton, K. (1976) *Second city politics: Democratic processes and decision making in Birmingham*, Oxford: Clarendon Press.

Powell, M. (1999) 'What's the big idea', *The Guardian*, 2 June.

Prior, D., Stewart, J. and Walsh, K. (1993) *Is the Citizen's Charter a charter for citizens?*, Belgrave Papers No 7, London: Local Government Management Board.

Rouse, J. and Smith, G. (1999) 'Accountability', in M. Powell (ed) *New Labour, new welfare state? The 'third way' in British social policy*, Bristol: The Policy Press, pp 235-56.

Stewart, J. and Davis, H. (1994) 'A new agenda for local governance', *Public Money and Management*, vol 14, no 4, pp 29-36

Tiptaft, N. (1945) *I saw a city*, Birmingham: Cornish Brothers.

Waldegrave, W. (1993) *The reality of reform and accountability in today's public service*, London: CIPFA.

EIGHT

Partnerships with the voluntary sector: can Compacts work?

Pete Alcock and Duncan Scott

Partnership working between the state and the voluntary and community sectors is an important, if sometimes less widely publicised, element of Labour's new agenda for the development and delivery of social policy; it has recently taken on a more formal guise through the introduction of Compact agreements between the sectors. However, translating the formal commitments within Compacts into practical partnership working is likely to require greater levels of understanding and commitment than has generally been the case in previous relations between the state and the voluntary and community sectors. It is also important to recognise the differences between the voluntary and community sectors themselves (see also Chapter Nine). This chapter describes the endeavours by the New Labour governments to formalise partnerships between statutory and voluntary sector organisations through the new mechanism of 'Compacts'; and explores the potential for partnership working through an analysis of the experiences of a small number of voluntary organisations. Attention thus focuses on these rather than on community action, but even here the clear message is that diverse needs and circumstances will not easily be captured within single regulatory frameworks.

The developing government agenda

The government has established a clear agenda for 'modernising' public services, particularly in the welfare field. This modernisation agenda is very much at the centre of the government's much trumpeted 'Third Way' for welfare reform, which involves, inter alia, a renewed commitment to 'partnership' between different providers in the welfare economy. It is now widely recognised, of course, that, despite the 'welfare state' reforms of the mid-20th century, which established the major public services for health, housing, education, income support and social care in the UK, there has always been a mix of providers – public, private and voluntary – supplying welfare services to citizens. This variation is usually referred to as the 'mixed economy of welfare' (see Chapter One).

However, a mixed economy of welfare is not the same thing as collaboration or partnership working. The latter terms imply joint involvement in service development and delivery, not just the use of providers from different sectors.

Beveridge (1948), often regarded as the architect of public welfare provision of the post-war period, was in fact a proponent of cooperation between public and other welfare providers, particularly voluntary sector agencies, although he saw the relationship mainly as one of complementary working rather than formal partnership. And, in practice, the public service agencies established in the 1940s did not work much in collaboration with voluntary organisations in planning and delivery services. Indeed, as in the case of tenants' associations and community advice agencies, the role of voluntary organisations was sometimes an oppositional or challenging one.

It is not just the lack of collaboration and partnership between public, private and voluntary agencies that is now of concern to the government. The new Labour administration is only too aware that public agencies have themselves developed in largely isolated 'silos' and do not have any tradition of co-working or even, in some cases, information-sharing. This 'silo' mentality is now openly challenged by the government's appeal for 'joined-up responses to joined-up problems' – a recognition that citizens and their communities in practice draw support and services from a range of public and other agencies and can rightly expect these agencies to respond in a coordinated way. It is the need for joined-up thinking that is one of the key drivers of the government's new-found commitment to partnership working; and included within the circle which is to be joined are voluntary sector organisations operating within, or upon, the welfare field.

For the Labour government, and for Prime Minister Tony Blair in particular, this re-engagement with the voluntary sector is part of an attempt to secure a renewed role for 'civil society' in combating the social problems afflicting British society at the end of the last century. Blair has clearly been influenced by American communitarians, in particular Etzioni (1993, 1997), who argue that the social problems of modern societies can only be addressed when citizens, acting collectively in their local communities, take on the responsibility for identifying and meeting social needs through voluntary action. Citizens therefore have responsibilities and obligations for giving, as well as getting; in acting collectively to do this, they will forge new social relations in between the state and the market:

> ... the work of the voluntary and community organizations is central to the
> Government's mission to make this the Giving Age. They enable individuals
> to contribute to the development of their communities. By so doing, they
> promote citizenship, help to re-establish a sense of community and make a
> crucial contribution to our aim of a just and inclusive society. (Blair, 1998,
> p 3)

The promotion of civil society is thus linked to the government's broader aim to promote social inclusion and reduce social exclusion. There is connection too with another developing policy agenda, the need to 'invest' in improving social capital. The work of American political scientists, such as Putnam (1993, 1995) and Coleman (1988, 1990), has demonstrated that poor social relations, as measured by low levels of voluntary and associational activity, are linked to a more general lack of 'trust' between citizens and public agencies and hence lower levels of democratic participation and social solidarity. They describe this as a loss of social capital and politicians such as Blair have responded by arguing that government should promote policy interventions to support associational activity and improve social relations.

Government is now therefore concerned to support policy programmes that promote *social* regeneration – or social inclusion, as it is often now referred to. To some extent, this is in contrast to the Thatcher governments of the 1980s, which saw the route to social progress through economic regeneration; this would be achieved by providing an environment in which private capital investment would be rewarded and economic growth would lead to social progress (see Chapter Eleven).

Since Labour came to power, a plethora of new area-based initiatives has been developed, alongside a continuation of the previous economic regeneration strategies. These new programmes include Sure Start, Action Zones for Employment, Education and Health, New Deal for Communities, Neighbourhood Renewal, Community Safety and other smaller initiatives. The commitment to partnership and participation runs clearly through them all, with the New Deal for Communities, for instance, promising to "bring together local people, community and voluntary organisations, public agencies, local authorities and business in an intensive local focus" on social problems (Social Exclusion Unit, 1998, p 54).

Devolution has also promoted a range of new commitments to partnership working. The Welsh National Assembly, for instance, is under a legal duty to work in partnership with the voluntary sector and has adopted a scheme "committed to recognising, valuing and promoting the voluntary sector as it builds a genuine partnership with the sector" (National Assembly of Wales, 2000, section 2.2). Within England, the new Regional Development Agencies have formal responsibility for promoting collaboration and have already begun to establish formal links with umbrella bodies representing voluntary sector agencies in their areas.

Nevertheless, commitments to partnership and participation, however formally expressed, do not automatically translate into harmonious and productive relationships between government agencies and voluntary and community organisations. In a review of past and current participation programmes, Foley and Martin (2000, p 480) refer to "community (non)involvement in urban regeneration". The more general challenges and limitations of partnership working discussed elsewhere in this book take on a particular form in the context of partnership working with the voluntary sector, where the tradition is often one of the late and reluctant inclusion of a partner who enters with unequal status and limited practical and political resources.

Of course, there are examples of long-standing and effective partnership working between public service agencies and voluntary organisations at national and at local levels. However, there is no consistent pattern of such successful collaboration. Indeed, the research discussed in this chapter, and other previous research in the field (Taylor, 2001), reveals a number of significant organisational and political obstacles.

Despite the recent acceleration and expansion of formal commitments to partnership working, there is still a significant legacy of paternalism within many public sector agencies – and among their political masters and mistresses. It is perhaps no surprise that, after a number of decades of developing, sustaining and then defending public services, many senior officers naturally feel defensive of their responsibilities and practices. These commitments to public service provision are often shared by politicians at national and local levels, who may not have entirely embraced the 'New Labour' Third Way for welfare policy. Foley and Martin (2000, p 486) comment that much depends upon the willingness of "local councils to cede power and control of resources, decision making and implementation processes to communities", though there is little evidence that this has happened to any significant degree in the past.

Power differentials are a dimension here. Real power is a positional good and, for partnership working to be based on redistribution of power between partner agencies, then some have got to lose in order for others to gain. This is not easily achieved. As well requiring changes in attitudes and activities by public sector agencies, it will require a willingness on the part of voluntary sector organisations or other community representatives to enter into partnership activity. This also involves challenging many traditions and shifting entrenched attitudes; for instance, only a fifth of residents in Best Value pilot areas stated that they would like to have more of a say in the running of local services (Martin et al, 1999). Furthermore, willingness to participate in partnerships must be backed by capability.

As discussed later in this chapter, the ability of voluntary organisations to engage effectively in partnerships varies not only in terms of their particular organisational commitments and capacity, but also with reference to contingent features of their wider working environment. These include the different or conflicting roles of stakeholders; unrealistic expectations about social entrepreneurs; the dilemmas of networking; and the often disruptive impact of external agendas. All these issues reveal that it is dangerous to dichotomise government and the voluntary sector; in terms of information, resources, work planning, capacity and commitment, there are as many differences as similarities in the potential of the voluntary sector to engage effectively in partnership activity.

This raises some very practical questions about how to engage voluntary organisations in partnership working. It also raises questions about the more formal relations with the voluntary and community sectors that are implicit – and increasingly explicit – in much current programme planning and partnership practice. Given the diversity and difference, and the resulting particular (even individual) limitations and contradictions, who can 'represent' voluntary and community organisations in the grand partnership bodies that are now proliferating within the various government programmes mentioned earlier?

> There are also thorny questions about whether a regional network can 'speak' for sometimes tens of thousands of groups. Who really knows what a mothers and toddlers group in Cranfield, Bedfordshire, for instance, or a drugs action charity in Teeside thinks? (Pollock, 1999, p 9)

Similarly, in a discussion of such developments in north-west England, Langslow (quoted in Pollock, 1999, p 9) points out that it was far from clear that people either within the government office or the body set up to lead local partnership planning "actually understood what the voluntary sector really was".

Long traditions of paternalism, limited and variable resources within voluntary and community organisations, and lack of knowledge and understanding across the sectors all pose formidable challenges to the development of partnership working. In a large part, of course, these challenges are not new – despite the greater urgency and profile that they may have acquired under new government policy programmes. They have already been acknowledged and addressed by policy makers and analysts concerned with the future of voluntary sector relations. It is to address just such issues that the Compacts arising out of the Deakin and Kemp Commissions were developed. It is also in order to inform such policy planning that our research into the experiences and dynamics of voluntary organisations was carried out.

Formalising relationships with the voluntary sector

The foundation stones of more formal and explicit relationships between government and the voluntary and community sectors were laid down in the Deakin Commission report (NCVO, 1996) for England and the equivalent Kemp Commission for Scotland (SCVO, 1997). The Commissions were initiated and serviced in England by the National Council for Voluntary Organisations (NCVO) and in Scotland by the Scottish Council for Voluntary Organisations (SCVO). These agencies operate as general intermediate or coordinating organisations, both within the voluntary sector and in relation to different arms of government. The Commissions were prompted by concerns about the alleged growth of individualism, coupled with a decline in civil society; and by fears that the increased development of voluntary sector-based service delivery in the 1990s was threatening the independence of many agencies (Lewis, 1999).

It was hoped that the Commissions' reports, based on extensive consultation with policy makers, practitioners and academics, would confer greater status and legitimacy on the voluntary sector as a whole and its coordinating, intermediate agencies in particular. Furthermore, it was hoped that the reports could be used to stimulate dialogue about new ways to consolidate voluntary sector relationships with government.

While there were many areas of overlap between the English and Scottish reports, subsequent commentaries have been dominated by a specifically English focus. The pre-election publication by the Labour Party, *Building the future together* (Labour Party, 1997), was implicitly generic. However, thereafter more devolved emphases emerged; for example, the first subsequent Home Office publication was explicitly subtitled *Compact on relations between government and the voluntary and community sector in England* (Home Office, 1998; emphasis added).

Several strands of thinking preface and underpin the formal mechanism of both national and local Compacts. These include a search for greater efficiency in the service delivery activities of voluntary agencies; a concern to connect more closely with and consult particular neighbourhoods and groups; and a principled commitment to involve consumers.

The first of these strands of thinking, the economic strand, developed out of transitional arrangements associated with the implementation of the 1990 NHS and Community Care Act. This required 85% of the funds to purchase community-based care services to be channelled via voluntary or independent for-profit agencies, at the same time as the new public management agenda was emphasising the importance of efficiency scrutinies. It was therefore hardly surprising that more explicit formal agreements became attractive: "… tighter regulation and the drive to build the capacity (or expertise) of non-governmental organisations are associated with standardisation, formalisation and professionalisation within the voluntary sector" (Harris, 2001, p 215).

Throughout the 1990s, these developments were closely linked to the prioritisation of market-based approaches, underpinned by quasi-legal service agreements between government and voluntary agencies termed 'contracts', which attempted to specify exactly what services were being purchased.

Deakin's focus was more general; he wanted government to agree a set of general principles about the need for closer relationships with a wide range of voluntary agencies – campaigning as well as service delivery ones. However, the very term used in his Commission's report – 'concordat' – assumed an underlying consensus that some critics (6 and Leat, 1996) asserted did not exist. Even the government of the day, in its response to Deakin, used similar arguments: "The Government does not believe that, given the diverse nature of voluntary organisations and activity, a formal concordat is a sensible or usefully achievable objective" (Department of National Heritage, 1996, p 2).

Other responses to the Deakin Commission expressed concern about the harmful consequences of formalisation and professionalisation, in particular the further marginalisation of volunteers (Russell and Scott, 1997). In addition, insufficient attention was paid to detailed empirical evidence about the very real contradictions associated with participatory strategies led by professionals from within formal state bureaucracies and more formal voluntary agencies such as the NCVO.

Nevertheless, a concordat approach – or Compacting, as it was now termed – was quickly taken up by the incoming Labour administration because it harmonised with policy rhetoric on inclusion and seemed to reinforce the 'politics of the middle' that had produced the election victory of 1997. The first Compact document outlined general principles and set the tone for its successors (Home Office, 1998). It was not legally binding, but implied a degree of authoritativeness because of the commitment shown by government. It focused on the allegedly distinctive value of voluntary and community groups and volunteers. This distinctiveness derives from functions such as innovation, advocacy and inclusion; principles such as partnership and transparency; the significance of black and minority ethnic involvement; and local diversity.

There is no doubt that central government took the idea of Compacts seriously. In the three years from mid-1997, there were extensive consultations, working groups and draft codes. For example, perhaps the key publication that marked the end of the initial phase of consultation (*Local compact guidelines*, WGGRS/LGA, 2000, p 2) proudly noted how the guidelines had emerged from "... two rounds of consultation, including four seminars attended by almost 300 people, and reflect the responses of 775 representatives from local authorities and voluntary and community organisations".

Assessments of the impact of local Compacts vary, but by late 1999, 10% of local authorities had a Compact and half of the rest planned to get underway during 2000 (WGGRS/LGA, 2000, p 24). The key indicator of 'impact' was the existence of a jointly negotiated protocol rather than, but not to the total exclusion of, changes in organisational practices. One set of case studies concluded, "In some localities, negotiations on Compacts were far advanced; elsewhere they were just beginning" (Craig, 2001, p 2).

Part of the problem of assessing the impact of Compacts is less to do with newness and uneven implementation, however, and more to do with organisational complexity. It is very difficult to identify how far and in what ways a local Compact (concerned with principles and relationships between local authorities and voluntary/community groups) differs from Local Strategic Partnerships (concerned with the coordination of public, voluntary, community *and* private sectors). Inevitably, there are fears that the coordination and evaluation of Local Strategic Partnerships and Compacts may become complex, if not confused (LGA, 2001).

The content of national (English) Compacts

There are three general publications outlining policy and practice on Compacts:

* General principles (Home Office, 1998)
* Consultation and policy appraisal (Home Office, 2000a)
* Funding (Home Office, 2000b)

... and three more specific publications:

* Black and minority ethnic voluntary and community organisations (Home Office, 2001a)
* Volunteering (Home Office, 2001b)
* Community groups (Home Office, 2002)

Figure 8.1 summarises what have been described as the 10 key undertakings of the national Compact (NCVO, 2001, p 9). The core national Compact documents, if considered superficially, appear to repeat familiar generalisations

Figure 8.1: Key undertakings of the national Compact

Compact publication	Key undertakings
1. General principles	• Lawful action; Charity Commission guidelines • High standards of governance • Quality standards • Effective cross-sector relations • User involvement • Annual review
2. Consultation/policy	• User/volunteer involvement
3. Funding	• Effective organisation • Effective monitoring/evaluation • Volunteer involvement in services

about inter-sectoral/organisational relationships; similar observations can be made about their local sisters and brothers.

The processes of Compact development have involved a considerable number of consultations at several levels. Nationally a ministerial group chaired by a Home Office minister and attended by up to 10 government departments has liaised with a voluntary and community sector working group; a reference group of 65 different voluntary organisations; a community sector coalition; and black voluntary and community organisations (Home Office, 1998, Annex A). At local levels, local authorities and/or Councils of Voluntary Service (CVS) have been initiators of steering groups and plenary conferences that have provided the formal arenas for processes of audit, debate and decision (WGGRS/LGA, 2000, pp 3-9).

By late 1999, 34% of English local authorities claimed to have a written policy on relationships with voluntary organisations, but only 10% had achieved a local Compact (WGGRS/LGA, 2000, p 24). Despite all the commitment and consultation, the most optimistic forecast is, therefore, that by the end of 2001 only about one third of English local authorities expect to have formal Compacts (NCVO, 2001, p 5).

Even enthusiastic participants in Compacting are likely to encounter dense ideological and organisational hurdles. Many local authorities find it hard to break out of a professional and bureaucratic mindset that views much voluntary and community activity as irretrievably complex and unmanageable. Where the more formal voluntary sector agencies can sustain paid workers, such as in a CVS, Citizens Advice Bureau (CAB) or church network, some of these anxieties and pessimisms can be displaced – the CVS or CAB director or the vicar can become a go-between or broker. Frequently, the community groups then still remain just over the horizon.

A further set of hurdles involves organisational dilemmas. These include joining up the different Compacts, partnerships and zones – at least on a metaphorical flipchart – so that major inefficiencies can be avoided. Additional problems concern overload, representation, resourcing, content, reviewing and development (Craig et al, 1999; Craig, 2001; see also Chapter Nine). Most inter-sectoral partnerships are neither adequately resourced nor prepared to become learning and change systems. They are more equipped to form committees, agree paper-based frameworks and conduct audits at arm's length. Until there is a greater dissemination and digestion of good practice about inter-sectoral learning and change, Compacts may tend to become one-dimensional, administrative devices around which more limited processes will be initiated and monitored.

The dynamics of partnership

Most local authorities have established a wide range of relationships with voluntary and community organisations, but there is often little sense that any one department or partnership body has either an overview and/or a strategic role in relation to the different organisations. Individual departments, such as education, social services or housing, will have their own voluntary sector links. Some may simply hold lists of contacts and basic details, while others pursue jointly negotiated policies, underpinned by dedicated resources, which explicitly and proactively seek to broaden and deepen relationships.

The 'silo' mentality, expressed in departmental separateness, remains a serious structural issue. Formal Compacting appears to make moves towards greater structural and organisational coherence, but there are few signs that the everyday dynamics and dilemmas of partnership are being sufficiently recognised, explored and resolved.

Commitment to partnership working, both formal and informal, requires an understanding of the realities and dynamics of daily life for both parties. Research carried out on the voluntary sector (Scott et al, 2000) revealed that the experiences of voluntary sector organisations were more complex and varied than some of the more zealous proponents of Compacting and partnership seemed to be aware. We tend to agree with those critics of the Deakin report who were cautious about assuming an underlying consensus underpinning government–voluntary relations; who identified as much government pragmatism and manipulation as rational benevolence; and who were sceptical of monolithic conceptions of sectors (Lewis, 1999, p 263). Despite the usefulness of principles and guidelines, we were persuaded that "... voluntary sector–governmental relations are subject to such vagaries and blurring that organisational 'positioning' in the relationship will vary often and readily" (Vincent and Harrow, 2000, p 17).

Our research was based on detailed qualitative case study material from eight voluntary organisations and employed a thematic approach, with each organisation illustrating one core theme – infrastructure, values and identity, social entrepreneurs, stakeholders and accountability, managerialism, strategic planning, networking or external agendas. Through lengthy interviews, incidents and contexts were identified that could provide a lens through which to analyse the confusion, complexity and contradiction of everyday voluntary action. As a result, we were able to contextualise beliefs and behaviour, to provide an understanding of the multidimensional and contradictory circumstances of the sector, the organisation, and even the individuals involved within these.

Furthermore, the research was able to use detail to reflect critically how:

> ... during the recent discussions about 'Compacts' between government and the voluntary sector there has been much welcome attention to the need for clear, explicit statements about institutional relationships. Yet, even as these various Compacts unfold, it is also clear how organisations find themselves (willingly or not) enmeshed in more informal relationships with the very same government departments. (Scott et al, 2000, p 7)

From the eight themes that structured the research, the focus here is on four which throw light on core elements of partnership working.

*   *Stakeholding* is often discussed at the design stage of Compacts, as attempts are made to identify different kinds of representation. The research found that stakeholding is not just about political connections, and that stakeholders find themselves caught in a mesh of often conflicting obligations.
*   *Social entrepreneurs* are the 'ball-bearings' of partnerships; their commitment and energy are often crucial in sustaining fragile relationships. The research concluded that as much attention needs to be paid to the support and development of the entrepreneurs as to the organisations from which they come.
*   *Networking* draws attention to the many linkages (often as many informal as formal, private as public) that both join *and* divide organisations. The study found that greater recognition needs to be given to the value of networking within the structure, processes and development of partnerships.
*   *External agendas* remind us that local partnerships do not operate in a vacuum; central government initiatives frequently disrupt the pattern and progress of local action. The continued strength of a local Compact will partly depend on there being joint, rather than unilateral, local responses to such external promptings.

From these themes two, more general, questions emerge:

*   What are the common experiences of voluntary sector workers, as members of agencies committed to such principles as stakeholding and as individual social entrepreneurs?
*   What kinds of linkages (informal and formal) do voluntary organisations make and seek to sustain with statutory agencies? Here the focus is on networking and external agendas.

Compacts and strategic partnerships depend on certain assumptions and common interests, so that across sectors it should be possible to encourage a deepening commitment to stakeholding. Our case study of KidsCare (a pseudonym, as are all subsequent names) represented a local voluntary agency with an explicit commitment to, and experience of, the strategic involvement of workers, volunteers and users. After a period of funding via a national charity, it became entirely funded through a contract with the local social services department. This new relationship marked a watershed. KidsCare was no longer entrusted with the complex task of reconciling the often divergent interests and concerns of different groups of stakeholders. As a result, a senior worker commented that she:

> ... had to go into advisory group meetings with users, knowing I had been gagged. This would have been unimaginable in the past – in a project driven by users.... I felt social services wanted us to be accountable to them – not to see users as the constituency to which we were accountable. (Scott et al, 2000, p 29)

The different stakeholders were clearly unequal, particularly in relation to sources of finance. As the statutory funder occupied the central strategic ground, so the instrumental, service delivery focus became more important than more elusive matters of democracy and participation. This underlines the need for stakeholders to confront likely conflicts of interest at the outset, and to be honest about priorities. Service delivery and social inclusion may not be *automatically* compatible.

Compacts need participants, partners or stakeholders in the plural. But, in the nature of so much collective inter-sectoral work, a lot depends on key individuals. Considerable attention is paid to their alleged flair, creativity and energy, but so often their specific organisational and wider operating worlds slip from view and can lead to unrealistic expectations and demands. Gwen (the project manager of Safety Works, an organisation that repaired and recycled nursery and safety equipment) experienced just this: "I was getting here earlier and earlier and I was taking work home at night.... kept waking up in the night and thinking I must do this and this and this" (Scott et al, 2000, p 20).

The fostering of new initiatives in the voluntary sector is likely to threaten the fragile shoulders of key individuals such as Gwen, unless a more multidimensional approach to their resourcing is adopted. Thus we need to direct attention to the real life pressures on the key voluntary sector 'ball-bearings', and ensure that the dedicated resources and support that they need are built into any partnership proposals. The weekly paperwork and meeting time associated with these processes of partnership can easily reach double figures, especially around the time of important conferences or document production. At these times, the very people who build up the most knowledge and expertise to support partnership activities are frequently most exposed, stressed and under-supported. Support need not be imported or expensive. It could be based on linkages between peer agencies and individuals; much of the time spent by voluntary sector entrepreneurs at inter-organisational meetings has a latent support function. Information exchange and alliance building, both reactive and proactive and underpinned by mixtures of shallow or deep connectedness, characterise the networks that are constructed here. For example, a worker from Money Advice Service (a local advice and campaigning organisation) explained why she took part in a strategy group:

> ... we want to be sure that our client group is represented.... It's a pain in the backside because sometimes I feel I could be doing much more productive work. But it's back to "if you're not there, you don't get to find out what's happening". (Scott et al, 2000, p 49)

Moreover, the 'finding out' is not always located in the formal and visible part of the meeting; even while large amounts of paper change hands and the Powerpoint presentation is flickering, much of the business depends on informal networking.

Voluntary sector participation in different kinds of networks, with peers and sponsoring agencies or individuals, is a demanding and time-consuming process. It requires release from everyday pressure but can deliver great benefits. When, therefore, agencies construct job descriptions and Compact documents are agreed, it will be important to allow time and space for network building – the 'social cement' of voluntary organisational life. On the other hand, artificially induced networks may be counterproductive. The answer is probably a light touch.

However, even with such a light touch, local authority sponsors of Compacts will need to extend their knowledge and understanding of the voluntary sector representatives who attend their meetings. In particular, they will need to conceptualise key representatives not simply in functional terms (director of X or representative of Y), but rather as social 'junction boxes', nodes in networks of individuals and agencies who may open up possibilities for policy experimentation:

> Loosely coupled networks may, moreover, be particularly appropriate in dealing with the most intractable public policy issues, where both the goals and the means to achieve them are problematic. (Painter and Clarence, 2000, p 481)

Thus Compact development, rather than remaining conventionally focused on *organisational* units, becomes extended instead to include a sense of the potential of different *networks*.

The strength of Compacts lies in their explicit and transparent commitment to collaborative working, and to the release of appropriate resources that might sustain this. They are the new 'front room' of statutory/voluntary relationships. Nevertheless, the emphasis on frameworks or codes of practice should not divert attention from the continued significance of the 'back rooms'. The experience of Family Friends, a voluntary agency that promotes the welfare of families with pre-school children, provided a salutary example of this. After a political lobbying of the local authority by voluntary agencies concerned to restore funding cuts:

> The outcome was the setting up of a sub-committee involving senior politicians, senior officers from all departments and voluntary sector representatives – to establish a corporate strategy on voluntary sector funding. As a result there will be clearer, more open procedures for funding. Everyone will use the same process. (Senior Coordinator, Family Friends, quoted in Scott et al, 2000, p 54)

However, at the end of the final meeting that agreed a strategy, one of the local authority officers hung back to initiate an informal funding deal with the coordinator, outside of the previously agreed process. Pressures from central government to increase work with disaffected families had tight deadlines and attractive financial carrots attached. Thus, even while a Compact-like process had been successfully concluded, the demands from another part of the state operated to contradict this.

Compacts cannot drive out such 'back room' activities. However, all the parties to Compacts need to identify the *systematic* interrelationship of all processes, both formal and informal, and to recognise that contradictions such as these can occur, whatever formal agreements may be in place.

Our qualitative case study material thus provides some glimpses of the unequal and contradictory pressures likely to be present within Compact or partnership building processes. To summarise:

- Stakeholding in practice reveals deep inequalities, with tensions between service provision and participative democracy.
- Social entrepreneurs are vital but prone to overload and burn out, especially when expected to carry individual burdens.
- The 'building bricks' of Compacts tend to be conceptualised as organisations represented by individuals; however, locating them within the concept of differentiated networks may be more developmental and sustaining.
- Local Compacts do not exist within a vacuum – the bigger picture, including central government initiatives, must also be recognised and incorporated into practice.

Conclusion – from contracts to Compacts

At the beginning of the 21st century, Labour government commitments to rebuild and reshape civil society through partnership working between the state and voluntary and community sectors have put the relationships between these two sectors at the heart of the policy planning agenda. As this chapter has discussed, however, these relationships are neither as simple nor as straightforward as some politicians and policy makers might assume. Building relationships with the voluntary and community sectors requires getting to know the organisations operating within these and finding out more about what makes them work effectively – or not.

These relationships are not new, of course. Negotiating the appropriate terms of engagement between the public and voluntary and community sectors goes back to Beveridge, and before. In one sense, therefore, the issue is not how to develop collaboration across these boundaries, but rather how to alter the balance of past forms. In such a rebalancing, past policies, experiences and fears are likely to continue to exert an influence on future developments. At the very least, these experiences and fears must be borne in mind by the new generation of partnership managers; more specifically, some ghosts may need to be exorcised.

Changes in the relationships between voluntary and community sector organisations and the state were experienced in the 1980s and 1990s. At this time, the pressure on policy makers was to reduce the role of the state as provider by shifting service delivery to non-government agencies through the contracting of welfare services – sometimes referred to as the 'contract culture'. Many, especially the larger and more established voluntary organisations, entered into contracts to deliver services, although this sometimes threatened to alter the nature of organisations that had in the past been characterised by less formal financial planning and organisational management (Russell et al, 1995; Russell and Scott, 1997; Billis and Glennerster, 1998, pp 79-9).

Contracts are still a major feature of service provision, and many voluntary sector organisations continue to play significant roles in the provision of contracted services. However, at the beginning of the 21st century it seems that *contracts* have been replaced by *Compacts* as the dominating feature of state and voluntary sector relations. In large part this reflects the changing policy agenda of the new Labour governments, which is much closer to the ideas of Deakin and Kemp than were the Conservative regimes. Labour's commitment to partnership is more formal, as the Compact developments imply, and its expectations of joint planning and delivery are more far-reaching (see also Chapter Nine). As Lewis (1999, p 265) discusses, Labour is also more aware of the distinctions between the voluntary and community sectors and the implications of this for collaborative activities.

Through these new Compacts, the government aims to capture and regulate the full range of collaborative relations between voluntary and community organisations and the state, both centrally and locally. The intention is that Compacts should be facilitative as well as regulatory, and that they should establish a framework for relations across the sector rather than being negotiated separately with each individual organisation. Nevertheless, as we have discussed, problems still remain within the new 'Compact culture'. Much of the literature on Compacts, including our own research, concentrates on tangible empirical features of local operational structures. Two caveats are necessary here. First, it is important to locate partnership working within a *structural* overview of contemporary governance – and, despite all the rhetoric of an egalitarian and redistributive kind, the Labour government is essentially a centralist one (Walker, 2000, p 18). Second, the *meanings* of partnerships need to be discussed alongside the visible practices. Commentators on comparable participatory strategies have alerted us to both the legitimising function of Compacts (cited in Harrison et al, 1997, p 14), and to the ways in which unequal power relationships are expressed in the mundane discourse of committee process and reportage (Cooke and Kothari, 2001, p 14).

The Labour government does want, and expect, something new and different from partnerships between the state and the voluntary sector; but translating this into practice is not a simple task. Compacts, like contracts, are based on the notion of negotiation and agreement and the sharing of goals and practices; yet the parties to these negotiations do not enter the Compact arena equally well equipped or with equal power. Inequality, as well as diversity, is an intrinsic feature of the voluntary and community sectors – indeed, the power, resources and influence of different organisations varies dramatically. However, in most cases the negotiations are likely to continue to be led by public sector agencies, some of whom have not fully embraced the new partnership agenda and remain defensive of traditional models of public service delivery. Moreover, within the voluntary and community sector itself, some larger (and particularly umbrella) organisations are much more likely to be round the table and participating in the talks than others. In practice, therefore, most voluntary and community organisations appear only belatedly, and perhaps reluctantly, in the formal processes of partnership building – and many do not appear at all. (This theme is taken up again in Chapter Nine.)

It was clear from our research that the different structures and operations of individual organisations result in different experiences of engagement with public agencies. These experiences were not always problematic, but they had their own dynamics that individual organisations, and often the individuals within these, sought to manage in their own way. It is these dynamics, and the fine-grained understanding that they give us of the workings of voluntary and community sector organisations, that will inevitably be the real stuff of the day-to-day development and delivery of collaboration and partnership.

Our research confirmed that the voluntary and community sector is highly diverse and differentiated (again, this theme is continued in Chapter Nine). This is one of the reasons why the contracts that were good for some could be either destructive or irrelevant to others. If the new commitment to partnership and collaboration seeks to embrace all through the medium of Compacts, then both the principles and the practice of 'Compacting' must be able to adapt to this variability and individuality. It may be a tall order for the architects (and the engineers) of Compacts to know what the mothers' and toddlers' group in Cranfield – or the KidsCare group or Money Advice Service – think; but if they do not, then any partnership working with them is likely to be ineffective. In the longer term, however, diversity and difference, if recognised and embraced appropriately, should be no barrier to partnership and participation – indeed, they are what make these new models of policy delivery so essential to truly effective policy practice.

References

6, P. and Leat, D. (1996) 'Inventing the British voluntary sector by committee: from Wolfenden to Deakin', *Non-Profit Studies*, vol 1, pp 33-45.

Beveridge, Sir W. (1948) *Voluntary action: A report on methods of social advance*, London: George Allen and Unwin.

Billis, D. and Glennerster, H. (1998) 'Human services and the voluntary sector: towards a theory of comparative advantage', *Journal of Social Policy*, vol 27, no 1, pp 79-99.

Blair, T. (1998) 'Message from the Prime Minister in Great Britain', *Compact between the government and the voluntary sector in Wales*, Cm 4107, London: The Stationery Office.

Coleman, J.S. (1988) 'Social capital and the creation of human capital', *American Journal of Sociology*, vol 94, pp 95-120.

Coleman, J.S. (1990) *The foundation of social theory*, Cambridge MA: Belknap.

Cooke, B. and Kothari, E. (2001) 'The case for participation as tyranny', in B. Cooke and E. Kothari (eds) *Participation: The new tyranny?*, pp 1-15, London: Zed Books.

Craig, G. (2001) 'Evaluating the significance of local Compacts', *Findings*, no 251, February, York: Joseph Rowntree Foundation.

Craig, C., Taylor, M., Szanto, C. and Wilkinson, M. (1999) *Developing local Compacts: Relationships between local public sector bodies and the voluntary and community sectors*, York: York Publishing Services.

Department of National Heritage (1996) *Raising the voltage: The government's response to the Deakin Commission report*, November, London: Department of National Heritage.

DETR/MAFF (Department of the Environment, Transport and the Regions/ Ministry of Agriculture, Fisheries and Food) (2000) *Our countryside: the future. A fair deal for rural England*, Cm 409, London: The Stationery Office.

Etzioni, A. (1993) *The spirit of community*, New York, NY: Simon and Schuster.

Etzioni, A. (1997) *The new golden rule: Community and morality in a democratic society*, London: Profile Books.

Foley, P. and Martin, S. (2000) 'A new deal for the community? Public participation in regeneration and local service delivery', *Policy & Politics*, vol 28, no 4, pp 479-91.

Harris, M. (2001) 'Voluntary organisations in a changing social policy environment', in M. Harris and C. Rochester (eds) *Voluntary organisations and social policy in Britain: Perspectives on change and choice*, Basingstoke: Palgrave.

Harrison, S., Barnes, M. and Mort, M. (1997) 'Praise and damnation: mental health user groups and the construction of organisational legitimacy', *Public Policy and Administration*, vol 12, no 2, summer, pp 4-16.

Home Office (1998) *Compact on relations between government and the voluntary and community sector in England*, Cm 4100, London: The Stationery Office.

Home Office (2000a) *Consultation and policy appraisal: A code of good practice*, London: Home Office.

Home Office (2000b) *Funding: A code of good practice*, London: Home Office.

Home Office (2001a) *Black and minority ethnic voluntary and community organisations: A code of good practice*, London: Home Office.

Home Office (2001b) *Volunteering: A code of good practice*, London: Home Office.

Home Office (2002) *Community groups: A code of good practice*, London: Home Office.

Labour Party (1997) *Building the future together*, London: Labour Party, February.

Langslow, P. (1999) *Winning friends and influencing people*, London: City University Business School.

Lewis, J. (1999) 'Reviewing the relationship between the voluntary sector and the state in Britain in the 1990s', *Voluntas*, vol 10, no 3, pp 255-70.

LGA (Local Government Association) (2001) *A new commitment to neighbourhood renewal: National strategy action plan and local strategic partnerships – frequently asked questions*, London: LGA.

Martin, S., Davis, H., Bovaird, A., Geddes, M., Hartley, J., Lewis, M. and Sanderson, I. (1999) *Best value baseline report*, Coventry: Warwick Business School.

National Assembly of Wales (2000) *A better Wales*, Cardiff: NAW.

NCVO (National Council for Voluntary Organisations) (1996) *Meeting the challenge of change: Voluntary action into the 21st century (the Deakin Commission)*, London: NCVO.

NCVO (2001) *The compact* (www.ncvo-vol.org.uk/main/gateway/compact.html), 20 January.

Painter, C. and Clarence, E. (2000) 'New Labour and inter-governmental management: flexible networks or performance control?', *Public Management*, vol 2, no 4, December, pp 477-99.

Pollock, L. (1999) 'Facing the realities of regionalisation', *NCVO News*, May.

Putnam, R.D. (1993) *Making democracy work: Civic traditions in modern Italy*, Princeton, NJ: Princeton University Press.

Putnam, R.D. (1995) 'Bowling alone: America's declining social capital', *Journal of Democracy*, vol 6, pp 65-78.

Russell, L., Scott, D. and Wilding, P. (1995) *Mixed fortunes: The funding of the voluntary sector*, Manchester: Manchester University Press.

Russell, L. and Scott, D. (1997) *Very active citizens? The impact of the contract culture on volunteers*, Manchester: Manchester University Press.

Scott, D., Alcock, P., Russell, L. and Macmillan, R. (2000) *Moving pictures: Realities of voluntary action*, Bristol/York: The Policy Press/Joseph Rowntree Foundation.

SCVO (Scottish Council for Voluntary Organisations) (1997) *Heart and hand (the Kemp Commission)*, SCVO: Edinburgh.

SEU (Social Exclusion Unit) (1998) *Bringing Britain together: A national strategy for neighbourhood renewal*, Cm 4045, London: The Stationery Office.

Taylor, M. (2001) 'Partnership: insiders and outsiders', in M. Harris and C. Rochester (eds) *Voluntary organisations and social policy in Britain*, Basingstoke: Palgrave.

Vincent, J. and Harrow, J. (2000) 'New distinctions and unexpected similarities: Comparing third sector relations with central government in Scotland and England', Paper to 4th Conference of the International Society for Third Sector Research, Dublin, 7 July.

Walker, D. (2000) *Living with ambiguity: The relationship between central and local government*, York: York Publishing Services.

WGGRS/LGA (Working Group on Government Relations Secretariat/Local Government Association) (2000) *Local compact guidelines: Getting local relationships right together*, London: NCVO.

NINE

Dangerous liaisons: local government and the voluntary and community sectors

Gary Craig and Marilyn Taylor

One of the many consequences of the growing emphasis on partnership over recent years has been an increasingly high profile for the voluntary and community sectors. Associated historically with choice, flexibility and the capacity to release new resources (donations, volunteers, mutual aid and self-help), they have also been seen as a way of reaching more marginalised groups in society and giving them a public voice. Through extending citizen involvement in both services and policy development, a healthy voluntary and community sector offers the potential for a variety of provision, catering for a diversity of need and bringing a wider range of resources to bear on the policy process.

In recognition of this role, the 1997 Labour government introduced a 'Compact' (see Chapter Eight for the background to Compacts) early in its first term, establishing a framework of principles for relationships between government and the voluntary and community sectors (Home Office, 1998). At the same time, emphasis on partnership and consultation with the sector across a wide range of new policies offered new opportunities for the voluntary and community sectors.

But while many organisations welcome the prospect that this partnership will bring the resources and energies of different sectors to bear more effectively on social problems, others are concerned about the impact on the autonomy of voluntary and community organisations. A cynical view might see partnership simply as a means through which a succession of governments have sought to transfer responsibility for welfare away from the state and, moreover, in a way that allows the state to continue to exercise control over policy and practice. This chapter reviews the experience of partnership between government and voluntary and community organisations in the key policy settings of regeneration and anti-poverty policy. It then examines more recent experience and, in particular, the potential strategic role of local Compacts, one of Labour's unique policy contributions, in addressing the problematic issues raised by partnership working. In doing so, we distinguish between the voluntary sector, which includes organisations employing paid staff and which are often formally incorporated; and the community sector, usually focused on communities of place or identity, which often operates without regular funding or paid staff.

The changing policy context

Partnership between government and the voluntary and community sectors is not new. Welfare was for many years highly dependent on philanthropy and mutual provision, both of which continued to play major roles until the post-war welfare state (Kendall and Knapp, 1996) and developed complementary and advocacy roles thereafter. Earlier urban and social policies, such as Labour's 1976 inner-cities strategy, anticipated more recent rhetoric and provided particular opportunities for the development of community organisations.

Nonetheless, after 30 years as a "junior partner in the welfare firm" (Owen, 1964, p 527), 1970s advocates of the voluntary sector argued that it should play a more central role in delivering welfare (Gladstone, 1979; Hadley and Hatch, 1981). Recession and the election of the Thatcher government were to offer a major new opportunity, with a shift towards a welfare market in which voluntary organisations became competitors alongside the private sector. Later in the 1980s, the idea of partnership re-emerged as voluntary organisations and service users became involved, as junior partners, in joint planning for community care alongside local and health authorities. The less stridently ideological Major governments also saw partnership with communities as a central theme of regeneration policy.

For many in the voluntary sector, these opportunities offered the possibility of greater recognition, a more even-handed relationship and more satisfactory funding conditions. But such opportunities came to be seen as a mixed blessing. As the frontiers of the welfare state were 'rolled back', some saw 'partnership' as code for 'incorporation', with government as the more powerful partner, dictating terms and putting the sector's distinctive characteristics at risk (Gutch, 1992). Indeed, Deakin (1996) argues that the most consistent theme in government attitudes towards the voluntary sector in the mid-1990s was the latter's usefulness in reducing costs. Meanwhile, experience of community participation policies suggested that little power was shared (Stewart and Taylor, 1995); indeed, some saw the promotion of community participation policies primarily as a means of incorporating dissent from critical 'outsiders' (Craig, 1989).

The 1997 Labour government promised to move from a contract to a partnership culture. At the same time, government discourse moved from an emphasis on poverty and deprivation in its social policies to a new language of social exclusion and social integration (SEU, 1998). Central to this debate was a recognition that services needed to work in new 'joined-up' ways if persistent problems of exclusion were to be addressed. A major theme of regeneration policy was the need to bring communities to the centre of neighbourhood renewal and other area-based policies. The Prime Minister argued: "... too much has been imposed from above, when experience shows that success depends on communities themselves having the power and taking the responsibility to make things better" (SEU, 1998, p 7).

The implications of involving voluntary and community organisations not only in project implementation but also in policy and strategic development were recognised both in longer lead-in times to government funding programmes like the New Deal for Communities and Sure Start and in the provision of resources for 'capacity building'. The inclusion of a Community Empowerment Fund in the National Strategy for Neighbourhood Renewal is the latest evidence of this commitment.

Partnerships in practice: the experiences of voluntary and community organisations

Partnerships in regeneration

Skelcher et al (1996) identify three phases of partnership associated with changing emphases in regeneration policy. The 1970s was the 'single-agency period', when the key role in developing and implementing urban policy agendas was taken by local authorities; the late 1970s/80s was the period when bilateral public-private partnerships dominated a policy approach concerned mainly with physical regeneration; and in the 1990s, multilateral partnerships of public, private, voluntary and community sectors contributed to a widening of the urban regeneration agenda to incorporate both economic and social foci, a remit which has been re-emphasised since 1997 (GOYH, 1997).

Conservative governments of the 1980s gave the private sector stronger roles in both urban regeneration and anti-poverty work. The priorities of single-purpose agencies such as urban development corporations (UDCs) or training and enterprise councils (TECs), dominated by private sector involvement, did not normally match the more consensual and corporate goals of partnership (Stewart, 1994). Even where partners were more or less equal in power, there was a tendency, observed in the first round of the Single Regeneration Budget (SRB) before many organisations began to understand partnership working, for some partnerships to collapse under competing priorities from differing partners (Littlewood and Winnett, 1997). Following more general attacks on the roles and functions of local government (Stewart and Stoker, 1989), partnerships in 1980s/90s urban regeneration initiatives remained dominated by private sector partners and central government policy (Mawson et al, 1995; Hastings, 1996; Lawless, 1996). The creation of local 'democratic' partnerships was considered neither necessary nor desirable – community involvement was seen as making 'counterproductive' demands (Brennan et al, 1998). It was hardly surprising that potential voluntary and community sector regeneration partners found themselves at the margins of bidding, of policy formation and as funding recipients. Voluntary and community organisations were there simply to implement policy made elsewhere (Robson et al, 1994; Hastings et al, 1996; Brennan et al, 1998; Pharoah et al, 1998; Taylor, 2000b), operating at best as 'peripheral insiders' (Maloney et al, 1994). A review of the impact of urban regeneration (Alcock et al, 1998) confirmed that the most deprived neighbourhoods, allegedly the targets of regeneration and partnership working during the 1990s, were effectively marginalised.

One recent study suggests that this remains the case (Anastacio et al, 2000), particularly where significant private sector interests remain involved in regeneration programmes. An initial evaluation of the New Deal for Communities (NCVO, 2000) has criticised partnerships involving voluntary and community organisations as being simply the territory over which long-standing inter-organisational tensions are played out, with local partnerships dominated by local authority priorities. Despite the shift in government thinking about regeneration towards the needs of deprived communities, it is still relevant to ask what benefits deprived communities have derived from partnership working? Research suggests that the rules of the game are set from above; the cultures and structures of public sector partners are not compatible with effective community involvement; and communities themselves do not necessarily have the organisational capacity and resources for effective involvement (Burns and Taylor, 2000; Chapter Eight in this book).

Partnership continues at present to be developed within existing structures, processes and frameworks of power – new rhetoric poured into old bottles. Public sector cultures are so engrained that power holders are often unaware of the ways in which they perpetuate unequal power relations through their language and procedures (see also Chapter Eight). There is little sensitivity to the fact that outsiders may find these processes difficult to penetrate, and little consideration of whether procedures should be changed or whether community participants might need preparation for their involvement.

Furthermore, experience in the UK and elsewhere suggests that where public money is involved, the requirements of formal accountability crowd out most other considerations. Perversely, while the money involved in partnership initiatives provides the incentive for partnership arrangements, it also obstructs them, focusing attention on spending money, rather than the need for a policy vision; and swamps agendas with procedural (and upwards) accountability issues. Local community members are aware of the ironies; while they are asked to substantiate a £1 claim for a bus ticket, they read of massive problems with fraud at the highest levels of the European Commission or the millions of pounds that are overspent on flagship projects like the Jubilee Line on London's underground system. Over and above the sense of unfairness is the fact that these disproportionate requirements exclude the very communities they are intended to support. Smaller organisations, already overworked, are put off by complex forms and monitoring systems and relationships with accountable bodies are soured. Even if smaller organisations do come on board, the demands of monitoring and accountability place power in the hands of those who can interpret the rules. They are also subject to preconceptions about which kinds of organisation are likely to be good managers.

The existence of special money can also set up conflicts between partners, both across and within sectors. Jeffrey (1997) drew attention to problems among even the most well-balanced and experienced partnerships within the voluntary and community sectors, when generally well-functioning systems broke down under the pressure of competition for funding. The demands of partnership, the lack of time and resources for community participants and the need to 'hit the ground running' make it extremely difficult to spread involvement throughout communities; too often, the work of community representation is concentrated on too few people. In many regeneration partnerships, the fact that the 'community' is predetermined from above also intensifies difficulties of representing the disparate interests that exist in any locality. This is a particular problem for black and minority ethnic communities, which are too often treated as if their interests are homogeneous and are rarely resourced in a way that can give voice to their many different members (Craig et al, 2002). Moreover, organisations working with the most deprived population groups have themselves historically been particularly marginalised. As a review of black community involvement in SRB put it, they were *'Invisible partners'* (Crook, 1995; LBGU, 1995). This marginalisation was reflected throughout the regeneration process from the initial planning, identification of needs and programme bidding, to the allocation and control of resources and service delivery. As we shall see, this situation has changed little.

Partnerships in local anti-poverty work

Local government anti-poverty work – strategic attempts to address local poverty issues – grew in scope throughout the 1980s and 1990s, partly in response to central government's failure to devise a coherent anti-poverty strategy. Partnership working, attempting to draw on the resources and skills of a range of local organisations, became a central feature of much of this work. Early evaluations of the scope of local government anti-poverty work (Alcock et al, 1995; Pearson et al, 1997) identified two approaches to partnership with local community organisations. Most local authorities felt that partners had to be engaged early on, to ensure wider ownership of any strategy. However, a minority of authorities rejected multi-agency working on the grounds that mixed policy agendas at the developmental stage of an anti-poverty strategy were not helpful.

Further distinctions emerged between partnerships that were generic and concerned with strategic development and service planning and those concerned with the implementation of specific anti-poverty initiatives. In the latter case, policies had effectively been devised before such partnerships were developed; local authorities expected voluntary and community organisations to deliver on specific projects or initiatives, rather than become engaged in generic or strategic policy developments, with longer-term implications for funding. Local community groups, increasingly identified in the literature and in policy pronouncements from the mid-1990s as important partners, were nonetheless reported relatively rarely to be potential partners in local anti-poverty initiatives – doubtless in part because many local authorities failed to grasp the important distinction between the voluntary and community sectors (Craig et al, 1999). Local voluntary sector agencies were the most common partner for both specific and generic arrangements, but predominantly for the former type.

Tensions were most evident in anti-poverty partnerships between private and public bodies, but research also suggests (Alcock et al, 1999) that the language of partnership was not matched by a sense within the voluntary and, in particular, the community sector, of sharing equal status and power with the statutory sector. Few local authorities had actively involved the voluntary sector in the conceptualisation of their anti-poverty strategies; even umbrella organisations such as voluntary sector or black and minority ethnic coordinating bodies were rarely invited to be involved beyond commenting on draft strategic plans. Local authorities saw individual voluntary agencies, particularly since the growth of the contract culture, more as organisations that would deliver services rather than contribute to anti-poverty policy development. Anti-poverty work also highlighted the disparity of power between partners, since voluntary sector agencies, mostly dependent on the local authority for funding, were usually unable to resist having their own work aligned to local authority anti-poverty objectives, a form of policy 'takeover'.

Other problems arose in defining the boundaries of the formally organised voluntary sector, particularly vis-a-vis the community sector. Community organisations generally had even less influence over the actions of local government (except by direct action) and less power. Even where some local authorities saw them as important potential partners, attempts at partnership were viewed rather cynically by community organisations. The failure of partnerships effectively to include community organisations – except as the target of policy – on anything like an equal footing has remained a key criticism of anti-poverty work in recent years.

Local authorities engaged in anti-poverty work have often argued that the difficulties of defining communities, or of identifying what they could regard as representative organisations, leads them to focus their work on deprived groups within the population, such as lone parents or members of minority ethnic groups. This sidesteps the problem of working with more traditional community groups; but the record of local authorities working with such groups as equal partners was generally no better, as we shall see. These more powerful partners committed to partnership working in regeneration or anti-poverty work needed to invest resources in community development strategies, upstream from major policy decisions, to develop capacity within communities to engage in the partnership process. Even so, community representatives drawn into the pressurised world of large-scale policy and resource decisions could still be drawn away from their constituencies.

Evidence suggested that anti-poverty strategies that involved partners at early stages of development seemed to differ from those developed within local government alone; the latter tended to display more paternalistic and insular characteristics. Successful anti-poverty alliances appeared to have been those that were created at an early stage, in which the notion of partnership had real meaning and where attempts were made to address the power imbalances between partners. Not only did such anti-poverty partnership working achieve what has been characterised as 'policy synergy' (Hastings, 1996). 'Budget enlargement' was also achieved; organisations working together produced added value, with an enhancement of available resources. However, the voluntary sector's attempts to be accepted as a real partner continued to founder on the rock of power relations. Since 1997, strategic local authority anti-poverty work has been reoriented to fit with the government's social exclusion agenda and strategic partnership working with the voluntary and community organisations has tended to be played out in other, newer, arenas. Will the lessons of partnership working be learnt?

Local Compacts: a framework for partnership?

In the past, voluntary and community organisations have found themselves marginalised in partnerships or, as the bruising experience of English local government reorganisation suggests, more or less completely overlooked when the interests of more powerful partners were at stake (Craig and Manthorpe, 1999). In Scotland and Wales, by contrast, comprehensive local government reorganisation stimulated the joint development of frameworks of principles to govern relationships between the sectors; in Scotland, from 1996 onwards, local authorities were required to develop consultative mechanisms involving the voluntary and community sectors. Reflecting these tensions, voluntary and community organisations across Britain have increasingly sought a structured partnership framework to protect their interests.

One of the recommendations of the Commission on the Future of the Voluntary Sector (NCVO, 1996) was that a 'concordat' should be established between government and the voluntary sector that would lay down basic principles for future relationships. The English 'Compact' was launched in 1998 (Home Office, 1998), followed by more detailed codes of practice (see Chapter Eight for details). Although there was no parallel recommendation for local 'concordats', it was recognised that most encounters between voluntary organisations and the state take place at local levels. In view of this, unless at least the principles of the national Compact were enshrined at local level, a national framework document would have limited value. Since the launch of the national Compact, pressure to develop local Compacts has increased and guidance has been drawn up as a framework for local negotiations.

Prior to the agreement of the national Compact, an increasing number of agreements or policies were already being developed on the relationship between local authorities, or their constituent departments, and local voluntary and community organisations. These varied considerably, both in content and in the extent to which they were developed in consultation with the local voluntary and community sectors (Craig et al, 1999). Research suggested that the value of such local agreements was as likely to be found in the *process* – the understanding that developed between the sectors during the negotiation of the agreement – as in the *product*, for example a final written statement. It also suggested that there was still a long way to go in actually putting these agreements and policies into effect. If this were to happen, adequate review mechanisms would be essential. Subsequent research (Craig et al, 2002) has followed the progress of local Compacts across England, Wales and Scotland. These Compacts have been developed during a period of rapid and profound change, with a complex array of new governance arrangements and partnership policies at local level. In theory, Compacts could provide the basis on which a wide range of new relationships between the sectors could be built. But in the real world, Compact negotiations have often been swamped by the urgent deadlines imposed on other reforms. Processes that could have been informed by a clear statement of procedures and protocols have gone ahead without this; and Compact development has tended to be left on one side while this has happened. In too many areas Compacts have become just another rather low-priority initiative.

Where Compact negotiations have gone ahead between the voluntary and community sectors and local public bodies, they have led in some areas to increased profiles for the former and to improved understanding of the breadth of voluntary and community sector activity. In some cases, new, strong and positive relationships have been built, underpinned by new resources. However, in other areas, changes of administration or key personnel have stalled the process. There are instances where funding cuts have been imposed without consultation, at exactly the same time as the Compact is being negotiated – hardly a recipe for trust. Compacts are most likely to be successfully developed where they are perhaps least needed – where a history of good working relationships exists between the partners.

The development of Compacts has been dependent on key personalities and the relationships between them. If one such individual moves on, the whole process can be jeopardised. This raises questions about how far Compact development is able to reflect the interests of all parts of the voluntary and community sectors, and how far commitment to a Compact reaches beyond key negotiators in the local authority. For Compacts to have legitimacy and authority, they need to reach deep into both sectors and, if that it is to happen, our research suggests that more resources may be needed. Those negotiating on behalf of public bodies need the authority to make their agreements stick; those in the voluntary and community sectors need the resources to convince their colleagues of the relevance of this seemingly rather abstract document. In particular, research suggests that, on the one hand, black and minority ethnic groups and smaller community organisations remain on the margins of the Compact process, while on the other hand, Compacts also need commitment from elected members who currently are conspicuously absent from most negotiations.

Compacts are likely to be more important for the voluntary and community sectors than for the public sector. While local authorities may see a Compact as a way of demonstrating to regional and central government that they take the voluntary and community sectors seriously enough to warrant approval and investment, it is the latter for whom the detail of the agreement is likely to make the difference. The balance of power, although tipped slightly, remains with the public authority. The success of Compacts will depend on how they work in practice; our research suggests that mechanisms for implementation and review are still lagging behind. It may be that success can be best judged by how far voluntary and community organisations are willing to push the Compact and complain when it is breached, in spirit or in fact.

Partnerships and power

There is a large body of literature outlining the processes necessary to enable local people to participate successfully in local initiatives and service programmes. Much of this literature relates to local regeneration projects and tenant participation in housing management schemes (for example, Stewart and Taylor, 1995; Cole and Smith, 1996; WECH, 1998). For example, effective strategic partnerships should involve local people from the outset; have an agreed and negotiated agenda with clear terms of reference; ensure that all partners are committed to community empowerment (Craig and Mayo, 1995); develop appropriate structures and procedures for community participation that are acceptable to all partners; and address issues of conflict and power (Taylor, 1995).

A common theme underlying all these principles is the need for a more equitable distribution of power in partnerships, which are generally dominated by 'top-down' working methods. This is most obvious where the disparity in power between partners is greatest: between local authorities with their structures, resources and paid staff on the one hand; and the most marginalised communities on the other – a clear illustration of the absence of equivalent status, which Hudson and Hardy argue in Chapter Four needs to underpin successful partnerships. Some of the chief barriers to redistributing power were identified in the earlier discussion on regeneration: the rules within which partnerships are framed; the funding-led nature of many partnerships; and the need to 'hit the ground running', which limits engagement to the few and better resourced. Local people can feel excluded from the processes of partnership working when they sense that they are ill-equipped to contribute, or where partnerships function only as ratifying bodies and important decisions are made through informal contacts elsewhere (Reid and Iqbal, 1996).

An analysis of power relations is therefore crucial to understanding the role and effectiveness of partnerships between government and voluntary and community organisations. Geddes and Martin (1996) suggested from their review of 1990s European partnerships that they might be seen not as marking a fundamental shift in relations between the state and civil society, but as yet another cheap way of managing urban problems (see also Pike, 1996). Geddes and Martin also observed that, while partnership working provided better coordination of policies among public regeneration agencies, the social and economic gains for local communities were less clear.

There is a prospect that this could change. Community involvement in local strategic partnerships (SEU, 2001) has the potential to promote forms of empowerment that differ greatly from the rather limited interpretation that has dominated consultation exercises and project implementation to date. Local Strategic Partnerships (LSPs), involving all key local stakeholders, are required to oversee neighbourhood renewal and work with local authorities to produce community strategies. Local authorities must facilitate the participation of communities and involve them centrally in neighbourhood management. However, even recent experience suggests that much still needs to change if the least powerful are to become central to these new partnerships and the voluntary and community sectors are to play their full part.

To change the rules of the game requires a major culture change within local and central government (see, for example, Taylor, 2000a); this has yet to be demonstrated in practice. But it also requires more realistic understandings of what, and how, voluntary and community organisations can contribute to partnership (what Hudson and Hardy refer to as 'clarity of purpose' in Chapter Four) and what support is needed to make this contribution. In this section, we focus on the latter. The power imbalance between local communities and their statutory partners is exacerbated by a number of factors: what is valued; how local communities are legitimated; how they are resourced; and what is expected of them.

First, senior figures in key public bodies (and some of the larger voluntary organisations) bring significant institutional and personal 'clout' to strategic partnerships. They can act on decisions and commit financial resources, a major element of power within a partnership climate that emphasises the importance of additionality and leverage. Partnership to date has rarely transferred assets to communities or invested to encourage them to develop their own. More recognition needs to be given to the assets that community partners represent – the knowledge, energy and hard work communities bring to renewal and other programmes.

The second issue is that of legitimacy. Community representatives are frequently challenged about their ability to represent diverse and disparate constituencies (see also Chapters Seven and Eight). However, this important question is rarely addressed to other partners, such as those from public agencies and the business sector (with marginal variations according to circumstances). These partners are rarely required to legitimise their involvement in the same way as community representatives. While communities are still expected to 'squeeze' their views through one or two representatives, public sector agencies (and business partners) rarely experience the challenges of representation that communities struggle with.

Commentators argue that strict enforcement of representation is less important than a partnership's ability to reflect local priorities (McFarlane, 1993; Taylor, 1995). This requires strategies that allow for both representative and participatory forms of involvement. It also requires recognition that, as Thake (1995) suggests, participation in community regeneration is something of a 'minority sport'; the demands that it places on those willing to participate can be formidable. Voluntary and community sector representatives have to negotiate involvement while coping with the demands of project and funding timetables; no one else is available to do their work while they are carrying out their representative roles. The lack of representativeness for which voluntary and community organisations are often criticised is created by the very systems in which they are involved: the lack of resources to support wider community involvement; the increased demands that are placed on them; and pressure to 'hit the ground running'. If they then lose touch with their constituencies, it is hardly surprising.

This raises the third issue of resources. What has been crucial in disempowering many community representatives is that they have not been backed by the levels of resources and organisational capacity available to other, more powerful, partners. Even umbrella organisations such as councils for voluntary service, expected to facilitate the representation of voluntary and community sector views across large areas, operate on a shoestring and are rarely resourced in a way that allows them to reach out to all parts of their constituency, especially the most marginalised. The most recent proliferation of partnerships simply exacerbates this problem. Communities are now reaching saturation point in terms of their ability to respond to successive partnership initiatives and there is an urgent need for infrastructure support, both to enable effective participation to develop and to explore alternative manageable methods for community participation.

If those willing to take on a representative role are to perform it effectively, resources need to be made available both to representatives and for infrastructure, to facilitate training, communication, outreach and accountability, especially in localities where there is a complex mix of local communities requiring a voice. If smaller organisations are going to field representatives, they need to be compensated for their involvement, so that their front-line work can be sustained.

It is probably appropriate that this support is independent of the local authority; in deprived communities, the relationship between local government and its electorate is not always easy (see Chapter Seven) and local authorities are often seen as part of the problem, not part of the solution (Alcock et al, 1995). Community development activities may lead to local communities challenging local authority decisions and, while many local authorities have made progress in developing 'community-friendly' approaches, there is still some way to go. Anti-poverty strategies have pressed for more sensitive service delivery in deprived communities; but for many people with low incomes, contact with local government frequently has predominantly negative associations linked to demands for rent, charges or the interventions of social services.

These difficulties are magnified within the most disadvantaged communities. This appears to be particularly true of black and minority ethnic communities, which are concentrated within the most disadvantaged urban areas (Modood et al, 1997; Dorsett, 1998; Craig, 1999). There is evidence that black and minority ethnic groups have been consulted in some regeneration and anti-poverty initiatives (LBGU, 1995), most notably in the inner London Boroughs and other major urban conurbations. As with local community members more generally, however, their involvement at strategic level has been limited and they have to date been largely excluded from access to policy development networks (Crook, 1995). Even where they have been included, the likelihood is that one representative is still, inappropriately, expected to act as the sole voice for diverse minority ethnic communities with divergent interests and experiences; a practice which reinforces exclusion processes (Craig et al, 1999).

It is important, therefore, that LSPs recognise the needs of black and minority ethnic communities and that this is reflected in appropriate representation and resources to enable their participation (an issue that strategic and umbrella voluntary sector organisations also have to face). Black and minority ethnic groups have hitherto felt that area-based regeneration activities have often not reflected their priorities (Skelcher et al, 1996). For these reasons, such communities did not feature largely in anti-poverty partnerships, although equality issues should, in principle, be an important feature of an anti-poverty approach to local government work. More recently, the Home Office *'Connecting communities'* (Home Office, 2000) and related programmes have made funding for black and ethnic minority groups available at local and regional levels, but doubt remains as to whether this funding will reach autonomous or critical local organisations. The general policy failure to support black and minority ethnic groups has been especially true in areas where there are not significant concentrations of black populations; here local authorities (and other policy makers) often argue that their sparsity requires no coherent policy response (Rai, 1995; Henderson and Kaur, 1999; De Lima, 2001). The ability of strategic partnerships to meet the needs of possibly the most vulnerable minorities – refugee communities – may be even more circumscribed, an area yet to be researched effectively.

Conclusions

The critical issues underpinning partnerships between local and central government and the voluntary and community sectors are those of resources and power. Organisations that are well-resourced in human and financial capital have expected ill-resourced community groups and relatively poorly resourced voluntary organisations to engage with them on equal terms, often within compressed timetables, in the context of complex, multifaceted programmes. This engagement appears tokenistic and oppressive to many voluntary and community organisations. Effective partnership working – taking the concerns and needs of local voluntary and community organisations seriously, rather than sucking them into the slipstream of policy programmes – requires them to be able to respond as far as possible on their terms and at a manageable pace, rather than at the speed determined by overarching political and policy imperatives (see Chapter Three). This, in turn, requires flexibility in budgeting and timetabling from government and its local agents. Moving from the rhetoric to the reality of partnership requires those holding power to engage in a major shift in thinking and practice (Taylor, 2000a).

A basis for real partnership requires better information and communication between local authorities and other public agencies, and the voluntary and community sectors; early engagement in any partnership process; effective resourcing; recognition of power inequalities between partners; specific attention to the needs of black and minority ethnic and other marginalised communities; clarity about the goals of partnership: compromise where appropriate; and, most of all, a recognition of the need for organisations within the voluntary and community sectors to protect their own role and purpose. Where major partners are subject to significant change, such as during reorganisation or adapting to major new legislative responsibilities, there should be transitional resourcing available to enable the voluntary and community sectors to cope with its consequences. This was a major issue with local government reorganisation, but has been also been evident during the process of regionalisation that left voluntary agencies struggling to respond to regional bodies and strategies.

Fears that the contribution of the voluntary and community sectors to policy development might be placed in jeopardy by the growth of the 'contract culture' may have been unduly pessimistic, but voluntary and community organisations often feel that they are very much 'unequal' partners, adjusting to or being driven by the cultures of more powerful public authorities. There are inherent tensions to be resolved in trying to reconcile the goals of public authorities and voluntary and community organisations: for example, between public accountability and the flexibility that many voluntary organisations seek to defend; between the requirements of public purchasers and the diverse missions that voluntary organisations seek to fulfil; and between representative and participatory democracy. There are also differences of emphasis within the sector: for example, between national and locally based organisations; between organisations with paid staff and those without; and between organisations providing services and those engaged in advocacy.

Continuing criticisms of partnership working are important, given that it is becoming ever more central to government regeneration policy, with the National Strategy for Neighbourhood Renewal (SEU, 2001). As partnership working extends, however, a clearer understanding is needed of the different contributions each partner can make and how they can best support and complement each other. Compacts may provide a basis for recognising and resolving these tensions, but there is a paradox inherent in Compacts. There is a sense in which they reflect mistrust between the sectors; a lack of security on the part of voluntary and community sectors vis-a-vis the local state; and a polarised world where the state is on one, more powerful, side of the fence, with the voluntary and community sectors on the other. As such, they may be perceived as a creature of the past rather than the future. The best indicator of progress might be when Compacts cease to be seen as a way to boost the position of the voluntary and community sectors in an environment disadvantageous to them and instead become incorporated into a process of a negotiation between equals towards common goals, building on trust rather than compensating for lack of trust. This might make them redundant. But there is potentially a still more significant role. The Compact idea and the process of mutual understanding it involves could be a valuable precedent as a framework for more extensive agreements and partnership working in general. The fact that other public authorities are also signing up to Compacts brings this prospect closer.

There are compelling reasons to enhance the effective involvement of voluntary and community organisations, not least to make strategic social, economic and environmental programmes more sensitive to local needs and to address one aspect of the 'democratic deficit'. The benefits of partnership will, however, be greatest where partners bring their own distinctive and autonomous strengths to the table. This has implications for the public sector partners as well as the voluntary and community sectors. For the former, as Taylor (1995) points out in relation to community participation, these 'new rules of engagement' will need to revisit some familiar questions: about procedures, structures and agendas for participation; about communication; and, most of all, about the relative power of various partners. This will involve providing adequate time and resources to the voluntary and community sectors and avoiding competitive bidding processes, which undermine partnership. Resourcing needs to be freed from the vagaries of political whim and based on an understanding within local government – still not always there – of the distinctive role of the voluntary and community sectors in identifying and meeting local needs.

For the voluntary and community sectors, making partnerships work means being clear about their own goals in seeking partnership (see also Chapter Four). It may mean having both 'insider' and 'outsider' strategies (Taylor, 2000b; Craig et al, 2001). But it will also mean ensuring that the most excluded are given access to the new opportunities that partnership provides. Perhaps the most important measure of the effectiveness of partnerships is whether the balance of power shifts towards the least powerful, in a sustainable way. New ways of thinking about representation are required and, for all partners, a special focus will need always to be maintained on the most excluded groups or communities.

Acknowledgements

The authors acknowledge the help of Professor Peter Alcock, Ms Sarah Pearson and Dr Mick Wilkinson with material on which parts of this chapter draw.

References

Alcock, P., Craig, G., Dalgleish, K. and Pearson, S. (1995) *Combating local poverty*, Luton: Local Government Management Board.

Alcock, P., Craig, G., Lawless, P., Pearson, S. and Robinson, D. (1998) *Inclusive regeneration*, Sheffield and Hull: DETR/Sheffield Hallam University/University of Lincolnshire and Humberside.

Alcock, P., Barnes, C., Craig, G., Harvey, A. and Pearson, S. (1999) *What counts? What works?*, London: Improvement and Development Agency.

Anastacio, J., Gidley, B., Hart, L., Keith, M., Mayo, M. and Kowarzik, V. (2000) *Reflecting realities: Participants' perspectives on integrated communities and sustainable development*, Bristol/York: The Policy Press/Joseph Rowntree Foundation.

Brennan, A., Rhodes, J. and Tyler, P. (1998) *A partnership for regeneration: An interim evaluation*, London: DETR.

Burns, D. and Taylor, M. (2000) *Auditing community participation: An assessment handbook*, Bristol/York: The Policy Press/Joseph Rowntree Foundation.

CDF (Community Development Foundation) (1996) *Regeneration and the community: Guidelines to the community involvement aspect of the SRB challenge fund*, 1996 edn, London: CDF.

Cole, I. and Smith, Y. (1996) *From estate action to estate agreement*, Bristol/York: The Policy Press/Joseph Rowntree Foundation.

Craig, G. (1989) 'Community work and the state', *Community Development Journal*, vol 24, no 1, pp 3-18.

Craig, G. (1999) '"Race", poverty and social security', in J. Ditch (ed) *An introduction to social security*, London: Routledge, pp 206-26.

Craig, G. and Manthorpe, J. (1999) *Unfinished business?: Local government reorganisation and social services*, Bristol/York: The Policy Press/Joseph Rowntree Foundation.

Craig, G. and Mayo, M. (eds) (1995) *Community empowerment. A reader in participation and development*, London: Zed Books.

Craig, G., Taylor, M., Szanto, C. and Wilkinson, M. (1999) *Developing local Compacts*, York: Joseph Rowntree Foundation.

Craig, G., Warburton, D., Taylor, M., Monro, S. and Wilkinson, M. (2001) 'Willing partners?: voluntary and community associations in the democratic process', Paper given to the Social Policy Association Conference, Belfast, July, mimeo.

Craig, G., Taylor, M., Wilkinson, M. and Monro, S., with Bloor, K. and Syed, A. (2002) *Contract or trust?: The role of compacts in local governance*, Bristol/York: The Policy Press/Joseph Rowntree Foundation.

Crook, J. (1995) *Invisible partners: The impact of the SRB on black communities*, London: Black Training and Enterprise Group.

Deakin, N. (1996) 'The devil's in the detail', *Social Policy and Administration*, vol 30, no 1, pp 20-38.

De Lima, P. (2001) *Needs not numbers: Rural racism in Scotland*, London: CDF.

Dorsett, R. (1998) *Ethnic minorities in the inner city*, Bristol: The Policy Press.

Fordham, G. (1995) *Made to last*, York: Joseph Rowntree Foundation.

Geddes, M. and Martin, S. (1996) *Local partnership for economic and social regeneration*, London: Local Government Management Board.

Gladstone, F. (1979) *Voluntary action in a changing world*, London: Bedford Square Press.

GOYH (Government Office for Yorkshire and the Humber) (1997) *Single regeneration budget challenge fund: Round 4*, Framework for Yorkshire and the Humber region, Leeds: GOYH.

Gutch, R. (1992) *Contracting: Lessons from the United States*, London: NCVO.

Hadley, R. and Hatch, S. (1981) *Social welfare and the failure of the state: Centralised social services and participatory alternatives*, London: George Allen and Unwin.

Hastings, A. (1996) 'Unravelling the process of "partnership" in urban regeneration policy', *Urban Studies*, vol 33, no 2, pp 253-68.

Hastings, A., McArthur, A. and McGregor, A. (1996) *Less than equal?: Community organisations and estate regeneration partnerships*, Bristol/York: The Policy Press/ Joseph Rowntree Foundation.

Henderson, P. and Kaur, R. (eds) (1999) *Rural racism in the UK*, London: SiA/ CDF.

Home Office (1998) *Getting it right together*, London: Home Office.

Home Office (2000) *Connecting communities, race equality support programmes*, London: Home Office.

Jeffrey, B. (1997) 'Creating participatory structures in local government', *Local Government Policy Making*, vol 23, no 4, pp 25-31.

Kendall, J. and Knapp, M. (1996) *The voluntary sector in the UK*, Manchester: Manchester University Press.

Lawless, P. (1996) 'The inner cities: towards a new agenda', *Town Planning Review*, vol 67, no 1, pp 21-43.

LBGU (London Borough Grants Unit) (1995) *Vision and visibility: Regeneration and ethnic minority communities in London*, London: LBGU.

Littlewood, S. and Winnett, C. (1997) 'In search of the X factor', *Regional Review*, July, pp 8-9.

Maloney, W.J., Jordan, G. and McLaughlin, A. (1994) 'Interest groups and public policy: the insider/outsider model revisited', *Journal of Public Policy*, vol 14, no 1, pp 17-38.

Mawson, J. et al (1995) *The single regeneration budget: The stocktake*, Birmingham: Centre for Urban and Regional Studies, University of Birmingham.

McFarlane, R. (1993) *Community involvement in city challenge: A policy report*, London: NCVO.

Modood, T. et al (1997) *Ethnic minorities in Britain*, London: Policy Studies Institute.

NCVO (National Council for Voluntary Organisations) (1996) *Meeting the challenge of change*, London: NCVO.

NCVO (2000) *New deal for communities, Phase 2 Report*, London: NCVO.

Owen, D. (1964) *English philanthropy 1660-1960*, London: Oxford University Press.

Pearson, S., Kirkpatrick, A. and Barnes, C. (1997) *Local poverty, local responses,*

Discussion Paper no 2, Sheffield and Hull: Sheffield Hallam University/ University of Lincolnshire and Humberside.

Pharaoh, C., Alexander, D.R., Kemp, K. and Smerdon, M. (1998) *Achieving the double bottom line*, West Malling: Charities Aid Foundation.

Pike, A. (1996) *In partnership: Subject to contract*, Swindon: Economic and Social Research Council.

Rai, D. (1995) *In the margins*, Social Research Paper no 2, Hull: University of Lincolnshire and Humberside.

Reid, B. and Iqbal, B. (1996) 'Redefining housing practice: interorganisational relationships and local housing networks', in P. Malpass (ed) *The new governance of housing*, Harlow: Longman.

Robson, B., Parkinson, M. et al (1994) *Assessing the impact of urban policy*, London: HMSO.

SEU (Social Exclusion Unit) (1998) *Bringing Britain together: A national strategy for neighbourhood renewal*, Cm 4045, London: The Stationery Office.

SEU (2001) *A new commitment to neighbourhood regeneration: The action plan*, London: The Stationery Office.

Skelcher, C., McCabe, A., Lowndes, V. and Nanton, P. (1996) *Community networks in urban regeneration – 'It all depends who you know …!'*, Bristol/York: The Policy Press/Joseph Rowntree Foundation.

Stewart, M. (1994) 'Between Whitehall and town hall: the realignment of urban regeneration policy in England', *Policy & Politics*, vol 22, no 2, pp 133-45.

Stewart, J. and Stoker, G. (eds) (1989) *The future of local government*, Basingstoke: Macmillan.

Stewart, M. and Taylor, M. (1995) *Empowerment and estate regeneration*, Bristol: The Policy Press.

Taylor, M. (1995) *Unleashing the potential*, York: Joseph Rowntree Foundation.

Taylor, M. (2000a) 'Communities in the lead: power, organisational capacity and social capital', *Urban Studies*, vol 37, nos 5-6, pp 1019-35.

Taylor, M. (2000b) 'Partnership: insiders and outsiders', in M. Harris and C. Rochester (eds) *Voluntary organisations and social policy: Perspectives on change and choice*, Basingstoke: Macmillan.

Thake, S. (1995) *Staying the course: The roles and structures of community regeneration organisations*, York: Joseph Rowntree Foundation.

WECH (Walterton and Elgin Community Homes) (1998) *Walterton and Elgin: From campaign to control*, London: WECH.

TEN

'Together we'll crack it': partnership and the governance of crime prevention

Gordon Hughes and Eugene McLaughlin

The emergent discourse of partnership in post-war crime control

Until the 1990s, anyone looking for a post-war history of crime prevention in the UK would, for the most part, have been forced to read about it in the margins and footnotes of texts on policing, courts and penalty. Traditionally, 'crime prevention' was deemed to be either the obvious, self-evident outcome of formal processes of criminal justice – the apprehension, prosecution, sentencing, punishment and reform of offenders – or 'unfocused' preventive activities associated with government-sponsored publicity campaigns about house and vehicle security (Gilling, 1997). Within the criminal justice system, the police had front-line responsibility for preventing crime, most obviously through law enforcement and the apprehension and prosecution of criminals.

With the publication of the report by the Cornish Committee in 1965, the case was presented for police forces to appoint specialist officers to encourage a more 'scientific' approach to crime prevention (Home Office, 1965). It was recommended that these officers should build and maintain relationships with private and public sector organisations to impress upon them the importance of taking responsibility for preventing crime. The Home Office Standing Committee on Crime Prevention was established in 1967 to coordinate national and regional crime prevention publicity. However, Weatheritt's overview of the status of crime prevention within the police in post-war Britain concluded that:

> Crime prevention has not become part of mainstream policing and the specialist crime prevention service has been left to languish in something of a policing backwater. There is evidence that a lot of specialist crime prevention work fails to make an impact. The arrangements for identifying and disseminating 'good practice' within the police service are rudimentary. Whatever the expressed commitment of senior officers and successive

governments to the view that prevention is the primary object of policing, the crime prevention job remains an activity performed on the sidelines while the main action takes place elsewhere. (Weatheritt, 1986, p 49)

In the wake of such criticisms, the beginnings of a partnership model of crime prevention can be discerned in the Home Office's *Review of criminal justice policy*, published in 1976 (cited in Gladstone, 1980). This review concluded:

> In view of the limitations in the capacity of the agencies of the criminal justice system to reduce the incidence of crime, the scope for reducing crime through policies that go beyond the boundaries of the criminal justice system merits particular attention. In recognition of this, work is already in hand exploring how the Home Office could involve other Government departments, local authorities and agencies outside government in the crime prevention field.... Work on the broader aspects of crime prevention should be pressed forward as speedily as possible. (cited in Gladstone, 1980, p 1)

A Home Office working group on crime prevention was conducting the work referred to as 'already in hand'. It had been established in 1975 to examine 'prevention' in the broadest sense, in order to identify the capacity for "influencing social policy for crime prevention purposes or for articulating the crime prevention dimension to other departments" (cited in Gladstone, 1980, p 7). The working group, according to Weatheritt (1986), attempted to find a means of integrating physical and social approaches to crime prevention within a framework that would persuade other government departments to participate in practical initiatives. It also considered how research could be applied to advance the philosophy and practice of crime prevention. The working group reviewed existing social and physical approaches to crime prevention in order to produce a more effective set of recommendations. However, it concluded that the Home Office did not have available to it sufficient knowledge about the broader aspects of crime prevention. Equally important, the working group noted that the Home Office had not "developed the right sort of intellectual framework to sustain ... a convincing or helpful approach to other departments or agencies on the crime prevention dimension of their policies" (quoted in Weatheritt, 1986, p 60).

It was in this context that the working party advocated what it defined as an 'opportunity reduction' or 'situational crime prevention' (rather than 'social' crime prevention)[1] approach, because this focused attention on 'the nexus of the criminal act itself'. Researchers needed to undertake a thorough analysis of the 'situation' in which an offence occurred in order to establish the conditions – opportunities, motivation and legislation – that needed to be met for an offence to be committed. Detailed analysis of the crime event would also identify the practical measures that would make it more difficult or impossible to fulfil each of these conditions (Gladstone, 1980; see also Clarke and Mayhew, 1980). The working party emphasised that:

> The situational approach should not be seen as providing new and certain answers on how to prevent crime or necessarily as supplying any fresh individual techniques. Rather it is intended to make up for the limited ability of the traditional approaches to meet the need for a broader based crime prevention initiative. It would facilitate the more systematic and coherent application of existing techniques, and would provide the framework in which present knowledge could be exploited and empirically tested, and the foundations in which new knowledge may be built up. (cited in Gladstone, 1980, p 10)

The case then was made for the need for a more systematic approach to crime prevention, premised on situational techniques of prevention. Here we can also see the seeds of the nascent discourse of partnership in crime control.

However, the 'new thinking' on crime prevention was confronted with stark realities. These realities arose from the election in 1979 of a Conservative government ideologically wedded to the idea that crime could be prevented and criminals controlled through sufficient numbers of police officers armed with the necessary legal powers, and backed by punitive sentencing and harsh penal regimes. As the 1980s progressed, despite the fact that criminal justice agencies enjoyed an unprecedented period of expansion and empowerment, both the official crime rate and the public's fear of crime escalated to unparalleled levels (Hough and Mayhew, 1983, 1985). However, Home Office officials, under increasing pressure from the Treasury to account for the dramatically increased 'law and order' budget, began to make headway in persuading ministers and key members of the policy community that a self-generated crisis of morale, legitimacy and resourcing was the logical outcome of a 'crime control' model of criminal justice. The sheer number of individuals entering and re-entering the system through the revolving door was threatening to paralyse the functioning of the courts. The knock-on effects of punitive sentencing were overcrowding in the prisons and demands from the prison service for more resources. The experience of incarceration was entrenching patterns of offending and increasing the likelihood of more serious offending on release. Spiralling rates of re-offending, increasing levels of victimisation and the growth of 'fear of crime' as an issue in its own right generated an all-pervasive mood of insecurity and fuelled demands for more police officers, tougher policing strategies and harsher sentences, which in turn propelled even more people into the system. A consensus was emerging within Home Office administrative circles and among academic 'policy entrepreneurs' that a pragmatic 'what works' settlement had to be pieced together that would redefine responsibility for the regulation of crime, create a cost-effective and efficient criminal justice system, depoliticise questions of crime and punishment and, most crucially for the purposes of this chapter, prioritise the need for crime prevention (Moxon, 1985; Home Office, 1988; Jones and Newburn, 1994). It was in this context of prioritising preventative approaches to crime that the turn to 'partnership' occurred.

The 1980s 'free market' in crime prevention and community safety and the rise of the discourse on partnership

In the aftermath of the Scarman Report, which followed urban disorders in Brixton, it is possible to identify three emergent models of crime prevention partnership: a 'mixed economy' model, a 'police led' model and a 'local authority led' model. In the context of the 1980s, these three models represented different attempts to establish the credibility of the partnership approach. All three models may be viewed as examples of partnership working to varying degrees, but they also imply different organisational and working relations, not least in terms of which – if any – agency is charged with the leadership role.

The 'mixed economy' model of partnership

In 1982 another Home Office-initiated, interdepartmental working group began deliberating on how to highlight crime prevention within central government departments and local authorities. The working group concluded that the preventive nature of all aspects of police work should be developed and expanded, that this work should involve collaborating with other agencies and that these other agencies should establish suitable administrative arrangements to facilitate such cooperation. These policy proposals were discussed further in a subsequent interdepartmental seminar hosted by the Home Office. Crime prevention circular 8/84, jointly issued by the participating departments, stated:

> A primary objective of the police has always been the prevention of crime. However, since some of the factors affecting crime lie outside the control or direct influence of the police, crime prevention cannot be left to them alone. Every individual citizen and all those agencies whose policies and practices can influence the extent of crime should make their contribution. *Preventing crime is a task for the whole community.* (Home Office, 1984, p 1; emphasis added)

A new Crime Prevention Unit was established within the Home Office to "light fires, to provoke crime prevention strategy activity as and where it could" (Tilley, 1993, p 3; see also Heal and Laycock, 1986). The Crime Prevention Unit subsequently disseminated its message through interdepartmental circulars, crime surveys, research activities, publicity campaigns, the Five Towns and Safer Cities programmes, Crime Concern, Neighbourhood Watch, Victim Support and police–community consultative committees. As Tilley (1993, pp 43-4) has detailed, located at the centre of the various initiatives was the 'situational crime prevention' framework:

1) crime is complex, with many features, causes, motivations and conditions;
2) given (1), it will not be possible for any agency on its own successfully to address crime prevention problems;

3) it follows from (1) and (2) that inter-agency groups are best suited to do crime prevention work;

4) crime problems, patterns, causes, conditions and motivations vary by type of crime, and across time and space;

5) it follows from (3) and (4) that crime prevention strategies will need to be tailored to distinctive local circumstances to be determined and managed by multi-agency partnerships;

6) given (5), for crime prevention to work it will be important to find out what the local circumstances are, so as to inform decisions about where crime prevention priorities lie and to develop possible strategies of amelioration;

7) if lessons are to be learned gradually about what works, both locally and in order to use resources efficiently, and more widely so that such trans-situational lessons as are possible can be learned, evaluations are needed.

In addition, the Home Office was involved in a number of schemes activated by the Department of Trade and Industry and the Department of the Environment, which also had a 'designing out crime' dimension, such as the Inner City Task Forces and the City Action Teams. The final set of Home Office anti-crime initiatives related to racial violence and harassment. Evidence from a variety of initiatives, collated in the aftermath of the publication of the influential Home Office (1981) *Racial attacks* report, revealed both high levels of harassment and intimidation and the inadequacy of the traditional police response. The interdepartmental Racial Attacks Group, which was convened in 1987, subsequently presented detailed proposals for proactive multi-agency responses to the problem of racial violence.

What is striking in retrospect about this 'mixed economy' model of partnership is the absence of any strategic role (never mind that of leadership) for local government. Responsibility was supposedly spread across the range of statutory, voluntary and private bodies. However, in practice, such partnerships were generally dominated by a police-driven discourse of crime prevention.

The 'police led' model of partnership

Certain senior police officers championed a more explicit police-led model of partnership. Although many forces preferred to do little more than pay lip service to such initiatives, the Scarman Report rekindled the debate about the desirability of 'community policing' as a distinctive police philosophy. For the Home Office, a 'low-key' version of 'community policing' had always been viewed as the vehicle to deliver situational crime prevention strategies, victim support schemes and police community race relations training. However, for John Alderson, then Chief Constable of Devon and Cornwall, it was the basis for a paradigm shift in policing, consistent with finding ways of bringing joint resources to bear in times of social change and economic deterioration (Alderson, 1979). Sir Kenneth Newman, the Commissioner of the Metropolitan Police, drawing on his experience of policing in Northern Ireland, insisted that the crime and social problems generated by, and concentrated within, multi-ethnic urban neighbourhoods were so complicated that they could not be addressed by the police acting on their own. According to Newman, it was no longer sufficient to think of framing policy responses in terms of traditional 'crime control'. The police needed to work in conjunction with other government departments, as a matter of urgency, "to lift the problems to a higher level of generality, encompassed by the expression 'social control', in a benign sense, in order to provide a unifying concept within which the activities of police and other agencies can be coordinated" (quoted in Gilroy, 1987, p 96). The police would also have to deploy new intelligence-gathering, surveillance and targeting techniques in these localities and develop contingency plans in the event of large-scale violent disorder. Hence Newman, like Alderson, was conceptualising the future policing of multi-ethnic neighbourhoods in governmental terms.

The 'local authority led' model of partnership

Local government-based police monitoring units supported this local authority model of crime prevention partnership most prominently. They contested the crime prevention agendas pursued by the Home Office and the police. Some units gained local and national notoriety for their attempts to block Home Office- and police-led multi-agency partnership initiatives and police–community consultative committees and for their campaigns for greater police accountability. However, although politically controversial, many of these units also established that, given their strategic capacities, local authorities had a central leadership role to play in tackling neighbourhood crime problems. As a result of their neighbourhood audits and group-based surveys and project work, the units gave voice to the special needs of victims of sexual, domestic, racial and homophobic violence. They also confirmed that sustained investment was needed to address the complex social and communal factors producing and/or concentrating high levels of crime, delinquency, disorder and fear in particular localities and estates. It is not surprising that these units tended to opt for the phrase 'community safety' rather than 'crime prevention' to describe the interrelated, non-police-defined range of problems and issues they were dealing with (McLaughlin, 1994).

As a result of these developing models of crime prevention and community safety partnership work, towards the end of the 1980s, a large number of anti-crime projects and programmes were in place across the country and a working consensus was emerging that 'partnerships', of some sort, were essential to developing and supporting a comprehensive, cost-effective crime prevention framework (Heal, 1987; Home Office, 1990; Graham and Bennett, 1995). However, despite local examples of 'good practice', there was also evidence that the pressing need for coordination, consolidation and formalisation of responsibility were being hindered nationally by the Conservative government's ideological commitments to, on the one hand, investing more resources in the traditional 'crime control' model; and, on the other, by its determination to expand market- rather than local government-led forms of service provision. In many neighbourhoods, the corollary of the chaotic 'free market' in crime prevention and community safety 'partnerships' was the proliferation of ad hoc agencies and numerous inter-organisational disputes about who should be the lead agency, about the purpose of the partnership and about funding arrangements (Gilling, 1996; Crawford, 1998; Hughes 1998). It has also been noted that throughout the 1980s the Home Office 'ducked' the issue of who should be tasked with taking lead responsibility, with the consequence that such responsibility tended to fall to the police (Newburn, 2001).

The Home Office Standing Conference on Crime Prevention Report

The Home Office Standing Conference on Crime Prevention Report of 1991 (the Morgan Report) has come to be viewed as both a key text and a crucial moment in the evolution of partnership approaches to crime. This working group was tasked, following the publication of the Home Office booklet *Partnership in crime prevention*, with considering and monitoring "the progress made in the local delivery of crime prevention through the multi-agency or partnership approach" (Home Office, 1991, p 10). For the Morgan Report, the concept 'crime prevention' was often narrowly interpreted and served to reinforce the belief that it was the sole responsibility of the police. 'Community safety', on the other hand, was open to wider definition and "could encourage greater participation from all sections of the community in the fight against crime" (Home Office, 1991, p 3). The working group confirmed that there was remarkably broad support for multi-agency partnerships. It noted that, despite the multitude of initiatives that it had observed, crime prevention remained a peripheral issue for the major agencies and a truly core activity for none of them. In other words, it was a classic example of what is now widely regarded as a 'wicked issue' for policy and practice. In order to correct this major defect, the report recommended that a number of key issues needed to be addressed – structure, leadership, information, durability and resources – in order to improve the organisation and delivery of multi-agency crime prevention strategies.

The Morgan Report went on to argue that the local authority was the natural focus for coordinating, in collaboration with the police, the full range of activities necessary for improving community safety. The report thus supported the idea that local authorities should be given the statutory duty and resources to coordinate local crime prevention and community safety initiatives.

Nevertheless, the Conservative government rejected the Morgan Report's key recommendations regarding both the proposed statutory role for local government and the reallocation of resources. Crawford (1998, p 41) argues that in the aftermath of the 'mothballing' of the report, the Conservative government became trapped "in the logic of its own limited vision: all it seemed capable of proposing was more of the same". In 1994 the then Opposition government published *Partners against crime* (Labour Party, 1994), which proposed to increase the number of special constables, expand Neighbourhood Watch schemes, encourage 'active citizens' to patrol their neighbourhoods and invest more resources in CCTV (effectively promoting a mix of the 'mixed economy' and 'police led' models). In November 1995 a National Crime Prevention Agency was established to agree a national agenda, disseminate good practice and develop innovative strategies for preventing and reducing crime. However, the new agency was "a pale imitation of the type of body envisaged by the Morgan Report" (Crawford, 1998, p 41) and was further evidence of the impoverishment of the Conservative approach to crime prevention and community safety. Strategic government thinking about crime prevention also moved back to the margins as a result of the hyper-politicisation of law and order in the early 1990s.

The politics of law and order

In January 1993, in the context of a news media fuelled panic about the UK's law and order crisis, the sound bite "tough on crime and tough on the causes of crime" was formulated by Tony Blair to signal a new (later termed 'Third Way') approach to crime (Blair, 1993). In the aftermath of the murder of two-year-old James Bulger by two 10-year-old boys, Blair gave voice to the multitude of public anxieties and fears and forged these concerns into a 'get tough' on youth crime philosophy. In various 'Third Way' speeches and position papers, Blair spelt out the importance of breaking through the either/or choices that had characterised the law and order debate of the 'Old Left' and the 'New Right'. Central to his vision was the espousal of the moral communitarian values of mutual obligation, self-discipline and individual responsibility (Hughes, 1996). Blair argued that rising crime rates were not inevitable and that the restoration of law and order could be achieved by rebuilding the foundations of a strong civic society through self-regulating families and re-moralised, cohesive communities; and by prioritising the needs and rights of victims and law-abiding citizens. Crime was morally wrong and New Labour would not seek to excuse or condone it. Individuals would be held responsible for their own behaviour and brought to justice and punished if they committed a criminal offence. Blair's ability to play the crime card for maximum electoral advantage in a highly volatile political and socio-economic context stoked an emergent Conservative backlash. At the Conservative Party conference in October 1993, an ever more desperate Michael Howard attempted to reclaim the ideological high ground of British criminal justice politics by unveiling a 'prison works' package of new criminal sanctions, tough minimum sentences and more prisons.

With the appointment of Jack Straw as shadow Home Secretary in 1994, it became apparent that New Labour was willing to go to considerable lengths to 'out-tough' the Conservative government on law and order issues (Downes, 1998; Sim, 2000). For example, in order to undermine politically the impact of the drop in recorded crime and an emerging post-recession economy, Straw fed and exploited the debate about the crime crisis by highlighting the need to implement New York Police Department style 'zero tolerance' policing strategies, to tackle what he described as an epidemic of 'low-level' disorder, incivility and anti-social behaviour. Furthermore, New Labour lent tacit parliamentary support to the increasingly illiberal and, many would say, irrational, Conservative proposals contained in the 1994 Criminal Justice and Public Order Act, the 1997 Crime (Sentences) Act and the 1997 Police Act.

In the countdown to the 1997 election, New Labour's remarkable transformation into the flag bearers of 'tough on crime' policies, smothered any meaningful political discussion of the party's proposals to tackle the underlying causes of crime. Considerably more attention was paid by New Labour to highlighting its short-term plans to reduce crime and disorder. Given its communitarian fears about the social fragmentation and de-moralisation wrought by neo-liberalism and the emergence of a significant 'underclass', New Labour gave notice that it was determined to implement crime and disorder reduction strategies, in order to re-establish social controls and norms of respectability. The reward for this promised communitarian crusade against criminality, crime, disorder and the tailoring of its policy headlines towards the fears of both its own core constituency and 'Middle England' was a series of opinion polls that indicated that, for the first time in the post-war period, Labour was consistently ahead of the Conservatives on the issue of law and order (Anderson and Mann, 1998).

The 'Third Way' on law and order

As many of the chapters in this book note, central to New Labour's modernisation project is the promotion of a 'joined-up' approach. *Modernising government*, launched in 1999, is intended to build policy coherence across government; institutionalise continuous improvement and innovation in policy making and service delivery; eradicate inefficiencies; and design out obsolete structures and practices. Partnership is central to this agenda:

> Distinctions between services delivered by the public and private sector are breaking down in many areas, opening the way to new ideas, partnerships and opportunities for devising and delivering what the public wants. We will build on the many strengths in the public sector to equip it with a culture of improvement, innovation and collaborative purpose.... Some parts of the public service are as efficient, dynamic and effective as anything in the private sector. But others are not. There are many reasons for this, and ... to help counter some of these difficulties, the Government is working in partnership – partnership with the new, devolved ways of government, and partnership with local authorities, other organisations and other countries. (Cabinet Office, 1999, pp 9-11)

In the field of criminal justice, New Labour is committed to reducing crime and disorder, fears of crime and disorder, and their social and economic costs; to dispensing justice fairly and efficiently; and to promoting confidence in the rule of law. Criminal justice professionals have been tasked with:

- deploying early effective interventions to divert those thought likely to offend from a life of crime;
- implementing fast-track, efficient procedures from arrest to sentence;
- improving services to victims and witnesses;
- enforcing court sentences more effectively;
- ensuring that the component parts of the system are performing to their maximum potential.

As with the rest of the public sector, virtually every Home Office document stresses the need for:

- consistent and mutually reinforcing aims and objectives;
- new funding mechanisms to direct resources strategically and effectively;
- the development of an 'evidence-based' approach to embed a 'what works' professional culture;
- the realignment of organisational boundaries to remove obstacles to 'joint working'; and the development of a performance management culture to enhance productivity.

Criminal justice agencies now publish business plans with specified aims, objectives, performance measures, efficiency targets and clearly defined outcomes. Police forces have been set five-year targets to reduce burglary and car crime; league tables on various aspects of police performance are commonplace. The Crown Prosecution Service has been instructed to overhaul both its relationship with the police and its management of cases, and courts have been instructed to reduce the time taken between the prosecution and sentencing of offenders. New penal establishments are being built with private money and run by the private sector. Moreover, a considerable amount of time, energy and resources are being spent 'tutoring' criminal justice and community safety professionals into accepting responsibility for managing, improving and accounting for their performance (Ekblom, 1998; Home Office, 1998; Hough and Tilley, 1998). Central to New Labour's plans to modernise all aspects of criminal justice is the emphasis on developing and employing incentives and levers to promote strategic coordination and collaboration, via 'joined-up' partnerships at national, regional and local levels. Notwithstanding the spate of partnerships that are being built across the criminal justice system, we would argue that it is with the 'wicked issue' of crime reduction that the institutionalisation of partnerships is most apparent.

New Labour's 'modernisation' of crime prevention partnerships

The case for the partnership approach to crime prevention was constructed by and for New Labour before the 1997 election. Prior to the release of the Morgan Report, discussed earlier in this chapter, the Labour Party had pulled together the experience of various local authority initiatives to argue the case for a partnership approach to crime prevention. In its earliest thinking, Labour supported the idea of a Crime Prevention Act, which would establish a Crime Prevention Council. This would require central and local government to integrate crime prevention into policy and budgetary decisions; and compel local authorities to establish Crime Management Committees and promote multi-agency approaches to neighbourhood crime problems (Labour Party, 1991). Not surprisingly, Labour enthusiastically endorsed the conclusions of the Morgan Report, that local authorities should have a clearly defined statutory responsibility for developing crime prevention partnerships with action plans and objectives. Moreover, New Labour further reinforced these proposals. For example, the party's pre-election position paper on crime prevention in the mid-1990s included the declaration that "monitoring progress and evaluating impact should be an automatic requirement of crime prevention and community safety activity. It is necessary to know what works, why it works, under what conditions it works and whether it is cost-effective" (Labour Party, 1996, p 19).

The 1998 Crime and Disorder Act (CDA) builds directly on this thinking by stressing that, for successful outcomes to be achieved, statutory responsibility for crime and disorder reduction and community safety should be devolved from the central state to a series of local partnerships, made up of statutory and independent agencies and privatised bodies. The CDA gave both local authorities and the police new duties to develop strategic partnerships in order to help prevent and reduce crime and disorder in their locality. This shared leadership approach sidestepped the issue of a single lead agency in crime prevention. Central government was not persuaded that the Morgan Report view of creating one agency as lead representative (namely the local authority) would be workable in practice. Rather, its views were that principles of partnership required joint working and collective responsibility. As a consequence, the CDA established that responsibility should lie jointly with the police and the district or unitary authority (or London borough) or, where two-tiered structures exist, with the county council (Newburn, 2001). There now exists a statutory duty on local authorities and police forces, in cooperation with probation committees, health authorities and police authorities, to formulate and implement strategies for the reduction of crime and disorder in their area. The most striking contrast with the previous models of partnership working is that post-CDA partnerships have a statutory footing in England and Wales. That noted, there remains a lack of adequate resourcing for the administration of partnerships alongside existing service delivery responsibilities. There is, as yet, limited research evidence on the workings and outcomes of these partnerships, but initial findings suggest that tensions and conflicts between partners remain. Furthermore, most partnerships have adopted a narrow crime and disorder reduction agenda rather than promoting a broader 'community safety' approach.

Since 1998 all 376 statutory crime and disorder partnerships have had to:

• carry out audits of local crime and disorder problems;
• consult with all sections of the local community;

- publish three-year crime and disorder reduction strategies based on the findings of the audits;
- identify targets and performance indicators for each part of the strategy, with specified timescales;
- publish the audit, strategy and the targets;
- report annually on progress against the targets.

Hence local strategies are, in theory, driven by a performance management agenda in which cost-effective measures for the realisation of specific outcomes and reduction targets are prioritised. This is neatly captured in the promotion of what are termed 'SMART' targets, that is targets that are 'specific', 'measurable', 'achievable', 'realistic' and 'time-tabled' (Audit Commission, 1999). In over half of all local strategies, these specific crime reduction targets related to vehicle crime, burglary and violent crime (Phillips et al, 2000). This clearly reflects the priorities of central government and the recommendations of the Audit Commission (Hughes, 2000).

Closely related to auditing is New Labour's commitment to funding 'evidence-based' projects and programmes. The routine operation of local crime and disorder reduction partnerships is massively affected by this 'evidence-based' paradigm of 'success' in policy and practice. The three-year Crime Reduction Programme, which is financed through £250 million made available following the 1999 Comprehensive Spending Review, is intended to build on the 1998 Crime and Disorder Act and 'harness' the activities of local crime reduction partnerships (Home Office, 1999a). It is premised on the conclusions of *Reducing offending* (Goldblatt and Lewis, 1998), a Home Office report that highlights those interventions most likely to provide the basis for a cost-effective, sustained reduction in the long-term rise in crime. Questions considered by the authors of *Reducing offending* included: how effective is an intervention and can the benefits be quantified; what evidence is available on the likely costs of implementation; what is the likely timescale for the costs and benefits; and how strong is the available evidence on effects, costs and timescales? The Crime Reduction Programme was extended in April 1999 with the announcement of an extra £153 million for CCTV initiatives and other interventions aimed at reducing vehicle crime. This 'evidence-led' approach was also to be applied to other related programmes that received funding under the first Comprehensive Spending Review, such as the £211 million allocated to drug use and related crime and the £226 million provided for 'constructive' prison regimes.

The Crime Reduction Programme is intended to make a significant contribution by ensuring that the Home Office is achieving maximum impact for money spent and that the impact is progressively improved. The programme hopes to promote innovation; generate a significant improvement in knowledge about effectiveness and cost effectiveness; and encourage the mainstreaming of emerging knowledge about 'best practice' (Home Office, 1999b). The Crime Reduction Programme chimes with the Audit Commission's emphasis on the need to act primarily on evidence-based research that establishes 'what works' and to ignore alternative approaches that are considered uneconomic and inefficient in preventing crime and disorder (Audit Commission, 1999).

New 'top-down' modes of accountability have been put in place to encourage greater transparency and to direct and monitor New Labour's reforms. In the establishment and development of crime reduction partnerships, extensive and prescriptive 'guidance' and 'training' has been provided through the increasingly synergetic services and materials provided by what may be termed the 'supra-local' partnerships of the Home Office, Audit Commission, Local Government Association, NACRO and Crime Concern. In turn, this work is monitored and 'policed' by the Home Office Policing and Crime Reduction Unit, together with Her Majesty's Inspectorate of Constabulary and the Audit Commission. Such bodies thus have a strategic remit in overseeing key aspects of all local crime and disorder partnerships. To supplement the work of these regulatory national bodies, during 2000 regional crime directors were appointed across England and Wales. Their key task is to oversee the links between local crime policy developments and those of the Home Office and central government. The Home Office has also insisted that each project be evaluated independently, to ensure that it contributes to realising the programme's overall objectives:

> By systematically recording and comparing the cost of inputs with the outputs and outcomes of an intervention, the analysis allows us to determine the economic efficiency of interventions. This allows more informed decisions on resource allocation between different policy options to be made and ... informs decisions on how to allocate scarce resources both within and between initiatives. It will also make this decision process more transparent by organising information on inputs, outputs, impacts and outcomes in a single comparative framework. (Dhiri and Brand, 1999, p 11)

Taken together, such developments have resulted in an ever more penetrative performance management regime, to which crime and disorder reduction partnerships must respond accordingly.

Conclusions

The purpose of this chapter was to trace the development of New Labour's partnership approaches in crime prevention. We progressed from a discussion of the chaotic 1980s and the struggle to establish the credibility of the partnership approach under successive Conservative governments to detailing how it has been formalised and 'modernised' under New Labour. What, then, are the distinctive features of 'Third Way' partnerships in the policy field of crime control and community safety? In many respects, it is too early in their evolution to be at all certain how they will become institutionalised. It is clear that they feed off past models of multi-agency partnership working, particularly developments under the Conservative administrations of the 1980s and 1990s. It is also apparent that the current political experiment of the 'Third Way' does not represent a total break with the past. Accordingly, the new 'Third Way' partnerships are likely to face continuing 'old' problems associated with earlier models of partnership working, such as inter-organisational conflict; differential power between partners; problems of blurred boundaries and loss of autonomy; and confusion over responsibility and accountability. Nonetheless, as Clarke and Glendinning warned in Chapter Three, partnerships in the new crime control complex have been subject to a marked intensification of the twin processes of managerialisation and audit regimes. Under New Labour, the idea of 'joining-up' has become a key organising idea in how social and criminal justice policies should be designed in response to contemporary levels of crime and disorder (Newburn, 2001). These contemporary partnerships are also closely intertwined with the communitarian impulse of New Labour, supposedly enabling government to come closer to the communities and neighbourhoods to which it is accountable and, more ambitiously, reinserting 'communities' into policy. As noted earlier, it is too early to predict the 'career' of such partnerships. However, there is a possibility that they will encourage the pluralisation of 'policing' in the broadest sense of the word. As Newburn (2001) notes, it is recognised by 'Third Way' governments that 'joined-up' thinking and practice is crucial in all policy areas, not least criminal justice. This key assumption is based on the recognition that the problems that government has to tackle are multidimensional in character and that the responses to these problems therefore need to be multidimensional and multi-agency in character. This represents a major challenge for all organisations. Here, the crucial development for the new partnerships may be the shift from 'multi-agency' to 'inter-agency' modes of working. Multi-agency relations involve agencies coming together in relation to particular problems without unduly affecting either the way each agency works or its rationale. By contrast, inter-agency relations interpenetrate and crucially affect the normal, internal working relations of the agencies involved (Crawford, 1998). Again, as Clarke and Glendinning argue in Chapter Three, it may be that the long-term 'success' of New Labour's partnerships in crime reduction and community safety will depend on the extent to which this cultural and organisational revolution is realised.

In the rest of this conclusion, we wish to highlight some of the issues emerging for practitioners in the field from New Labour's 'modernisation' of 'partnership' approaches to crime prevention. First, for understandable reasons, those working within the crime reduction/community safety partnerships are remarkably uncritical, in public at least, of what is a highly prescriptive top-down approach; this contrasts with the assumptions (see Chapters Two and Four) that partnerships involve a degree of equality between the partners. New Labour's declared commitment to pragmatism, in the form of 'what works' and 'knowledge-based' practice, is obviously a welcome relief from the New Right's dogmatic insistence on 'competition'. In addition, the Home Office is providing very clear guidance on how to measure 'success' and 'progress'. But is this conducive to undertaking imaginative crime prevention, never mind community safety work? It is becoming increasingly obvious that 'success' in the reduction of crime and disorder is, in the short term, largely synonymous with what can be counted, audited and easily targeted. The pressure to deliver 'what works' and to minimise risks ensures that 'tried and tested' (situational) crime prevention initiatives will be prioritised over more ambitious (social) crime prevention programmes.

Second, in the long term, is 'partnership' really the framework through which a multitude of overlapping disciplinary techniques is being impressed upon criminal justice professionals? New Labour's intention is to replace 'old' criminal bureau–professional arrangements with multifunctional integrated partnerships whose performance will be dominated by the requirement to produce ever more arduous measurable and quantifiable outputs and cost-effective outcomes. Professional practice is also being shifted more and more towards a technical process in which risk assessment is determined by standardised statistical prediction models (Hughes, 2001). Third, an ever-present challenge confronting these partnerships is whether they will be able to manage New Labour's desire to manufacture headline-grabbing authoritarian 'tough on crime' initiatives to placate right-wing tabloid and mid-market newspapers (McLaughlin, 2001). In the countdown to the 2001 election, New Labour moved further right in its law and order rhetoric in an attempt to substantiate its 'tough on crime' credentials and raise the bidding for the law and order vote. Hence, a serious question to be answered is whether innovative crime prevention and community safety work can be mainstreamed when New Labour remains committed to a 'war on crime' discourse that requires resourcing for more 'cops, courts and corrections'. The final question worth posing is what are the implications for democratic accountability of the appearance of new forms of corporate governance (see Chapter Three). The crime reduction and community safety partnerships, when joined-up with the other partnerships discussed in this book, are part of an emergent, seemingly 'depoliticised', network of local governance that, as we have illustrated, is accountable first and foremost to the central state. Hence, for all the discussion of the need to consult local communities, there is every possibility that crime reduction work will not necessarily reflect the concerns of local communities.

Note

[1] Whereas situational crime prevention focuses on reducing the opportunities for crime in targeted places and events by means of specific techniques, social crime prevention is focused on questions of causation and is aimed at changing social environments and the motivations/dispositions of offenders (Hughes, 1998).

References

Alderson, J. (1979) *Policing freedom*, London: Constable Books.

Anderson, P. and Mann, N. (1998) *Safety first: The making of New Labour*, London: Granta.

Audit Commission (1999) *Safety in numbers: Promoting community safety*, London: Audit Commission.

Blair, T. (1993) 'Why crime is a socialist issue', *New Statesman and Society*, 29 January, pp 27-8.

Cabinet Office (1999) *Modernising government*, London: The Stationery Office.

Clarke, R.V. and Mayhew, P. (1980) *Designing out crime*, London: HMSO.

Crawford, A. (1998) *Crime prevention and community safety: Politics, policies and practices*, London: Longman.

Dhiri, S. and Brand, S. (1999) *Analysis of costs and benefits: Guidance for evaluators*, London: Home Office.

Downes, D. (1998) 'Toughing it out: from Labour opposition to Labour government', *Policy Studies*, vol 19, no 3/4, pp 191-8.

Ekblom, P. (1998) *Community safety and the reduction and prevention of crime – A conceptual framework for training and the development of a professional discipline*, London: Home Office.

Gilling, D. (1996) 'Policing, crime prevention and partnerships', in F. Leishman, B. Loveday and S.P. Savage (eds) *Core issues in policing*, London: Longman.

Gilling, D. (1997) *Crime prevention*, London: University College London.

Gilling, D. and Hughes, G. (2000) 'Initial findings from a national survey of community safety officers', Paper delivered at the British Criminology Conference, Leicester, July.

Gilroy, P. (1987) *There ain't no black in the Union Jack*, London: Hutchinson.

Gladstone, F.J. (1980) *Co-ordinating crime prevention efforts*, Research Study No 62, London: Home Office.

Goldblatt, B. and Lewis, P. (eds) (1998) *Reducing offending*, Home Office Research Study 187, London: Home Office.

Graham, J. and Bennett, T. (1995) *Crime prevention strategies in Europe and North America*, Helsinki: HUENSI.

Heal, K. (1987) 'Crime prevention in the United Kingdom: from start to go', *Home Office Research and Planning Unit Research Bulletin*, vol 24, pp 9-15.

Heal, K. and Laycock, G. (eds) (1986) *Situational crime prevention*, London: HMSO.

Home Office (1965) *Report of the committee on the prevention and detection of crime*, London: Home Office.

Home Office (1981) *Racial attacks*, London: HMSO.

Home Office (1984) 'Crime prevention', Circular 8/84, London: Home Office.

Home Office (1988) *The costs of crime*, London: Home Office Standing Conference on Crime Prevention.

Home Office (1990) 'Crime prevention: the success of the partnership approach', Circular 44/90, London: Home Office.

Home Office (1991) *Safer communities: The local delivery of crime prevention through the partnership approach* (The Morgan Report), London: HMSO.

Home Office (1998) *Guidance on statutory crime and disorder partnerships*, London: Home Office.

Home Office (1999a) *Criminal justice system: The strategic plan for 1999-2000 to 2001-2002*, London: Home Office.

Home Office (1999b) *Reducing crime and tackling its causes*, London: Home Office.

Hough, M. and Mayhew, P. (1983) *The British crime survey*, London: Home Office.

Hough, M. and Mayhew, P. (1985) *Taking account of crime*, London: Home Office.

Hough, M. and Tilley, N. (1998) *Auditing crime and disorder: Guidance for local partnerships*, Police Research Group Paper 91, London: The Stationery Office.

Hughes, G. (1996) 'Communitarianism and law and order', *Critical Social Policy*, vol 16, no 4, pp 17-41.

Hughes, G. (1998) *Understanding crime prevention: Social control, risk and late modernity*, Buckingham: Open University Press.

Hughes, G. (2000) 'In the shadow of law and disorder: the contested politics of community safety', *Crime Prevention and Community Safety*, vol 2, no 4, pp 47-60.

Hughes, G. (2001) 'Crime and disorder partnerships: the future of community safety?', in G. Hughes, E. McLaughlin and J. Muncie (eds) *Crime prevention and community safety: New directions*, London: Sage Publications.

Jones, T. and Newburn, T. (1994) *Democracy and policing*, London: PSI.

Labour Party (1991) *Tackling the causes of crime: Labour's crime prevention policy for the 1990s*, London: Labour Party.

Labour Party (1994) *Partners in crime*, London: Labour Party.

Labour Party (1996) *Tackling the causes of crime: Labour's proposals to prevent crime and criminality*, London: Labour Party.

Laycock, G. and Tilley, N. (1995) 'Implementing crime prevention', in M. Tonry and D. Farrington (eds) *Building a safer society: Strategic approaches to crime prevention*, Chicago, IL: University of Chicago Press.

McLaughlin, E. (1994) *Community, policing and accountability*, Aldershot: Avebury.

McLaughlin, E. (2001) 'Questioning 'what works': tThe rationalisation, re-moralisation and the hyper-politisation of crime control', in A. Edwards and G. Hughes (eds) *Community crime prevention:Theory, research, politics and practice*, Cullompton: Willan Publications.

Moxon, D. (ed) (1985) *Managing criminal justice*, London: HMSO.

Newburn, T. (2001) 'Community safety and policing: some implications of the Crime and Disorder Act 1998', in G. Hughes, E. McLaughlin and J. Muncie (eds) *Crime prevention and community safety: New directions*, London: Sage Publications.

Phillips, C., Jacobson J., Considine, M. and Lewis, R. (2000) 'A review of audits and strategies produced by Crime and Disorder partnerships in 1999', Home Office briefing note, London: Home Office.

Scarman, Lord (1981) *Report into Brixton riots*, London: HMSO.

Sim, J. (2000) 'One thousand days of degradation: New Labour and old compromises at the turn of the century', *Social Justice*, vol 27, no 2, pp 168-92.

Straw, J. (1998) 'New approaches to crime and punishment', *Prison Service Journal*, no 116, pp 2-6.

Straw, J. (1999) *The Government's crime reduction strategy:The Home Secretary's preface*, London: Home Office.

Tilley, N. (1993) 'Crime prevention and the safer cities story', *Howard Journal of Criminal Justice*, vol 32, no 1, pp 40-57.

Weatheritt, M. (1986) *Innovations in policing*, London: Croom Helm.

ELEVEN

Regeneration partnerships under New Labour: a case of creeping centralisation

Jonathan S. Davies

Introduction

During the 1990s, 'local governance' became the dominant paradigm through which local political processes are studied. The concept of local governance acknowledges that local government is no longer the dominant institution in local politics (see Chapter Seven). Rather, it is one organisation among many collaborating in a complex framework of governing (John, 1997, p 253). Within the local governance debate, there has been considerable scholarly interest in regeneration partnerships, particularly the relationship between local authority and business elites. This chapter joins that debate, arguing that partnerships are evidence of a governing strategy aimed at giving central government greater leverage over local politics. To use the terminology of Rhodes (1999), regeneration partnerships are top-down or hierarchical institutions, rather than bottom-up institutions characterised by networking and trust.

According to the Local Government Association (LGA), regeneration is the "promotion of the social, economic and environmental well-being of an area" (LGA, 1998). This is an inclusive definition of regeneration, in which education and the environment are inseparable from economic development. This chapter therefore looks at the Single Regeneration Budget (SRB), which encourages multidimensional regeneration projects, and recent initiatives in the sphere of education (see also Chapter Twelve). While the partnerships in question often involve community representatives, church leaders and voluntary sector groups, the focus is specifically on interactions between local authority and local business elites, the relationship at the heart of partnership initiatives over the past decade. The chapter argues that, with important differences in emphasis, New Labour is following an evolutionary policy trajectory based on the direction established by the previous Conservative governments in the early 1990s. Hilary Armstrong, Minister for Local Government and Regions in the first (1997-2001) Labour government, has commented that "it is vital that we lose the skills of battle and find the skills and organisation of partnership" (see Stoker, 1999, p 17). However, this chapter will conclude that central government policy initiatives, while they have succeeded in generating bureaucratic partnerships, have inhibited the development of collaborative synergy. The chapter further argues that local regeneration partnerships are part of a centralising tendency, where central government is trying to increase its influence over those actors it sees as having a part to play in regeneration. If 'New Labour' is serious about partnerships with local government, it will have to relax financial controls and allow much greater freedom for local people to determine the goals they wish to pursue. In short, talk of a 'Third Way' in the politics of regeneration is premature. Rather, policy has continued along an evolutionary path established by the Conservatives in the early 1990s, with talk of a central–local partnership echoing initiatives from the last Labour period in government during the 1970s.

The chapter is organised into five main sections. It begins with a brief summary of the way urban policy has encouraged regeneration partnerships since the late 1960s. Comparisons are then drawn between this period and recent developments under 'New Labour'. The third section uses evidence from four case studies in Yorkshire and Humberside to show how collaboration is driven by downward pressures, and how the internal dynamic of local collaboration between local authorities and the business sector remains weak. This evidence is indicative of the further centralisation of urban policy and increasing regulation of local politics by the centre. The fourth section considers what added value, or collaborative synergy, can be attributed to partnership working. The final section characterises regeneration partnerships as central government policy instruments, arguing that if government is serious about creating strong, autonomous local partnerships, it will need to allow localities greater flexibility in deciding regeneration priorities.

Urban policy 1969-97

Urban policy is the targeting of resources by government to problems that it regards as peculiar to, or concentrated in, towns and cities. It can focus on places or people and on single or multiple issues. In recent times, urban policy has attempted to tackle the economic and social effects of decline in the former industrial heartlands of the UK. The present era of urban grants for regeneration began with the 1969 Local Government Grants (Social Need) Act. The late 1960s were an era of housing developments characterised by high-rise blocks, which still blot our landscape today, and badly planned or non-existent community facilities. They were also characterised by racial tension, inflamed notoriously by Enoch Powell's 'rivers of blood' speech. Under the Act, government gave out grants to local authorities on the basis of 'special social need' in urban areas. One of these grants was the Urban Programme, designed to encourage investment through land and building improvements and support revenue costs for social projects (Parkinson and Wilks, 1986).

The Inner Urban Areas Act, passed in 1978, created seven Inner City Partnerships (ICPs) within the Urban Programme, which encapsulated the partnership approach of the Wilson and Callaghan Labour governments. ICPs were intended to generate closer collaboration between government and the private sector and improve central–local collaboration. However, they failed in these objectives, falling instead under the control of Whitehall, government ministers and local government officials (Bailey et al, 1995, p 45; Barnekov et al, 1989, p 157). The ICPs were fatally undermined with the election of the Conservative government in 1979. By 1981, the Tory government had a new agenda for urban policy and the ICPs withered on the vine.

The 1980s were the era of 'privatism' (Barnekov et al, 1989). The urban riots of the early 1980s led British politicians and civil servants to look overseas, particularly to the United States, for policy initiatives involving the business sector. In 1982, a British version of the US Urban Development Action Grant (UDAG) was introduced in the form of the Urban Development Grant (UDG) (Wolman, 1992, pp 31-2). The objective of the UDG was to lever private sector funds into inner cities by means of government grants (Boyle, 1985). Throughout the 1980s, the role of business in urban policy was enhanced and that of the local authority was undermined. The Urban Development Corporation (UDC), the 'flagship' urban policy during this period (Burton and O'Toole, 1994, p 162), was dominated by private sector interests and it marginalised local authorities from economic regeneration. Lawless (1994, p 1304) describes the policy statement *Action for cities* (HMSO, 1988) as the "high tide of anti-collectivism towards the cities".

By 1990, the government had changed its position, calling for a "spirit of co-operation, of partnership between all of those involved in central and local government, including local business" (Department of Environment, cited in Lawless, 1994, p 1304). This policy shift was based partly on a new confidence in the compliance of Labour local authorities. But the effective exclusion of local government from urban policy had also been criticised by sources close to the government, including the Audit Commission and Business in the Community (Le Gales and Mawson, 1994, p 84). By 1991, this 'exclusive' approach to regeneration was widely perceived to be failing (Le Gales and Mawson, 1995, p 222).

The introduction of City Challenge in 1991 was therefore a watershed in government policy, marking a shift in political attitudes and the introduction of initiatives that encouraged local authorities to establish partnerships to compete for targeted regeneration funds. City Challenge was based on the idea that substantial and lasting urban regeneration requires partnership between all the key players. It therefore placed local authorities back into the centre of urban policy, focusing on infrastructural development and market investment (Oatley and Lambert, 1998, p 111). City Challenge lasted until 1994 when it was replaced by the SRB, probably the most significant urban policy initiative under the Major government. The SRB combined 20 regeneration programmes, including City Challenge, and was described as the new 'flagship' regeneration programme. Government thinking behind the SRB had three strands: partnership; integration of economic and social issues; and competition. It thus represented a move away from City Challenge and a move towards today's axiom that economic and social ills have to be tackled in tandem – thinking that informs the current government's social exclusion programme. The first three annual rounds of the SRB were concerned with generating local partnerships to address economic and social difficulties. The Labour government was elected in May 1997, during Round 4.

Urban policy after 1997: New Labour and 'joined-up thinking'

Fresh SRB guidance was issued by the new government. It asked for a stronger emphasis on social 'need', based on criteria defined in the Index of Local Deprivation (ILD) (DETR, 1998b) or on special local circumstances. It also demanded a greater emphasis on tackling the 'needs of communities in the most deprived areas' and greater collaboration between local partnerships and regional offices (GOYH, July 1997). Subsequent guidelines for the SRB went further, demanding a 'strategic' or 'comprehensive' approach to addressing regeneration needs, and requiring bids to address a range of issues identified by the government's new Social Exclusion Unit (DETR, 1999).

This approach to the SRB was centred on the idea that regeneration is enhanced when regeneration problems are tackled in a comprehensive and cross-cutting way. Regional guidance for Round 5 of the SRB enhanced the new emphasis on 'extensive and multiple deprivation', with a formal commitment to allocate 80% of resources to those areas falling within the worst 50 local authorities in the 1998 ILD (DETR, 1998a, 1999). The government identified three main problems with the previous Tory approach to the SRB. First, it highlighted a lack of community capacity, that is a lack of 'quality' people engaging in the partnership process. To alleviate this problem, 10% of the SRB was top-sliced to assist local capacity-building initiatives. Second, it argued that the focus on local initiatives had led to an absence of strategic thinking, contributing to uneven economic performance between the regions. Third, it was acknowledged that the onus on local partnerships to match outputs to criteria set out in SRB guidelines had generated a heavy bureaucratic burden. The government therefore promised that in future it would take account of the need for a balance between flexibility and decentralisation on one hand, and monitoring and management of public money on the other. Whether this will occur remains to be seen. The government has now decided to end the SRB in April 2002, when SRB resources will be subsumed within the budgets of the new Regional Development Agencies (RDAs). In 2001-02, RDAs will be responsible for making SRB bids to the government on behalf of their regions (DETR, 2001).

How committed, then, is New Labour to a central–local partnership and to the development of local regeneration partnerships? On taking office, the Blair government signalled a new central–local partnership and the end of what the government described as the adversarial policies of the Conservative years (Stoker, 1999, p 17). The Local Government Association's (LGA, 1998) *New commitment to regeneration* initiative is indicative of this approach. *New commitment* is supposed to be an overarching framework within which local partnerships, including SRB partnerships, will work. On paper, *New commitment* is evidence of a new willingness on the part of government to experiment with local government-led policy initiatives. It was developed by the LGA based on research undertaken by Le Gales and Mawson (1994). Shortly after the 1997 election, New Labour agreed to a pilot scheme involving 22 local partnerships. The objective of the scheme was to explore different ways of improving partnerships between actors at the local level and, more importantly, between central and local government. It involved time-limited agreements between partners, including central government, each of whom is required to stipulate their contribution to the partnership. On the other hand, the 1999 Local Government Act (HMSO, 1999) granted even stronger powers to central government in the event of perceived failure, including the right to enforce outsourcing. This is evidence that the government still mistrusts local political leaders (Stewart, 2000, pp 95-6) and it is questionable, therefore, how far recent measures represent a commitment to decentralisation. It is arguable that they empower only those authorities that are in step with government thinking.

As a central plank of the government's approach to regeneration, changes in education policy and the structure of local education partnerships are a good example of this tendency. School–industry links were formalised with the establishment of Education Business Partnerships (EBPs) in 1990 (see also Chapter Twelve). These partnerships drew together a range of school–industry projects in a single umbrella organisation comprising local education authorities, training and enterprise councils (TECs) and other local organisations. EBPs shared the common goal of improving employability among young people. They were a key vehicle for education–industry links in the early to mid-1990s, but under New Labour two new initiatives seem set to supplant them.

In November 1998, the then Secretary of State for Education David Blunkett announced plans for strategic Lifelong Learning Partnerships for the governance of post-school education, as a contribution to the government's agenda for regeneration and social inclusion: "In a world of increasing global competition, education and training are the best economic policy we have" (DfEE, 1998). Learning is "an essential part of regenerating our communities and bringing social justice for all our people" (DfEE, 1999b). A *National partnership protocol* was drawn up in November 1998, establishing a national framework and creating the conditions in which local partnerships could develop. The broad objectives for Learning Partnerships are to widen participation in learning, increase attainment, improve standards and meet the skills challenge.

The White Paper, *Learning to succeed: A new framework for post-16 learning* was published later in 1999 (DfEE, 1999a). It proposed to establish a Learning and Skills Council for England, supported by up to 50 local councils, to replace the system of TECs. These councils plan and coordinate post-16 education; assume responsibility for further education funding; take over the funding of modern apprenticeships and national traineeships; and ensure that an effective partnership network exists to support work-related learning for the pre-16 age group. A key role is envisaged for employers both on the national and the local councils, with business constituting the biggest single group on the national body. The

White Paper argued that local learning partnerships will complement local learning councils. It is intended that the local learning councils will consult with the learning partnerships, thereby avoiding duplication and providing a mechanism for accountability. It was claimed that they would not 'impose' another layer of partnership locally, but rather 'subsume' existing arrangements, building on what was already in place. Whether or not these initiatives duplicate each other is a matter for further research. But they are evidence of the increasing and complex regulation of local politics.

In summary, New Labour policy toward local regeneration partnerships is characterised by both continuity and change. Continuity is visible in the emphasis on developing relationships between local government, business and other sectors. Change is visible in the development of a more 'holistic' emphasis in regeneration programmes designed to generate joined-up thinking in local partnerships; and in the commitment by central government to work in partnership with local government. However, despite paper commitments to a stronger partnership with local government, recent initiatives in education suggest the centre is tightening its grip on important aspects of urban policy. Two key themes can be identified. First, the government is keen to enhance the role of business elites in urban policy. Business leaders are to be given a much greater role in education than before. Second, it is further bureaucratising the partnership process, creating collaborative institutions to implement a largely predetermined agenda. The mechanisms for Lifelong Learning Partnerships and Learning and Skills Councils are suited to top-down hierarchical relationships, not to networking based on trust (Rhodes, 1999).

Regeneration partnerships in Yorkshire and Humberside

What impact, then, have these policies had on the development of local partnerships and is it possible to identify a 'New Labour' effect? This part of the chapter considers these questions, drawing on material from four studies of regeneration in Yorkshire and Humberside, Barnsley, Rotherham, Hull and North East Lincolnshire, undertaken over two years from early 1998. The cases are good examples of partnership building under similar economic and political conditions.

It became clear during the research (Davies, 2001) that it is useful to distinguish between partnership 'types'. Stoker (1998b, 1998c) identifies three types of partnership: principal–agent relations; inter-organisational negotiation; and systemic coordination (see also the typologies discussed in Chapter Two). The first category involves purchaser–provider relationships, such as the contracts associated with competitive tendering and Best Value. Regeneration partnerships cannot be characterised in this way, as they do not involve legally binding agreements. The second category involves negotiation and coordination between parties through the blending of capacities. This is the sort of arrangement typical of SRB partnerships (Oatley and Lambert, 1998). The third category goes further, establishing a level of "mutual understanding and embeddedness", to the extent that organisations develop a shared vision and joint working that leads to the establishment of self-governing networks (Stoker, 1998a, p 22).

The research (Davies, 2001) aimed to determine how far the relationship between local authority and business elites in regeneration partnerships conformed to the categories of hierarchy or network; and whether collaborative synergy, or added value, could be identified from this aspect of partnership working. Other actors were not central to the research, although the conclusions may apply equally to local authority relationships with other actors. The findings were based on a variety of sources, including interviews with elites from each local authority, Chambers of Commerce, TECs and local industry. Interviews were also undertaken with government ministers and officials, representatives of regional organisations and the LGA. Other important sources included local studies archives, internal documentation provided by the participants and the Internet.

The main conclusion of the research, across all four localities, was that the endogenous dynamic, or 'internal glue', to local partnership working was weak. An ideological commitment to partnership between local political and business elites existed to a greater or a lesser extent in all areas. However, the more detailed the examination of the partnerships, the less substantial they appeared to be. Business participation, in particular, was symbolic. There were a mere handful of local business activists involved, and while they agreed that partnership was a good thing in principle, they were cynical about partnership working in practice. The process of bidding for government grants had generated formal links between local government and business, but these were shallow and did not depend on local synergy. The following sections consider why this was the case. They appraise the role of the SRB in the development of partnerships and consider local responses to government-sponsored education partnerships. It is argued that partnerships have yet to deliver tangible added value and that responsibility for this failure lies with the bureaucracy imposed by central government (Davies, 2001).

The influence of the Single Regeneration Budget on local partnership practices

The SRB was held to be the most influential factor in all four areas, affecting partnership structure, partnership objectives, partnership activities and partnership relations. In each area, a public–private partnership was established in the early 1990s to bid for government funds. Some partnerships started with City Challenge, others with the SRB, but each evolved along similar political lines. The partnerships tended to concern themselves initially with economic regeneration, later developing a wider social and economic regeneration agenda, following first the trajectory of City Challenge and later the SRB. Recent changes in partnership structure and orientation were universally attributed to developments in the SRB. In practice, this meant a greater focus on integrated economic and social regeneration, a theme that underpins New Labour's social exclusion agenda and that has been visible in the SRB guidelines issued since May 1997. The overriding perception of those responsible for developing strategies for bidding to the SRB was that they are driven more by changing central government priorities than by local aspirations.

Given that the SRB was a key influence on the development of local priorities for regeneration, how important was it in generating and sustaining partnership work? The common view was that it represented an important stimulus for local partnership activities and the glue to partnership working. But while it played an important role in stimulating and maintaining partnerships, it was also universally criticised for its prescriptiveness and for the bureaucracy it generated. This criticism had a particular edge in partnerships that were attempting to develop comprehensive regeneration strategies encompassing economic and social objectives. In these cases the SRB was perceived to have *undermined* local governing capacity, preventing local actors from developing their own approaches by tying them up in complex bids for projects and in evaluation. The bureaucracy in partnership working was a key factor putting off business leaders from participation in partnerships. The terms 'initiativitis' and 'partnership fatigue' were used frequently to describe a feeling among business activists and local authority elites that too much time was spent in committee rooms doing the government's bidding.

The influence of the SRB is therefore contradictory. It is responsible for maintaining partnership focus and sustaining partnership activity; it has pushed local authorities into formalised partnerships; and it offers business an incentive to participate. At the same time, it saps local energies, leaving little room for local ideas and aspirations. It has disempowered local politicians and strategically minded business leaders, tying them up in bureaucracy and hampering attempts to carve out local strategies. While resources from the SRB are vital for local regeneration projects, they impede the development of capacity *within* the partnerships it has shaped. This situation was described as 'local administration, not local governance'. It was also apparent that neither central government nor local activists had thought about what business leaders could, or should, contribute to partnership working. Local activists acknowledged that there was no recent history or culture of partnership working within the business community and consequently a clearer role was needed for business leaders, together with an incentive structure to generate wider business participation.

Education and lifelong learning

A further objective of the research was to determine how education fitted into the overall regeneration agenda by studying partnerships dedicated to education–business links and those linked directly to the wider regeneration process. The research discovered two main trends: first, some partnership activities were fragmenting; and second, the recent education initiatives discussed above had generated concerns that local autonomy is being further eroded.

The research showed that EBPs were disintegrating or coming under severe stress. In three instances, the EBP had been wound up and in the fourth, its future was under discussion. The failure of the EBPs was attributed locally to difficulties in the relationships between the local authority and the TEC and and a corresponding absence of common commitments to partnership objectives. EBPs were perceived to have outlived their usefulness, no longer fulfilling the strategic role for which they were established. The National EBP network confirmed that EBPs were becoming unsustainable because of unreliable levels of local commitment, local turf wars and the lack of a reliable national funding stream (National EBP Network, 1999).

What of DfEE proposals for another raft of partnerships? Business and local authority leaders were sceptical. Like the SRB, the local Learning and Skills Councils and Lifelong Learning Partnerships were perceived to be too prescriptive. It was feared that central government proposals, however worthy in their intentions, would distort local objectives and undermine existing partnerships. In one case, it was claimed that the existing 'strategic' education partnership, an integrated branch of the wider SRB partnership that had been successful in the past, could lose both its 'helicopter vision' and its 'cradle to grave' ambitions for education. This reflected an anxiety that the problems associated with prescriptiveness and bureaucracy in the SRB were being replicated in the new education partnerships.

Added value in partnership?

It might be argued that it is irrelevant whether government policy imposes tight constraints on local partnerships if, as a result, local capacity for tackling local problems is enhanced. How far have partnership initiatives achieved positive outputs? Le Gales and Mawson (1994, p 112) note that it is difficult to produce measures for political outputs such as solidarity, coordination and cohesiveness. These words are 'motherhood and apple pie' concepts, which partnerships are supposed to engender. The process of evaluating partnership synergy was not aided by the absence of systematic thinking in the four study localities about this issue. Notwithstanding these difficulties, it is possible to evaluate partnership activities on a qualitative basis. Stoker (1997, p 19) argues that it is necessary to consider not only the 'doing' of governance (inputs), but also the impact of governance – its achievement of social purpose (outputs). Cropper (1996, pp 83-4) distinguishes between 'constitutive' value, an input-related concept reflected in expressions of purpose and individual capacities; and 'consequential' value, reflected in claims about the efficiency, output and legitimacy of collaboration. However, he recognises that organisations, in this case partnerships, can also be valued for what they are and what they represent, for "direct personal gratification and for group integrity and perpetuation, rather than for what, instrumentally, they can do" (Cropper, 1996, p 90). In this sense, added value is intangible and unquantifiable (Huxham, 1996, p 177). Evaluation should not, therefore, be limited to material outputs, although in the case of regeneration these are the mark of success. Hastings (1996, p 259) distinguishes between resource synergy as a materialistic concept and policy synergy, indicative of a process by which new insights or solutions are produced from differing perspectives. Added value, broadly conceived, can therefore be conceptualised in three ways: as resource gain (allowing for a broad definition of 'resource'); as enhanced strategic capacity achieved through deliberation; and as a simple belief that cooperation is inherently good (Cropper, 1996). Local partnerships in the study were evaluated against the objectives for collaboration as understood by local activists and, more speculatively, against the question of whether they could be achieved by the local authority or the private sector alone, were government grants to be reallocated to one party or the other (see for example, Harding, 1998, p 71).

Overall, there was a general predisposition in favour of partnerships, in the sense that the term carried positive connotations and that good working relationships with other actors were viewed as a worthwhile aspiration. This predisposition was much stronger in the local authorities than the business sector and was associated with the abstract principle of collaboration rather than the practice of bureaucratic SRB partnerships, where scepticism and cynicism were pervasive. Thus, procurement of governmental funds tended to be the only material achievement claimed for these partnerships. In each case, understandably, grants were perceived as an indicator of partnership success. But there were senior figures in local government who believed that monies allocated through the SRB would have been better spent by the local authority. For them, partnerships were necessary rather than virtuous, a means to the end of much-needed public investment. Otherwise, partnership achievements were characterised in terms that were vague and soft, including the 'feel-good factor', 'synergy' and a 'different perspective on problems'. These claims have to be accepted or rejected at face value, depending on whether partnership is perceived as a positive route to regeneration or not. But the impact of soft values on regeneration outputs could not be quantified by local actors and there was in any case widespread cynicism that positive outcomes could be attributed to partnerships.

Some local activists acknowledged that the local partnerships had failed to evaluate their achievements. It is easy to assume that partnership generates added value in a political–ideological culture that assumes it will. Indeed, one local survey pointed out that hopes and practices become intertwined where added value in partnerships is concerned (Davidson, 1998). Nevertheless, evidence that SRB partnerships had produced outputs that could not have been achieved had the same resource been allocated to a single organisation was minimal. However, partnership working is still relatively new and it would be unfair to judge it on the basis of relatively new initiatives. Harding (1998, p 87) believes that the 'partnership movement' will continue to 'gain strength' in the coming period. If he is right, evaluation of collaborative advantage undertaken in 2010 could reveal more positive results, particularly if a future government takes a less prescriptive approach to urban policy. But at present, there are few visible outputs that can be attributed with confidence to partnership activities.

Partnership and governance failure

Recent studies of local partnerships have neglected the possibility that they may contribute to governance failure; that is, the failure to achieve governing objectives. In other words, the very process of collaboration may, in some circumstances, be responsible for the failure to achieve agreed governing objectives and for the consequent fragmentation of partnerships. Models such as that developed by Stoker and Mossberger (1994) and Bassett (1996), show that partnerships can suffer from internal conflict. But the local governance debate, while recognising the likelihood of governance failure (Jessop, 2000), has underplayed the extent to which partnerships themselves generate centrifugal or fragmentary tendencies. Stoker (1998c, p 24) argues, following his co-authored study of Detroit (Orr and Stoker, 1994), that local governance failure is crucial to understanding the new world of governing. Scepticism about the quality and efficacy of local partnerships is similarly crucial. It cannot be assumed that partnership provides an unqualified answer to the problem of coordination posed by the proliferation of taskforces and quangos (Barker et al, 1999).

Cropper (1996, p 82), furthermore, argues that the survival of alliances depends on their ability to create and to command value. The case studies illustrated the wisdom in this simple point. Building partnerships can be difficult (Stone, 1989) and the process of collaboration can generate more costs than benefits, contributing to governance failure (Jessop, 2000). It is unsurprising, therefore, that the case studies threw up instances where partnerships foundered, thereby providing a basis for better inter-organisational relations and, potentially, more effective governance. One example was that of EBPs, discussed above. Whatever the reasons for this, the fragmentation of the EBPs resulted in a situation where school–industry links were being managed almost exclusively by the TECs. This solution was viewed positively by all parties, including the LEAs. In this case, the 'partnership' whole generated less than its constituent parts, a situation that was redressed by the disaggregation of the partnership.

The perception that there is no added value in partnership work was often cited by business as a reason for non-participation. Partnership activity was felt by outsiders to require effort that was disproportionate to the potential gain. One company claimed that its local authority had no idea about private sector needs and that it could not hope to influence the inward investment decisions of major companies, a key objective for economic regeneration. This example illustrates a failure to collaborate rather than a failure of collaboration, but it indicates that even for large businesses, the costs of collaboration can outweigh the benefits. Negative views of this kind could also be indicative of the reasons why a wider segment of the private sector has not become involved in partnership. Quite simply, they may not think that partnerships work.

These examples support a broader observation; that partnerships can have negative sum effects on governance, as well as zero and positive sum effects. If the management of education–business links by one organisation is more effective than a costly partnership, then partnership fragmentation can result in better governance. It may enable the parties concerned to get on with fulfilling their tasks without the distraction of obligations to other parties and without problems of achieving coordination. It may also liberate the potential for flexible networking, without the costs imposed by bureaucratic partnerships. Hence, the dominant ideology in government, that partnerships always make a positive contribution to regeneration activities, is questionable.

Regeneration partnership as a policy instrument

To reiterate, the level of strategic autonomy within SRB partnerships was inhibited by extra-local political forces. These partnerships had not generated synergy. Rather, they were symbolic, driven not by local economic and social imperatives, but by extra-local demands. Furthermore, they did not produce tangible added value. One reason for these shortcomings is that local regeneration partnerships were over-regulated by a range of government policy instruments (see Chapter Three). If the case of education is typical, then the use of these instruments to regulate partnership activities is increasing (see Chapter Twelve).

The regulation of partnerships is not only about bringing local government and business together; it is also about attempting to draw local stakeholders, including business, into supporting and carrying out the government's agenda for regeneration. This point is given implicit support by John and Cole (1998, p 384), who argue in their study of Leeds that, due to collaboration, local business is "more subject to the balance of public decisions than before". It could be, for example, a way for government to gain influence over the market by drawing the private sector into its regeneration strategy, as well as being a means of marketising local politics. According to Atkinson (1999, p 67), government advice helps to incorporate partnership activists into the "linguistic market and products which dominate urban regeneration, creating an appreciation of what is appropriate and likely to be valued". The central–local partnership, therefore, is as much about bringing local actors into a relationship with government as it is about bringing them into partnership with each other. But partnerships are not, strictly speaking, organs of the state; they are policy instruments or implementation agencies for the centre (Peters, 1998; Pierre, 1998). Since the early 1990s, central government has delegated responsibilities for economic regeneration to the locality. But it has done so in a way that enables it to retain its influence through the construction of heavily regulated partnerships. In this sense hierarchy, rather than network, is dominant in the local politics of regeneration (Rhodes, 1999).

What, if anything, might be done by those who wish to generate stronger, self-sustaining partnerships? Stephen Elkin (1987, p 177) warns that too much central control over the finances of local government inhibits the vital, deliberative city. His perspective has strong resonance in the UK. As was argued above, the very structure of the SRB inhibits the development of local partnership synergy (see also Morgan et al, 1999). One obvious answer, therefore, is for central government to trust local government more and enter more fully into the spirit of partnership talked about by Hilary Armstrong (Stoker, 1999, p 17). The structure of partnerships must be redesigned to facilitate local innovation and autonomous action. This would involve allowing partnerships greater latitude in deciding what government money should be spent on; for example, by abandoning the bureaucratic structure of the SRB altogether, allocating the funds to local authorities on a needs basis and trusting them to devise appropriate local partnership mechanisms. Time will tell whether subsuming SRB funds into the budgets of the RDAs will have this effect. Either way, if local regeneration partnerships are to become instruments of *local* governance, defined by Rhodes (1996) as autonomous self-organising networks, central government will have to relax its grip on local politics and find ways to persuade local business elites to commit themselves to the partnership approach. This is not being done at present because central government does not trust local authorities (Davies, 2000, 2001; Stewart, 2000, p 95-6), despite the rhetoric of partnership.

Conclusions

New Labour perceives regeneration as requiring 'joined-up thinking' and its agenda for the further expansion of the partnership culture into the domain of education, discussed in detail in Chapter Twelve, is a clear indication of this thinking. It is also an indication of the highly prescriptive nature of government regulation of local politics. The Blair government has continued the centralising tendencies of its predecessor, despite its commitments to central-local partnerships and to relaxing the bureaucratic burden imposed on localities. Its prescriptions for regeneration policy and partnerships, through guidelines (in the case of the SRB) and through legislation (in the case of *Modern local government*, DETR, 1998b), appear closer to the concept of government by control than to governance by negotiation and trust. However, the more insistent the government is about what partnerships should do, how they should be funded, and who should be involved in them, the more difficult it seems to be for mutually enriching collaboration to develop (Morgan et al, 1999; Davies, 2000, 2001). Of course, what the government really wants to do is debatable. If it wishes to pursue regeneration by increasing its influence on local politics, it is arguable that current approaches are working. But if, on the other hand, it wants to generate strong, self-sustaining local partnerships to lead the regeneration process, it is failing. These processes cannot be described as distinctively 'New Labour', if this term means an approach distinguishable from both Old Labour in the 1970s and the Major government of the early 1990s. The government's strategy is more a 'middle way', reviving the 1970s idea of a central-local partnership and combining it with an integrated, or cross-cutting, regeneration effort pursued through the top-down, public-private partnerships that were introduced by the Major administration.

It is too early to be sure whether new initiatives, like *New commitment* (LGA, 1998) and RDAs will lead to a relaxation of the constraints on partnerships and, if so, whether they can become self-sustaining. With a second Blair administration now underway, it is difficult to know whether central government will continue to centralise, or whether it will trust local authorities to a greater extent. In these circumstances, the evolution of local partnerships will interest scholars for the foreseeable future.

References

Atkinson, R. (1999) 'Discourses of partnership and empowerment in contemporary British urban regeneration', *Urban Studies*, vol 36, no 1, pp 59-72.

Bailey, N., with MacDonald, K. and Barker, A. (1995) *Partnership agencies in British urban policy*, London: UCL Press.

Barker, T., Byrne, I. and Veall, A. (1999) *Ruling by taskforce*, London: Politico.

Barnekov, T., Boyle, R. and Rich, D. (1989) *Privatism and urban politics in Britain and the United States*, Oxford: Oxford University Press.

Bassett, K. (1996) 'Partnerships, business elites and urban politics: new forms of governance in an English city?', *Urban Studies*, vol 33, no 3, pp 539-55.

Boyle, R. (ed) (1985) 'Leveraging urban development: a comparison of urban policy directions and programme impact in the United States and Britain', *Policy & Politics*, vol 13, no 2, pp 175-210.

Burton, P. and O'Toole, M. (1994) 'Urban development corporations: post-Fordism in action or Fordism in retrenchment?', in R. Smith and J. Raistrick (eds) *Policy and change*, Bristol: SAUS Publications, University of Bristol, pp 155-72.

Cropper, S. (1995) 'Collaborative working and the issue of sustainability', in C. Huxham (ed) *Creating collaborative advantage*, London: Sage Publications, pp 80-100.

Davidson, N. (1998) *City Vision stakeholder survey 1988*, Hull: University of Hull/Humberside TEC.

Davies, J.S. (2000) 'The hollowing-out of local democracy and the "fatal conceit" of governing without government', *The British Journal of Politics and International Relations*, vol 2, no 3, pp 414-28.

Davies, J.S. (2001) *Debating urban regime theory: Local politics and regeneration partnerships in the UK*, Aldershot: Ashgate.

DETR (Department of the Environment, Transport and the Regions) (1998a) *1998 index of local deprivation (Regeneration research summary no 15)*, London: DETR.

DETR (1998b) *Modern local government: In touch with the people*, London: The Stationery Office.

DETR (1999) *Single regeneration budget round 5: Regional framework for Yorkshire & the Humber*, London: DETR.

DETR (2001) *Single regeneration budget guidance to Regional Development Agencies on approval of successor schemes to the SRB in 2001-2*, London: DETR.

DfEE (Department for Education and Employment) (1998) *National partnership protocol*, London: DfEE.

DfEE (1999a) *Learning to succeed: A new framework for post-16 learning*, London: DfEE.

DfEE (1999b) *Lifelong learning partnerships: Remit*, London: DfEE.

Elkin, S.L. (1987) *City and regime in the American Republic*, Chicago, IL: University of Chicago Press.

GOYH (Government Office for Yorkshire and the Humber) (July 1997) *Single regeneration budget challenge fund: Round 4: Supplementary national guidance*, Leeds: GOYH.

Harding, A. (1998) 'Public–private partnerships in the UK', in J. Pierre (ed) *Partnerships in urban governance: European and American experiences*, Basingstoke: Macmillan, pp 72-96.

Hastings, A. (1996) 'Unravelling the process of "partnership" in urban regeneration policy', *Urban Studies*, vol 33, no 2, pp 253-68.

HMSO (1988) *Action for cities*, London: HMSO.

HMSO (1999) *Local Government Act 1999*, London: The Stationery Office.

Huxham, C. (1996) 'The search for collaborative advantage', in C. Huxham (ed) *Creating collaborative advantage*, London: Sage Publications, pp 176-80.

Jessop, R. (2000) 'Governance failure', in G. Stoker (ed) *The new politics of British local governance*, Basingstoke: Macmillan, pp 11-32.

John, P. (1997) 'Local governance', in P. Dunleavy, I. Gamble, I. Holliday and G. Peele (eds) *Developments in British politics 5*, Basingstoke: Macmillan.

John, P. and Cole, A. (1998) 'Urban regimes and local governance in Britain and France: policy adaptation and coordination in Leeds and Lille', *Urban Affairs Review*, vol 33, no 3, pp 382-404.

Lawless, P. (1994) 'Partnership in urban regeneration in the UK: the Sheffield central area study', *Urban Studies*, vol 31, no 8, pp 1303-24.

Le Gales, P. and Mawson, J. (1994) *Management innovations in urban policy: Lessons from France*, London: Local Government Management Board.

Le Gales, P. and Mawson, J. (1995) 'Contracts versus competitive bidding: rationalizing urban policy programmes in England and France', *Journal of European Public Policy*, vol 2, no 2, pp 205-41.

LGA (Local Government Association) (2 April 1998) *The new commitment to regeneration*, Local Government Association Circular, 22 June.

Morgan, K., Rees, G. and Garmise, S. (1999) 'Networking for local economic development', in G. Stoker (ed) *The new management of British local governance*, Basingstoke: Macmillan, pp 181-96.

National EBP Network (1999) Interview with Jane Ritchie, Secretary, National EBP Network, July.

Oatley, N. and Lambert, C. (1998) 'Catalyst for change: the city challenge initiative', in N. Oatley (ed) *Cities, economic competition and urban policy*, London: Paul Chapman Publishing, pp 109-26.

Orr, M.E. and Stoker, G. (1994) 'Urban regimes and leadership in Detroit', *Urban Affairs Quarterly*, vol 30, no 1, pp 48-73.

Parkinson, M. and Wilks, S. (1986) 'The politics of inner city partnerships', in M. Goldsmith (ed) *New research in central–local relations*, Aldershot: Gower, pp 290-307.

Peters, B.G. (1998) 'With a little help from our friends: public–private partnerships as institutions and instruments', in J. Pierre (ed) *Partnerships in urban governance: European and American experiences*, Basingstoke: Macmillan, pp 11-33.

Pierre, J. (1998) 'Conclusions', in J. Pierre (ed) *Partnerships in urban governance: European and American experiences*, Basingstoke: Macmillan, pp 187-99.

Rhodes, R.A.W. (1996) 'The new governance: governing without government', *Political Studies*, vol xliv, pp 652-67.

Rhodes, R.A.W. (1999) 'Foreword: governance and networks', in G. Stoker (ed) *The new management of British local governance*, Basingstoke: Macmillan, pp xii–xxvi.

Stewart, J. (2000) *The nature of British local government*, Basingstoke: Macmillan.

Stoker, G. (1997) 'Urban political science and the challenge of urban governance', Paper presented to Conference at Ross Priory, 8-10 October.

Stoker, G. (1998a) 'Governance as theory: five propositions', *International Social Science Journal*, vol 155, pp 17-28.

Stoker, G. (1998b) 'Public–private partnerships and urban governance', in J. Pierre (ed) *Partnerships in urban governance*, Basingstoke: Macmillan, pp 34-51.

Stoker, G. (1998c) 'Theory and urban politics', *International Political Science Review*, vol 19, no 2, pp 119-29.

Stoker, G. (1999) 'Introduction: the unintended costs and benefits of new management reform for British local government', in G. Stoker (ed) *The new management of British local governance*, Basingstoke: Macmillan, pp 1-21.

Stoker, G. and Mossberger, K. (1994) 'Urban regime theory in comparative perspective', *Environment and Planning C: Government and Policy*, vol 12, pp 195-212.

Stone, C.N. (1989) *Regime politics: Governing Atlanta 1946-1988*, Lawrence, KS: University Press of Kansas.

Wolman, H. (1992) 'Understanding cross-national policy transfers: the case of Britain and the US', *Governance*, vol 5, no 10, pp 27-45.

TWELVE

Education Action Zones

*Marny Dickson, Sharon Gewirtz, David Halpin, Sally Power and
Geoff Whitty*

At its launch in January 1998, the Education Action Zone (EAZ) initiative was presented as "the centrepiece of Labour's modernisation agenda" (DfEE official, cited in Carvel, 1998). Six months later, the first 25 EAZs were formally announced as the "standard bearers in a new crusade uniting business, schools, local education authorities and parents to modernise education in areas of social deprivation" (DfEE, 1998a). Over the following two years the scheme was expanded to include a further 48 'second-round' zones. Like a number of New Labour policies, including Employment Zones, Health Action Zones (see Chapter Six) and New Deal for Communities, EAZs are area-based initiatives that seek to develop integrated solutions to complex social problems within regions of social disadvantage. The aims of EAZ partnerships are, broadly, to raise educational standards and tackle social exclusion in areas of 'educational under-performance'. A typical EAZ consists of around 20 schools (usually two or three secondary schools plus their feeder primaries) and receives government funding of between £500,000 and £750,000 per annum for a period of three to five years. Zones are expected to raise £250,000 additional sponsorship in cash or 'kind' from the private sector[1].

While EAZs are managed on a day-to-day basis by an appointed director, each EAZ is formally governed by an Education Action Forum (EAF), a statutory body set up through powers established by the 1998 School Standards and Framework Act. The EAFs are required to include one appointee from each of the governing bodies of participating schools (with the caveat that any of the governing bodies can decide they do not wish to be represented) and one or two members appointed by the Secretary of State. In addition, the EAF may add to its membership parents, students and representatives of the local "business and social community". EAFs are also urged to ensure that there "is an appropriate gender balance among the members" and that "significant minority communities within the EAZ are represented" (DfEE, 1998d, para 2.4.10). EAFs have a statutory responsibility for formulating, implementing and monitoring a detailed local 'action plan', to be implemented over a period of three to five years. In this plan they are expected to set and meet performance targets for both student achievement and student behaviour. In order to achieve their targets, EAZs are encouraged to experiment with 'innovative' approaches to teaching and learning (DfEE, 1999).

The promotion of partnerships between the private, voluntary, public and community sectors is a central feature of EAZ policy (Jones and Bird, 2000). The particular conception of partnership on which the policy is based is clearly defined in the EAZ handbook, which states that:

> Both the title and the composition of the Action Forum are intended to underscore the importance of a partnership approach to achieving improvements across the community. In other words, the intention is that there should be consensus on the action to be taken, a willingness to pool ideas and resources towards the achievement of a shared goal, and joint ownership of the successes and failures of the project. (DfEE, 1998c, para 2.1.3, section 2)

The assumption in the initial bidding guidance was that there would be a small number of main partners who put forward the EAZ proposal, which would "typically include one or more of the following: a parent group, a local education authority (LEA), a training and enterprise council (TEC), a business or a community or voluntary organisation" (DfEE, 1998b, p1), as well as at least one representative from the participating schools. Other organisations were "likely to be actively involved once a zone is running" (DfEE, 1998b, p 1). It was hoped that EAZ partnerships would "draw in local and national agencies and charities involved in, for example, health care, social care and crime prevention" (DfEE, 1997, p 4) and that EAZs would 'link up' with health and employment zones and projects funded by the Single Regeneration Budget.

A new kind of partnership?

The notion of partnerships in English education is not new, but traditionally the key 'partners' have been central government, local education authorities and teacher organisations. EAZs can be seen as part of a wider trend towards reducing the power of these historic partners (especially local education authorities and teachers) in favour of what the government argues are broader, more inclusive partnerships. However, the EAZ policy represents a hybrid of divergent approaches (Gewirtz, 1999; Power and Whitty, 1999) and this has led to competing claims about its nature and significance. Critics from the Right, for example, claim it embodies 'old thinking' on positive intervention (Skidelsky and Raymond, 1998), while those from the Left fear it to be a 'Trojan horse of privatisation' that is considerably more dangerous than previous reforms (STA, 1998).

In some respects, the policy does look rather like earlier initiatives that were also designed to address persistent low educational achievement in areas of multiple disadvantage, such as the Educational Priority Areas (EPAs) introduced in the wake of the 1967 Plowden Report (Halsey, 1972). Certainly, the EAZ policy aims to concentrate additional resources in schools located in areas of social and economic disadvantage. Like the EPAs and some of the urban development initiatives of the 1970s – such as the Comprehensive Community

Programme – and the early 1990s – in particular City Challenge (since incorporated into the Single Regeneration Budget) – EAZs are also supposed to have a multi-sector focus. Thus, in one sense, EAZs (alongside Health Action Zones, Employment Zones and other 'joined-up' initiatives) can be viewed as the latest in a series of policies designed to target resources on areas of disadvantage and counter the strict demarcation between different areas of welfare provision that has been seen as a contributory factor in the marginalisation of key sections of the population (Becker, 1997; Cochrane, 2000).

However, the policy also contains organisational and managerial features that bear a close resemblance to Conservative initiatives of the 1980s, such as Enterprise Zones, Urban Development Corporations and City Technology Colleges (CTCs) (Whitty et al, 1993). These policies were based on the assumption that private enterprise and market forces could succeed in regenerating socio-economically distressed areas (or, in the case of CTCs, that they could succeed in creating good urban schools), where public sector bureaucracies had consistently failed. As with these earlier Conservative initiatives, the private sector is expected to play 'a central role' in both funding and managing EAZs (DfEE, 1997, p 4). Moreover, although in its documentation the DfEE emphasised collaboration rather than competition, EAZ status has been awarded on the basis of a competitive bidding process, a means of resource allocation also favoured by Conservative governments of the 1980s and 1990s. The EAZ policy has also left intact the quasi-market structure, established following the 1988 Education Reform Act, which sets schools in competition with each other for student recruitment.

Despite these obvious continuities with earlier policies, it is possible to identify some potentially novel features of EAZ partnerships. First, although the multi-sector focus is not new, EAZs are expected to draw together a broader range of services than previous initiatives (Cochrane, 2001, personal communication). For example, the DfEE documentation mentions the possibility of zones working with social services, libraries, health, housing, Youth Offending Teams and crime prevention agencies to set up "'one stop shops' combining education with advice and support to pupils and their families" (DfEE, 1999, p 14).

However, it is the public–private dimension of the EAZ partnership agenda that has been presented as perhaps the most 'groundbreaking' aspect of the policy (Hallgarten and Watling, 2001). In itself, business involvement in English state schooling is not new. Schools have long been dependent on income generated from the private sector (Benn and Chitty, 1996), and partnerships between businesses and schools that give students the opportunity to engage in what is now called 'work-related learning' have a long history. In addition, the CTC initiative allowed businesses to run schools independently of LEAs. However, while the Conservatives' CTC initiative gave private sector organisations the power to run *individual* state schools, the EAZ policy represents the first occasion in which businesses have been encouraged to take a lead in managing *groups* of schools. In the initial EAZ bidding guidance, the DfEE expressed a particular desire to support zones that were 'primarily business-led'

(DfEE, 1998b, p 2). This guidance also paved the way for governing bodies of EAZ schools to use the EAF to 'act as Agents on their behalf', a development that raised the prospect of a 'business-led' forum contracting to provide educational services within local zone schools. More radically, the guidance allowed for the governing bodies of EAZ schools to cede their powers altogether to the local forum, thus giving individual zone forums control over delegated school budgets.

It was the expectation that businesses were to play a lead role in the running of zones, coupled with a reduced role for governing bodies, that led a number of observers to suggest that the policy represents part of a wider effort to establish new (privatised) forms of educational governance with reduced powers for LEAs and teachers (for example, Hatcher, 1998; STA, 1998). These critics have suggested that the involvement of businesses in EAZs, and the concomitant marginalisation of LEAs and teacher unions, is likely to *reduce* local autonomy and accountability. However, others have chosen to emphasise the potential for EAZs to offer more inclusive modes of educational governance. Such commentators have suggested that EAFs could provide significant testing grounds for innovations in the local democratic control of state-funded schools (Halpin, 1999).

In practice, however, although EAZ policy texts may give the impression that EAZs represent a significant development in the history of business involvement in schooling, the vast majority of established zones have been LEA-initiated and DfEE claims about the numbers of 'business-led' zones have been overstated (NUT, 2000; Hallgarten and Watling, 2001). A variety of business partners are involved in EAZs, from multinational and national corporations to small local industries. The nature of their business interests varies, from supermarkets and professional football clubs to management consultancies and specialist education businesses. Organisationally, they range from straightforward profit-making businesses to not-for-profit companies. However, it is perhaps significant that the only private company involved in leading a first-round zone was a not-for-profit education company, and that two out of the three 'business-led', second-round zones are led by trusts set up by companies for educational purposes.

Moreover, none of the governing bodies of schools in either the first- or second-round zones has so far ceded its powers to its local forum. Furthermore, nationally it is clear that "the amount of genuinely new money that the private sector has contributed to EAZs has undershot expectations" (Hallgarten and Watling, 2000, p 26). The latter finding was perhaps foreseeable, given evidence from the CTC initiative, which suggests that raising large amounts of sponsorship from the private sector can be exceedingly difficult (Walford and Miller, 1991; Whitty et al, 1993). In any event, few zones (only 12 at the time of writing) have managed to secure the expected £250,000 per year from the private sector and most sponsorship has taken the form of 'in kind' contributions rather than cash (NUT, 2000; Mansell, 2001).

In the remainder of this chapter, we draw on empirical data from an ongoing ESRC-funded project, which is examining the origins, implementation and effects of the EAZ policy[2] in order to explore how the zone partnerships are working in practice. We begin by examining the operation of EAZ partnerships at a strategic level. We analyse the assumptions about the membership and purposes of the EAFs that were embedded in the successful applications for first-round zone status and draw on observational and interview research to explore the decision-making practices of zone forums. In doing so, we examine whether EAFs do indeed offer the possibility for a more participatory politics of education, or whether they act to restrict local participation. We will then consider the initiatives being piloted at school level, paying particular attention to those sponsored by private sector partners, in order to reflect on the consequences of these 'new' partnerships for their intended beneficiaries – under-attaining schools and their students. Finally, we highlight some of the tensions in the EAZ policy, particularly those relating to the goal of 'joined-up working'; the use of a business derived model of resource allocation; and the unreformed education quasi-market setting in which the zones are situated.

Strategic partnerships in practice

EAZ guidance clearly specifies the legal responsibilities of EAFs, particularly in relation to their financial obligations; it addresses technical issues, such as how often meetings should take place; and it provides instructions relating to the appointment of the chair and the delegation of various responsibilities to sub-committees of the EAFs. The guidance is, however, largely silent on how meetings should be managed and conducted (DfEE, 1998c).

Our reading and analysis of the 25 successful applications for zone status in the first round (discussed in more detail in Dickson et al, 2001) shows that, while these defined a variety of purposes for their respective EAFs, most were interpreted in terms of 'strategic', 'management' and 'monitoring' responsibilities. The majority of aspiring EAZs stated that they intended to establish some kind of executive group that would meet fairly frequently (often monthly) to make and act upon decisions, thereby reducing the role of the EAF to one of providing 'ultimate' approval.

The size of EAF membership spelt out in the bids varied from around 20 members to over 50. The emphasis in most forums on individual institutional representation means that the voice of the participating schools was the one most likely to be represented and heard at forum level. While head-teachers' voices and the interests of business tend to be well represented, other constituents struggled for recognition. Less than a third of the first 25 zones, for example, stated in their original bids that their forums would have either direct parent or student involvement; just nine mentioned teacher representatives, and only three highlighted the role of teacher trades union officials. Strikingly, only a handful of bids made explicit commitments to involve the wider public and only two described the EAF's role as one of increasing opportunities for local democracy.

The EAZ bids did make explicit commitment to cross-agency activities drawing together representatives from public, private and voluntary sectors.

However, there is less explication of just how these forms of integration are to effect any change. The representation of welfare providers *other* than those in education is relatively absent; the private and voluntary sector organisations that are represented tend to concentrate on areas involving the provision of educational services or work-related training (Power, 2001). This suggests that, despite the recognition within the EAZ applications of the complex, multifaceted nature of disadvantage and the need for multi-sector strategies, the responses of EAZs tend to be relatively one-dimensional.

Decision-making practices of the forums

This section draws on research conducted in two zones – Nortown, a first-round zone and Tolside, a second-round zone (both pseudonyms). Thirty-two EAF and executive board meetings have been observed over the course of three years and this observational data is supplemented by interviews with 16 forum members across the two zones. The composition of the EAFs, their meeting cycles and their relationships with other committees vary between the two zones. However, despite their differences, there are strong similarities in the nature of their operations.

In relation to representation, while *some* EAZ partners and other interests have formal positions on the two EAFs, their composition does not reflect the character of either of the zone communities. In numerical terms, head-teachers and business partners are well represented (even if they do not necessarily attend), while teachers are proportionately under-represented. There is very limited involvement of either parents or local voluntary and community group representatives on the forums; moreover, the related executive boards and working committees (each consisting of around 10 members in total) tend to have even fewer, if any, classroom teachers and community or voluntary group representatives. Both EAZs have found it difficult to tap into existing voluntary or community groups and organisations – let alone develop innovative forms of engaging previously excluded groups.

In Nortown, it is particularly noticeable that community representation is heavily skewed away from the character of the district in which the zone is located – a highly multi-ethnic population living in poor housing in an area of high unemployment. Rather than reflecting these characteristics, as the DfEE bidding guidance enjoined, the majority of forum members are white, male and in professional or managerial positions. In Tolside, the gender composition is more even (due to the high numbers of primary head-teachers represented), but no non-white forum members have been present at any of the observed meetings.

In terms of function, despite the formal responsibility of EAFs to provide their zone with 'strategic direction' (DfEE, 1999, p 7), in practice it appears that both strategic and operational decisions are frequently made elsewhere. In both zones, EAF meetings primarily serve as a venue at which decisions and overall progress are *reported* rather than debated and the framing of the agenda leaves little time for open discussion or the introduction of new issues. As the director of Tolside acknowledged, "[the forum] simply confirms policy". This perception was expressed more forcefully by other forum members in this zone, one of whom (a parent representative) described the forum's role as one of "rubber-stamping".

In both zones, the minutes of previous forum (and executive board) meetings and the agenda are often circulated only a few days before the meeting. The same applies to the distribution of reports, some of which are tabled at the meetings. This practice — often a result of the huge amount of paperwork required by the DfES (Department for Education and Skills) — leaves insufficient time for most EAF and executive board members to digest what is sometimes quite technical and almost always voluminous material, or reflect on its implications. Perhaps unsurprisingly then, the members who have the most knowledge of, and involvement in, managing the zone on a day-to-day level dominate these meetings, in terms of both time and authority. In Nortown, the LEA is particularly dominant; in Tolside, it is the EAZ officials who are mostly to the fore. The specialist knowledge, expertise and bureaucratic power invested in these roles, in addition to the informal power the officials are able to wield behind the scenes, allows them literally to set the agenda, decide which issues to 'report back' and frame the nature of any discussion.

EAZ policy appears to have created a new and significant managerial position in the form of the EAZ director. While formally accountable to EAFs, EAZ directors appear much less accountable in practice, either to their individual forums or to the local communities that they are meant to be serving. To some extent, this may be due to external constraints, in particular the speed with which EAZs have been implemented. In addition, because EAZs are given priority access to numerous other new government initiatives, EAZ directors are under pressure not only to apply for any and all additional resources, but also to spend them within exceedingly tight time frames. This not only reduces the scope for developing autonomous local initiatives, but also seems to encourage immediate and unilateral action by EAZ directors on a fairly regular basis. This is not to say that power and influence remain constant, either over time or even over the course of a given meeting. In Nortown, business partners contribute to discussions on a regular basis, usually in the form of raising issues and occasionally challenging the contributions of the LEA representatives and the zone director. Their voice, however, is not a privileged one. Even so, the relatively high level of involvement in EAF and executive board discussions by the business and/or head-teacher partners far outweighs that of the community representatives, including parents, whose contributions are minimal in both zones. This finding replicates what is known of the workings of school governing bodies (Deem et al, 1995).

Attendance levels at forum meetings in both zones are low, frequently running at less than 50% and in some instances falling below quorate. In Nortown, attendance levels over the course of 1999 declined, with marked reductions apparent among all but the LEA partners. There are indications that for at least some EAF members, the tailing-off of attendance is due to a decreasing sense of engagement with the forum. As one community representative put it, "I felt that everything that I'd said had fallen on deaf ears, we hadn't achieved anything, hadn't gone anywhere really ... the other community people that are on the Forum, they're not anymore. They have all gone". The problem of involving 'lay' people is not unique to EAZs. Nevertheless, their forums have yet to find ways of overcoming the barriers created by professional discourse. A lapsed forum member recalled, "you can often be browbeaten by what they're talking about. I often missed the plot about what they were talking about".

Of course, there may also be more prosaic reasons for low levels of attendance. For example, in their research into the factors affecting the contributions and attendance of the business members on school governing bodies, Thody and Punter (2000) found that key constraints included lack of time and the distance of the school from the person in question's place of work. EAFs appear to be relatively unstable, reliant on the voluntary involvement and commitment of individual members of staff in key organisations. When these staff change jobs or, as seems to happen often, they obtain internal promotion, the links weaken and may even fade altogether. In Nortown, the attendance of some business partners faltered following the departure of key individuals who were initially heavily involved in the EAF but who subsequently moved to new jobs.

Despite the patterns we have identified in relation to different levels of participation and the influence of various groups, it is difficult to map the overall relative influence of the various EAZ partners from our existing observational data. As the following quote from a Nortown parent governor illustrates, the apparent reliance on networking outside of EAF and executive board meetings privileges some EAZ partners over others: "... people had their own agenda.... Me being what they called 'lone parent representative' didn't have the connection between people". Parents and other community representatives who lack access to formal and informal networks are particularly disadvantaged in situations where strategic and operational decisions are made outside official EAZ meetings. Our findings suggest that EAFs sometimes serve as an exercise in impression management, rather than as a vehicle for frank and open debate of the direction being taken by these two zones.

While much of the literature associated with EAZs has focused on the strategic and managerial implications of the new partnerships, there has been little attention paid to the nature and impact of partnerships at the school level. Given that EAZ partnerships were established to modernise education in areas of social deprivation and tackle social exclusion (DfEE, 1998a), it seems pertinent to examine their impact on participating schools and their consequences for the distribution of resources.

The nature and impact of 'partnership' initiatives in schools

Here we present data drawn from three first-round EAZs that appeared to be piloting particularly interesting or 'radical' curriculum innovations – Brickly, Seaham and Wellford (all pseudonyms). We concentrate on initiatives sponsored by the private sector, primarily because of the controversy surrounding private sector involvement in EAZs, although the focus also reflects an apparent paucity of inter-agency public and voluntary sector initiatives in these schools. (The introduction of a new counselling service in some Seaham schools, provided by a local NHS mental health trust, was the only initiative of this type uncovered at the time of our fieldwork.) The analysis is based primarily on interviews with head-teachers and teachers, supplemented by conversations with pupils and by classroom observations that were conducted in four schools within each EAZ. Each zone had been operating for around a year prior to the fieldwork, which involved spending up to a week in each of the 12 schools visited.

At the time of the fieldwork, EAZ-related business contributions took three principal forms within the 12 case study schools:

- **Cash** Contributions varied widely across the three zones, but direct cash donations formed a very small proportion of overall business sponsorship.
- **Equipment and materials** Businesses in Wellford provided sponsored curriculum materials to support various curriculum enrichment schemes. However, the most significant donation of this type was in Brickly, where an ICT company provided all zone schools with additional ICT equipment.
- **Human resources**
  Curriculum Enrichment Partnerships with professional football clubs, local artists and drama groups led to 'football fun days' and visits to and from theatre groups in all three zones. With the exception of the Arts programme in Wellford, most of these initiatives were short-term and small-scale, involving only a small proportion of zone pupils. All three zones introduced or increased the number of vocational GNVQs offered and arranged a small number of additional work experience placements in some or all of their secondary schools.
  Managerial Services A management consultancy firm provided managerial and financial advice to the zone director in Seaham. In Brickly, a private company provided an attendance monitoring service to some zone schools.
  Mentoring All three zones were intending to establish a business mentoring scheme involving some zone head-teachers and/or pupils. A small number of business volunteers in Seaham and Wellford were involved in listening to children read in some local primary schools.

There were large discrepancies in levels of private sector sponsorship between the three EAZs. This is indicative of a national context that favours zones with the good fortune to be located near large, sponsorship-minded local employers. Indeed, levels of business involvement are to a large extent dependent on factors outside the control of any given EAZ. In addition, private sector contributions of all kinds are subject to fluctuation over time because of the vagaries of local economies and changes in company personnel. By definition, EAZs are situated within economically depressed areas and in many cases their fundraising efforts are hampered by the dearth of large local employers. But even where large national or multinational EAZ partners are present, this is in itself no guarantee that their contribution will be proportionally large. Large-scale business sponsorship by one company seems to act as a spur to others; conversely, a failure to attract big contributions appears to be self-perpetuating. An important consequence of this local variation, therefore, was a massive disparity between the amounts of private sponsorship that different zones were able to raise. Among the 25 first-round zones, one raised £400,000 in private sector contributions, while nine raised less than £20,000 in the financial year 1998–99 (NUT, 2000).

While levels of business contributions in two of our three study zones were among the highest nationally, they were not immune from the types of 'creative accounting' practices that Hallgarten and Watling (2001) have identified as widespread. These include the overvaluation of 'in-kind' contributions and the recycling of public, private and voluntary sector money by the re-labelling of existing schemes as 'EAZ-related'. Indeed, the Seaham director admitted to meeting his sponsorship targets for the first year in large part by re-labelling a host of pre-existing initiatives.

Given the broader context of widespread business involvement in English state schooling, it is difficult to claim that these 'new' public–private partnerships had a major additional effect on the curriculum of any of the 12 zone schools. Indeed, few of the initiatives identified by the three EAZs involved 'partnership' at all, if this implies more than straightforward commercial sponsorship within a public sector organisation. Furthermore, almost all of the schemes that did go beyond straightforward sponsorship were part of already established national or local schemes. While some schools were subject to additional initiatives, which placed business personnel or commercially sponsored curriculum materials in the schools, the scale of any direct business involvement in terms of curriculum initiatives, attendance at meetings, visits to schools, mentoring or work placements was small.

Because of the relatively small amounts of money allocated to any given EAZ innovation, almost all zone initiatives – whether school-based or zone-wide – have involved some form of targeting or selection, either by the students themselves or by their teachers. Initiatives that involve direct private sector involvement (such as work experience placements in Wellford) were often accessed by a small number of relatively 'able', well-motivated pupils. This raises questions as to whether the interventions are reaching those most in need. This situation appears to reflect both the desire of businesses to associate themselves with 'high achievers' and head-teachers' consciousness of how best to represent their school to the outside community.

Moreover, it appears that, through their eagerness to attract additional resources to their schools, teachers may lose a degree of control over the types of curriculum materials that their children are exposed to. In the case of Wellford's 'Football and Reading' initiative, which used sexist imagery, and its 'Supermarket Maths Trail', with its promotional orientation, the class teacher did not see the material before it was used with her students. We also observed the work of 'business reading mentors', whose competence to assistance in the learning process was questionable. Second-round zones, which are eager to attract DfES 'matched' funding to support core services, are in an even poorer position to negotiate for high-quality, relevant private sector contributions and instead are likely to feel under pressure to accept whatever types of support local businesses are willing to offer.

New partnerships take time to become established and we are aware that levels of business involvement have increased in at least one of the three zones since the fieldwork was conducted. In addition, although EAZ-related public–private partnerships initially had an apparently limited direct effect on the overt curriculum of the 12 zone schools we studied, this is not to say that they are having no impact on the wider teaching and learning environment. It is clear that some companies are using EAZs to pilot products and services that they aim to introduce elsewhere, such as in Brickly, where the company providing an attendance monitoring service has since expanded the service to cover non-EAZ schools in this district. Similarly, the company that donated ICT equipment to all Brickly schools promptly received large orders from other EAZs and, more recently, from non-EAZ schools.

Joined-up thinking? EAZs, the bidding culture and the quasi-market

As mentioned earlier, due to the logic of 'joined-up thinking', EAZs are given 'priority access' to funding from a number of other DfES initiatives. Zone schools are also frequently in receipt of funds from other sources, including the Single Regeneration Budget, the New Opportunities Fund and the European Social Fund. Our early evidence suggests that, in practice, the bidding culture within which zones are enmeshed may actually increase the fragmentation of provision, because the coexistence of many small-scale, tightly bounded projects can appear to lack coordination and lead to a confusion of responsibilities between EAZ, LEA and school personnel. Having constantly to bid for additional resources also places a significant time burden on both EAZ directors and head-teachers. Recognition of the importance of additional fundraising has led at least two of the five case study zones discussed in this paper (Tolside and Brickly) to consider hiring an 'income generator' to specialise in attracting funding from public and private sector sources. Similarly, a secondary school in Seaham has appointed a partially EAZ-funded deputy head-teacher to generate additional income and manage externally funded projects.

One of the key aims of EAZs is to foster 'collaboration not competition' between local schools. However, there are inequalities in access to resources, not only between EAZs but *within* zones as well, as levels of school-based funding are at least partially dependent on head-teacher expertise, time and inclination to bid for the additional resources available from the menu of projects on offer. This diversity in access to funding highlights the difficulties of encouraging schools to behave collaboratively in the context of a bidding culture.

Similarly, although a number of zone head-teachers have nevertheless spoken positively of the 'cooperative climate' fostered within their EAZ, certain schools have used the additional EAZ learning support they have been offered at least partly to improve their position within performance 'league tables' and the local quasi-market. The most resource-effective way to do this is not to target the most disadvantaged pupils, but to focus on those who are deemed to be capable of meeting an assessment benchmark (Gewirtz et al, 1995; Gillborn and Youdell, 2000; Gewirtz, 2002). In Wellford, for example, one of the primary schools studied held an 'invitation only' Easter school for 'borderline pupils' immediately prior to the compulsory national Standardised Attainment Tasks (SATs). Similarly in Brickly, one of the primary schools provided mentoring support for pupils who were 'just below' gaining level four SATs, while the secondary school allocated resources to allow senior members of staff to work with 'able but underachieving pupils' who were 'just below' gaining the required number of A-C grades at GCSE. There is evidence that targeting of resources on students deemed to be on the borderline of assessment benchmarks is a widespread practice (Gillborn and Youdell, 2000). However, there are additional pressures on EAZ schools as the DfES is measuring the success of EAZs in part by the performance of their students in national tests. Thus there is a particularly strong incentive for EAZ schools, keen to secure funding beyond the initial three-year period, to focus on those students whose performance will make a difference to their overall league table positions. While such strategies may be an 'efficient' use of EAZ resources for schools in competition for local pupils, this does raise significant equity concerns.

Conclusions

At the time of their announcement, EAZs were presented as new kinds of partnerships, bringing together groups of schools, parents and local private, voluntary and community organisations, including agencies from different welfare sectors, to tackle disadvantage and raise standards in schools (DfEE, 1997, p 4). However, although the government encouraged the involvement of a range of different partners, "a central role for business" (DfEE, 1997, p 4) was envisaged from the outset. While school–business partnerships have a long history, we have argued in this chapter that what appeared to be new and distinctive about EAZs was that they offered the private sector an opportunity to be involved in the running of *groups* of schools. The assumption was that private sector partners would contribute both material resources and the skills needed to help solve the kind of intractable problems faced by socio-economically disadvantaged communities that, despite repeated attempts, the public sector acting on its own had been unable to solve (Jones and Bird, 2000). Another distinctive feature of the policy, as represented in DfEE documentation, was the emphasis placed on the benefits of broad-based, multi-sector, coordinated action as a means of tackling various manifestations of social exclusion such as youth crime, truancy and school exclusions (DfEE, 1999).

However, our early empirical evidence suggests that in assessing the distinctiveness of EAZ partnerships, it is important to distinguish between what is stated in the policy documentation and the practice. Although both central government documentation and the EAZ bids themselves emphasise the value of multi-sector working, we found little evidence of concrete multi-sector initiatives impacting at the level of individual zone schools at the time of our fieldwork. Difficulties in establishing multi-sector working were exacerbated by the bidding culture associated with EAZs, which militated against coordinated action at both strategic and operational levels. The bidding culture could both discourage consultation between zone partners and promote a fragmentation of provision. This could lead to an unwieldy proliferation of small-scale, short-term projects that were difficult to manage and could give rise to a confusion of responsibilities between the different agencies involved. (Indeed, the problems of fragmentation, confusion and duplication associated with area-based initiatives have been recognised by another government department, the Department for Transport, Environment and the Regions, which has commissioned research to foster greater coordination between such initiatives (Cochrane, 2000).) But it is not only multi-sector working that is difficult to achieve within a competitive context. Despite EAZ efforts to encourage collaboration between schools, competition for pupils within local education markets may ultimately hamper inter-school cooperation. Market forces also encourage schools to target resources on the students deemed to be at the borderline of assessment benchmarks, particularly schools that are subject to additional EAZ performance targets.

In contrast to the paucity of multi-sector initiatives, we did identify a range of private sector ones. However, these schemes tended to be targeted at a small proportion of students, often those deemed to be the most able or motivated. More generally, the nature and limited scale of private sector initiatives cast doubts on suggestions that businesses have the willingness, energy, creativity or know-how radically to transform the provision of education in socially disadvantaged areas (see Barber, 1998, cited in Jones and Bird, 2000). It is perhaps as a consequence of this that the far-reaching commercialisation of the school curriculum feared by critics of the policy (STA, 1998; Wilby, 1998) has not materialised. Nor have we uncovered evidence to suggest that business involvement in EAZ activity is leading to a diminution in the role of other interest groups, as some critics had also feared (Hatcher, 1998; STA, 1998). On the other hand, as presently constituted, the EAFs we have been observing do not appear to be examples of the kind of 'little polities' envisaged by some. Nor currently are there signs that the EAZs in question are beginning to provide "the capability citizens need for the task of regenerating civil society" (Ranson, 2000, p 263). This issue has particular significance, given the important symbolic role EAFs were meant to play in legitimating EAZs as new, more inclusive partnerships for planning and delivering local services. If anything, what we discern is a further consolidation of managerial interests, notably those represented by the LEA, EAZ managers and the head-teachers of participating schools. Finally, the research has highlighted problems of sustainability, which emanate from the fact that private sector contributions are liable to fluctuation as a consequence of changing local economic conditions and changes in company personnel.

The lukewarm stance on EAZ policy now emanating from the DfES means that there will not be a third round of EAZs and none of the existing 73 will be renewed after the end of its five-year initial funding. Instead, zones deemed to be successful will be integrated into the Excellence in Cities (EIC) initiative – another area-based intervention designed to raise educational standards in areas of disadvantage, which was introduced after the EAZ policy. Unlike EAZs, where the private sector was supposed to take a lead role, EIC programmes were always meant to be LEA-led and controlled. However, other new forms of public–private partnership have emerged since the launch of the EAZ policy and these are likely to expand in the future. These include the privatisation of national government services, such as the administration of performance-related pay; the outsourcing of LEA services to private companies; the involvement of private firms (some of which have minimal experience in education) in running 'failing' LEAs; and fixed-term contracts with private (for-profit and not-for-profit) companies and charities to run state schools (Hatcher, 2001). At the same time, a number of small EAZs (58 at the time of writing) have been established as part of the EIC initiative. Like the large EAZs, small zones are meant to have a multi-sector focus and to secure private sector sponsorship, although, unlike the large EAZs, they operate within traditional LEA structures. It is yet to be seen whether those who are promoting and implementing these new forms of 'partnership' have learnt any of the lessons of the large EAZ experiment – or indeed of previous attempts to harness private sector funds and energies to the provision of state schooling or to coordinate action across welfare sectors.

Notes

[1] First-round zones were guaranteed £750,000 government funding per year for three years. Second-round zones are only guaranteed government funding of £500,000 per year, with a further £250,000 available annually to match funds raised from the private sector.

[2] ESRC reference: R000238046.

References

Barber, M. (1998) *The Guardian*, 7 January.

Becker, S. (1997) *Responding to poverty: The politics of cash and care*, London: Longman.

Benn, C. and Chitty, C. (1996) *Thirty years on: Is comprehensive education alive and well or struggling to survive?*, London: David Fulton.

Carvel, J. (1998) 'Labour revolt on private schools plan', *The Guardian*, 7 January.

Cochrane, A. (2000) 'New Labour, new urban policy?', in H. Dean, R. Sykes and R. Woods (eds) *Social Policy Review 12*, Luton: SPA, pp 184-204.

Deem, R., Brehoney, K. and Heath, S. (1995) *Active citizenship and the governing of schools*, Buckingham: Open University Press.

DfEE (Department for Education and Employment) (1997) *Education action zones: An introduction*, London: DfEE.

DfEE (1998a) '£75 million boosts radical education action zones to raise standards', DfEE Press notice, 23 June.

DfEE (1998b) *Guidance on completing the form*, London: DfEE.

DfEE (1998c) *Handbook for education action zones*, London: DfEE.

DfEE (1999) *Meet the challenge*, London: DfEE.

Dickson, M., Gewirtz, S., Halpin, D., Power, S. and Whitty, G. (2001) 'Education action zones and democratic participation', *School Leadership and Management*, vol 21, no 2, pp 169-82.

Gewirtz, S. (1999) 'Education action zones: emblems of the "third way"', in H. Dean and R. Woods (eds) *Social Policy Review 11*, Luton: SPA, pp 145-65.

Gewirtz, S. (2002) *The managerial school: Post-welfarism and social justice in education*, London: Routledge.

Gewirtz, S., Ball, S.J. and Bowe, R. (1995) *Markets, choice and equity in education*, Buckingham: Open University Press.

Gillborn, D. and Youdell, D. (2000) *Rationing education: Policy, practice, reform and equity*, Buckingham: Open University Press.

Hallgarten, J. and Watling, R. (2000) 'Zones of contention', in R. Lissauer and P. Robinson (eds) *A learning process: Public–private partnerships in education*, London: IPPR.

Hallgarten, J. and Watling, R. (2001) 'Buying power: the role of the private sector in education action zones', *School Leadership and Management*, vol 21, no 2, pp 143-58.

Halpin, D. (1999) 'Democracy, inclusive schooling and the politics of education', *International Journal of Inclusive Education*, vol 3, no 3, pp 225-38.

Halsey, A.H. (ed) (1972) *Educational priority, EPA problems and policies, 1*, London: HMSO, 241.

Hatcher, R. (1998) 'Profiting from schools: business and education action zones', *Education and Social Justice*, vol 1, no 1, pp 9-16.

Hatcher, R. (2001) 'Getting down to business: schooling in the globalised economy', *Education and Social Justice*, vol 3, no 2, pp 45-59.

Jones, K. and Bird, K. (2000) '"Partnership" as strategy: public–private relations in education action zones', *British Educational Research Journal*, vol 26, no 4, pp 491-506.

Mansell, W. (2001) 'Private sector cold-shoulders fledgling EAZs', *Times Educational Supplement*, 27 July, p 2.

NUT (National Union of Teachers) (2000) *An analysis of first round EAZ accounts 1998-1999*, London: NUT.

Power, S. (2001) 'Joined up thinking? Inter-agency partnerships in education action zones', in S. Riddell and L. Tett (eds) *Education, social justice and inter-agency working: Joined up or fractured policy?*, London: Routledge.

Power, S. and Whitty, G. (1999) 'New Labour's education policy: first, second or third way?', *Journal of Education Policy*, vol 14, no 5, pp 535-46.

Ranson, S. (2000) 'Recognising the pedagogy of voice in a learning community', *Educational Management and Administration*, vol 28, no 3, pp 263-79.

Skidelsky, R. and Raymond, K. (1998) *Education action zones: The conditions of success*, London: Social Market Foundation.

STA (Socialist Teachers Alliance) (1998) *Trojan horses – education action zones: The case against the privatisation of education*, London: STA.

Thody, A. and Punter, A. (2000) 'A valuable role? School governors and the business sector, 1996-1997', *Educational Management and Administration*, vol 28, no 2, pp 185-98.

Walford, G. and Miller, H. (1991) *City technology college*, Buckingham: Open University Press.

Whitty, G., Edwards, T. and Gewirtz, S. (1993) *Specialisation and choice in urban education. The city technology college experiment*, London: Routledge.

Wilby, P. (1998) 'This may be the end of the LEA show', *New Statesman*, 20 March, pp 24-5.

THIRTEEN

Public–private partnerships – the case of PFI

Sally Ruane

Introduction

Provision of public infrastructure has not escaped Labour's partnership philosophy. Although originally viewed as a mechanism for levering private finds into public sector development, the Private Finance Initiative (PFI) was reconceptualised as a form of public–private partnership in the earliest days of the Labour administration. By January 2001, three major hospital developments had been built and opened for business under PFI. A further 20 had reached financial close and work had begun on site.

This chapter explores the meaning and practice of partnership through an analysis of PFI and its troubled development in the NHS. Specifically, it focuses on the character and meaning of PFI partnerships for the NHS Trusts engaged in them. It begins with an examination of the initiative's early struggles and the determination with which Labour has sought to salvage it. The chapter considers the aims of the participating parties and the difficulties NHS Trusts encounter in achieving these aims. It concludes with an analysis of the nature of the evolving partnership. This endures well beyond contract signing and persists throughout the lifetime of the contract, typically 30 or more years. Thus, any conclusions here can only be preliminary and speculative, focusing on the setting-up stages.

The discussion is based on a broad range of documentary material: official guidance from the Department of Health and Treasury Taskforce; 'oppositional' material provided by organisations such as Unison; academic critiques, including those published by the Department of Public Policy at University College London; professional commentary and observation, such as that found in the *British Medical Journal*; and general and specialist press coverage. Additional observations are based on information obtained through interviews with 11 NHS Trust managers involved in various stages of eight first-wave PFI schemes. Although these accounts are not 'balanced' by the views of private sector partners, they nevertheless provide powerful insights into the problematic character of these deals as partnerships.

The development of PFI

The origins of PFI in healthcare lie in Conservative Chancellor Lamont's Autumn Statement of November 1992. This sought to attract private funding to resolve problems of under-investment in public infrastructure across a range of sectors, within a context of strict public expenditure controls. Public sector bodies seeking capital investment were encouraged to consider private finance possibilities. In 1994, this option became a requirement. Rather than merely providing (that is, building) upfront assets, as had hitherto been the case, the private sector was now invited to design, build, finance and operate services for the public sector, which would confine itself to identifying necessary 'outputs' (for example, the number of patients to be treated or the range of treatments).

Under the Major administration, the rationale for PFI in the NHS was presented as securing more effective achievement of service objectives; more efficient use of public money; and better value for money and quality, through the use of competition. Schemes would be approved only where value for money through ongoing efficiency savings superior to that of the 'public sector comparator' (a notional public rival) could be demonstrated; where risks could be shared; and where the purchase could be seen to be affordable and consistent with NHS (Trust) objectives (DoH, 1997). The private sector could achieve this through the experiences, skills and innovation it could bring to bear.

Disappointing progress in the early stages of PFI policy led to a series of political interventions, including subsidies and hasty legislation to reduce the costs and risks to interested private companies. However, these initiatives proved insufficient to combat excessive red tape and private sector fears arising from, ironically, the operation of the internal market, in which competitive forces left potential new providers with no guarantee that their services would be purchased. By the time the Labour government assumed office, no major deals had been signed. Indeed, over 40 large-scale hospital investment schemes languished at various stages of development. Initially opposed to PFI as the 'thin end of the wedge of privatisation', the Labour Party reversed its position prior to the May 1997 election and came into office firmly committed to making it work. The new government brought a fresh vigour and enthusiasm to the job, rapidly implementing a number of measures formally reported in the Bates Review of June 1997 (HM Treasury, 1997), but long advocated by the proponents of PFI. By late 1997, a Treasury Taskforce had been established to develop policy statements and technical guidance and the 1997 NHS (Private Finance) Act had clarified the legal powers of NHS bodies to enter agreements and secured the ring-fencing of payments to PFI providers. The Capital Prioritisation Advisory Group had identified 13 'first (PFI) wave' schemes; and greater emphasis was placed on continuity and collaboration, as competition in the internal market was replaced by longer-term service agreements. Between 1997 and 2000, the Treasury Taskforce produced a plethora of detailed and often prescriptive guidance, drawing particularly on the advice of the National Audit Office (Broadbent and Laughlin, 2000).

If the actions of New Labour were characterised by an urgency and enthusiasm never quite demonstrated by the Conservatives, its rhetorical construction of PFI was also more zealous and evangelical. Like its Conservative predecessor, the Labour government saw PFI as a way of accessing 'private managerial, commercial and creative skills' as well as private finance; it retained the focus on securing value for money through 'significant performance improvement' and 'efficiency savings' brought about by these innovative management skills. Like the Conservatives, Labour sees PFI as transforming the role of government bodies from being owners and operators of assets into purchasers of services from the private sector. However, under Labour, PFI is also explicitly recast as a principal mechanism in the government's new commitment to public–private partnerships (PPPs). This is seen most clearly in the newly established Treasury Taskforce's confident exposition of the philosophy, framework and principles of PFI, published in the early months of the Labour government – *Partnerships for prosperity: The private finance initiative*. For Labour, the PPP approach, and PFI specifically, represents a burying of "the old battles – public sector versus private sector, employee versus employer and state regulation versus the free market" (Treasury Taskforce, 1997, p1). In the new order, investment and partnership are the keys to economic success. An ideological equivalence of public and private is implied, in which government objectives are to be achieved through the use of *all* resources and skills available, public and private. Deals must and can be good for both sides. Indeed, Labour goes further than its predecessor, since, not content with asserting the superiority of the private sector, it proclaims an 'absolute identity of interest' of the two:

> The private sector wants to earn a return on its ability to invest and perform. The public sector wants contracts where incentives exist for the private sector to deliver services on time to specified standards year after year. In that, the public sector shares an absolute identity of interest with private financiers whose return on investment will depend on these services being delivered to those standards. (Treasury Taskforce, 1997, p 1)

Thus, although not conceived of as partnership at its inception, PFI has been reconceptualised as such under Labour. Partnership is a prerequisite for economic success, since long-neglected infrastructure requires value for money renewal in a context of tight public spending (Treasury Taskforce, 1997) and PFI remains the most common model for this task. With the passage of time, it has become clear that traditional Treasury funding of NHS schemes is all but impossible to obtain. In practice, despite all the talk of the 'private finance *option*' and the 'public sector comparator', PFI has become the 'only game in town', with little more than 10% of funding for new hospital developments since 1997 coming from the Treasury (www.doh.gov.uk/pfi/schemes).

Initially justified by Labour as a pragmatic step, the determination, speed and scope of PFI policy in the face of critical analysis underline this as an ideological project. Although the Andersen Report (2000), which concluded that PFI appeared to offer excellent value for money, is cited as evidence of PFI's superiority, the report's methodology has been criticised as fundamentally flawed

(Pollock and Vickers, 2000). The government did not wait for the conclusions of the Institute for Public Policy Research's Commission on PPPs (IPPR, 2001), suggesting that its outcome could be either ignored or anticipated. Indeed, *The NHS Plan* (DoH, 2000) injected further life into PFI by promising 100 new hospitals by 2010, as well as developments in primary and intermediate care – the largest construction programme ever in the NHS. Significantly, by 2010, around 40% of the total value of NHS estate will be less than 15 years old, and the majority of this is likely to have been developed through PFI, despite projected increases in public funds for capital development (DoH, 2001) and the growing significance of other forms of development and ownership (C 15, 2001; Pollock et al, 2001). This significant leap forward can be seen as part of a broader restructuring of public–private relations in healthcare. An historic 'concordat' between the NHS and the private health sector laid the basis for the planned use by the NHS of private health facilities, thereby institutionalising the outsourcing of clinical services. Meanwhile, the IPPR report on *Public– private partnerships* (IPPR, 2001) confidently recommends no 'no-go' areas for the involvement of the commercial and voluntary sectors in service provision.

The partners and their aims

In the large-scale, new-build NHS hospital schemes considered here, the 'partnership' is between the NHS Trust and a consortium of private companies. After inviting expressions of interest from private consortia, discussions flesh out the details of the Trust's requirements and of the rival bids. The preferred bidder is chosen, paying particular attention to risk transfer, value for money and affordability. Final discussions focus on the details of the transaction and meeting the requirements of funders. After contract signing and financial close, the contract requires long-term management, providing the basis for an ongoing managerial and operational relationship between the public client and private provider.

The typical consortium consists of a large construction company, experienced in handling complex tenders and responsible for the construction and probably the design of the new development; a 'hard facilities management' (hard FM) company undertaking maintenance, repair and estates management; a 'soft FM' company delivering 'hotel' services, such as catering, laundry and cleaning; and a financial institution that contributes to the financing of the deal. The facilities management companies may be subsidiaries or sister companies of the construction firms or may belong to some larger group that is involved in other PFI projects. The principal players in PFI, such as Carillion, Sodexho Alliance and Granada Compass, are large international companies.

Although these distinct components have different roles to play, technically the NHS Trust's partner in negotiation, agreement and contract management is an overarching body called the 'special purpose vehicle' (SPV). It is this body that is ultimately liable and to which the NHS Trust makes (usually monthly) payments for the use of the amenities supplied by the consortium. Additional services, such as sterile supplies, patient record systems and equipment maintenance, may also be part of the deal. As a tactic in the macro-economic battle to reduce the Public Sector Borrowing Requirement, new assets are kept off the balance sheet of the NHS Trust, first through assigning ownership to the consortium and, more recently, by assigning freehold to the Trust with a head-lease/sublease arrangement. Contracts are typically of around 30 years' duration (though some stretch to 60 years), after which most hospitals will revert to full NHS Trust ownership or a new PFI agreement might be reached.

The goal of the NHS Trust is to secure a new development that will allow it to deliver sufficient high-quality healthcare over the next few decades; a rationalised facility capable of providing 21st century services in a safe patient environment, which avoids the costs of duplicated services arising from multi-site arrangements. The Trust needs to obtain this on a value-for-money basis at an affordable price. The goal of the consortium is to increase its long-term security by engaging with the new opportunities created by state policy to pursue new profit-making avenues opened up through public sector collaborations. The consortium, or more specifically, each component company, seeks to make profit by supplying a range of healthcare-related services and charging for their use. The compatibility of these aims would appear to depend on the private sector's ability to cut costs while maintaining or enhancing quality.

Are PFI deals enabling Trusts to achieve their objectives?

PFI has made available to Trusts resources that they would not otherwise have been able to access, given the Treasury's reluctance to borrow to invest or raise taxes on income. At the time of writing only a handful of hospitals have been built and opened. However, drawing on the new guidance and expertise developed under Labour, PFI does appear to be succeeding in producing single-site developments offering rationalised amenities for healthcare, taking advantage of modern design knowledge and techniques, and offering the prospects of a safer environment for patient care. These schemes have generally been welcomed by Trust managers as promising facilities that are far superior to those they replace, given the dated and often inadequately maintained capital stock of the NHS. By making available in one go more cash than would have been available under a traditional Treasury option, developments have been completed in a single phase rather than staged over several years. Additionally, some mangers see the built-in provision of ongoing (life-cycle) maintenance as a great improvement on the traditional 'build and walk away model'.

However, these new facilities have been obtained at a cost. Despite the reassurances provided by the Department of Health regarding the economics of PFI schemes (www.doh.gov.uk/pfi/quanda.htm), and accepting the necessarily speculative character of evaluation at this stage, serious concerns have been raised by critics, including academic analysts and NHS managers. The economics of PFI schemes have been seriously questioned. An analysis by Gaffney and colleagues (1999) contrasts the annual charge to Trusts (for use of the building) of 9-18% of the original construction costs under PFI, with the

3-3.5% interest rate paid for Treasury borrowing. Indeed, subsidies were made available to first-wave schemes to help meet such costs. Trust managers were generally reluctant to talk about precise costs, although in some instances cost constraints had resulted in the scale and scope of the deal being reduced (for example, fewer beds and fewer services covered). One manager questioned the assumptions on which bed numbers had been calculated. Two Trust managers strongly endorsed the claim made by Gaffney et al (1999) that the accounting procedures prescribed by the NHS Executive and the Treasury strongly and unfairly tilts the playing field to the advantage of the private option. Both of these managers explicitly denied that their deals had represented value for money, despite the appearance of this through the prescribed accounting process.

Furthermore, all deals to date have been very costly to set up, in terms of both money and time. A number of NHS managers reported that negotiations with their management counterparts in the private consortium had been gruelling and time-consuming; indeed, all the deals so far signed have taken years to bear fruit. Private negotiators were seen as highly skilled and experienced, driving a hard bargain and, particularly with construction companies it was noted, 'scooping up every last crumb' of possible profit. Trust managers' keen awareness of the burden of their responsibilities to both the Trust Board and the patient population they served, contrasted sharply with their own perceived lack of experience and negotiation know-how. The frustrations and difficulties they faced, many of which stemmed from lack of previous NHS experience of these sorts of contracts, were referred to by some as 'the blind leading the blind'. Some NHS teams lacked the necessary skills; even where expensive consultancy expertise was bought in, this in itself was not always sufficient to safeguard the best interests of the Trust. Indeed, some NHS managers suggested that private companies deliberately sought to exploit the lack of experience and indeterminacy in healthcare.

Trust managers had to learn quickly to adopt different negotiating positions, discern posturing from real 'bottom line' positions and to convince themselves psychologically that their adversary was only human too. They also had to recognise the profit motive of their negotiating opposites and, beyond this, to accept the *legitimacy* of that profit motive. For some, it was implied, there was an initial reluctance to do so. Managers contrasted their own emphasis on value for money with their adversaries' focus on profit. Their own comparative vulnerability at the negotiating table, combined with an awareness of the profit imperative, led some managers to believe that vigilance was required to avoid being caught out should the other side try to 'pull a fast one'. For example, one manager complained that negotiators for the consortium had tried to build inflation into the model twice; another claimed the Trust had been asked to pay twice for a risk. Trust managers were not always successful in retrieving such errors.

Risk features as a major difficulty for negotiators on both sides. As mentioned previously, projects are to be evaluated on appropriate risk transfer. That is, all risks entailed in such a complex project must be identified, assigned financial value and then allocated to either the Trust or the consortium. In some instances, the consortium's reluctance to accept risk has created, and continues to offer the prospect of, conflict between the parties. Private sector companies were seen as keen both to avoid and to evade liability. In negotiation, they were perceived as highly risk-averse, even though risk transfer was proclaimed as one of the great benefits of PFI. One NHS Trust manager believed this was in part a consequence of the character of the construction industry, which tends, as a whole, to be fairly confrontational; "everybody tries to do everybody else out". This meant that private sector negotiators would accept risk only if they were certain they could pass it on to a subcontractor.

Evasion was possible because the details of contracts are often open to competing interpretation. In addition, one manager described how the facilities management companies in his scheme had "evaded to some extent their responsibility" by trying to insist on a "failure reporting system" (for instance, where standards of cleaning or maintenance did not come up to scratch) that was so complex and longwinded that a nurse on a busy ward would not be able to use it – "a marvellous way of getting out of it". Such instances left managers in the unenviable position of feeling that they could, in future, be held to account for activities and events over which they felt they had little or no control; "The Trust will carry the can".

This concern about liabilities was related to a further worry; the quality of the services to be delivered by private companies. Although there was general agreement among managers on the superior character of the new or prospective facilities over the old, this was not unqualified. The PFI process impeded straightforward and direct discussions between Trust management and staff on the one hand and the design team on the other. Although a welcome cost-containment strategy, this approach almost certainly contributed to some of the design errors reported by managers in the early stages of contract negotiation. Design problems were perceived by some managers as inevitable in any new hospital construction and not a feature peculiar to PFI. Indeed, several managers commented scathingly on the paucity of hospital-specific expertise evident among the private teams. Furthermore, there have been well-publicised design problems in early developments, such as the Cumberland Infirmary (Mathiason, 2000).

Another quality concern related to the proposal by private companies to run services with far fewer staff than were currently employed to provide those services; for instance, by underestimating the amount of routine general maintenance required even in a new building. Although this example reflects concern about hard FM, most concern surrounding quality related to 'soft' services. PFI schemes appeared to have in place a system of *self*-monitoring: that is, the component parts of the consortium monitor the standards at which their own services are delivered and complete a scoring sheet to record those standards. Some managers described these measures as detailed and comprehensive, although, it appears, less detailed than had been the case under Compulsory Competitive Tendering (CCT). It was then up to Trusts to devise a way of checking that the scores given were accurate. Several managers could see this as a potential problem. Detailed payment mechanisms had been created to penalise poor standards, but even the manager most positive about PFI could not 'promise' better hotel services, *even though* the specification in the contract was higher than before.

Another manager had already experienced the 'havoc' of private soft FM services. He put the problem down to a mindset geared to a purely profit orientation rather than an understanding of the needs of a hospital. He also identified the cheapness of the soft FM bid ("making the affordability stack up") and the inability of the Trust to establish requisite staffing levels as key factors in the genesis of the crisis. Above all, he was appalled at the impact on clinical staff who, he believed, could not be expected to carry out their clinical work without adequate support services.

Managers themselves rarely used the term 'partnership'; nor did they appear to conceive of their relationships with their counterparts in those terms. Indeed, some managers were distinctly scornful of 'partnership talk'. One manager remarked:

> "We keep saying we're working in partnership but we're already seeing that this is a building contract and building contracts the world over are no different. They'll want their pound of flesh. And it's a very nice, emotional word saying we're working in partnership. You're in a contract."

Another manager commented on partnership as a word "that brings a smile to most people's faces". Other managers similarly demonstrated a strong degree of scepticism, one describing as 'amusing' the contractor's invitation to 'trust'. There is little evidence of (NHS) managerial trust of the private sector operators. And yet the very same managers appeared to shy away from zealous surveillance of standards, preferring instead a softly-softly approach to checking as better for 'working relationships'. One made a rare allusion to 'partnership', explicitly linking this to a regime of contract compliance that looks lax or 'soft':

> "The trick, though and this is where you are back to partnership, if this is going to work, the company has got to be responsible to the Trust for standards with the Trust dipping in occasionally to check. But not doing it the whole time. I believe that would be too much."

Quite how you 'know' the company is not performing unless you check often enough is not clear from his account. Many penalty regimes appear to kick in when several score points have been lost. Ascertaining this may require more than an occasional 'dipping in'. Another manager, however, who had already had considerable experience of poor soft FM services, took a very different line, insisting that strong Trust monitoring was essential to prevent the provider cutting corners.

Reflections on the character of 'partnership' in PFI

The first observation to make about the nature of these relationships is how unequal the partners appear to be. One Trust manager believed that the secret of a good partnership was two strong parties: "If you have a strong party and a weak party, you get domination and the law of the jungle prevails". However, several managers believed NHS partners were not yet as strong as they should be. This was partly because of a lack of relevant expertise and skills within the NHS. Many NHS managers did not have adequate negotiating experience and had been slow to understand the sort of team necessary to undertake such a venture; one manager complained that, at the time of his appointment, the contract under negotiation had been like "a sieve with big holes in it". Several managers could link such weaknesses with policy-level factors. For example, some managers believed that a prior 'hollowing out' of the NHS had left them significantly weaker 'partners'. Because design skills had tended to be concentrated at regional level, local managers only ever had an "arm's-length understanding of what happened in capital planning". However, even regional expertise had been lost, leaving the NHS devoid of the necessary skills. Within the process of PFI itself, as functions were transferred some NHS managers expected to find their ability to monitor quality hampered by precisely the loss of personnel and information that monitoring required.

Furthermore, these partnerships were virtually compulsory; if Trusts wanted a new hospital, they had to do business with the private sector. Moreover, although managers felt their own lack of skill and know-how left them vulnerable in negotiation, they rarely viewed any deficiencies in private sector skills as advantageous, since these were usually precisely the skills that Trusts needed and were unable to access in any other way. Even more fundamentally, the unequal character of the partnership is underscored by the public and political accountability of public sector managers (Farnham and Horton, 1999). This was alluded to by the manager who believed the Trust would 'carry the can' even where service failure had been caused by the private partner's inadequate performance.

Hastings (1996, p 259), modifying Mackintosh's (1992) earlier conceptual framework, discusses the benefits of partnership to be derived through "resource synergy" (a "*combining* of resources and efforts"; emphasis added), or through "policy synergy" (a product of the *distinctiveness* of parties which makes possible innovative policy developments). NHS managers see access to resources for capital development as the great benefit of PFI, but this benefit is obtained only in the context of a political decision *not* to fund public investment in NHS infrastructure. Other synergy benefits, such as improved design, are difficult to attribute specifically to PFI. Given the diversity of hospital functions and the uniqueness of each hospital, a design team would have to listen to staff working within the institution, whether its client was a Trust or private consortium. Indeed, it could be argued – as one manager did – that such collaborative working could be obstructed by the design team's accountability to a client other than the hospital itself. Furthermore, some managers interpreted 'our staff as having to show their staff what to do' as evidence of the latter's incompetence, rather than evidence of synergy benefits. At the least, then, one can conclude that some managers are sceptical about claims for both resource and policy synergy.

What might have more applicability here is the notion of 'transformation', defined as a "process of partnership whereby partners seek to change or challenge the aims and operating cultures of other parties" (Hastings, 1996, p 262). In PFI, this transformation process appears to be unidirectional, with the private capitalist partner threatening the public sector ethos. It is possible to discern a dynamic at work in the relationship between public and private; the private sector moves forward to take advantage of public sector weakness and the public sector responds. As the public sector body acquires growing commercial confidence and knowledge – as it 'learns the game' – the room for private sector advantage (profit) is delimited. The standardisation of contracts (Treasury Taskforce, 1999) and other publications issued by the Treasury Taskforce (now succeeded by Partnerships UK (Ruane, 2001)) are supposed to assist in the learning of this game and most managers did believe the process of PFI procurement would get easier as a result of such guidance.

However, it is worth thinking about what learning this game means. Some managers insisted that the way forward for the NHS lay in a greater acquisition of commercial skills, know-how and experience. One manager linked lack of previous Compulsory Competitive Tendering (CCT) experience in his Trust with a lack of commercial skills in dealing with business. Managers described a process of changing their perceptions, of learning to see things from the other side's (that is, the private sector's) point of view. They had to 'learn quickly', develop commercial skills and bodies of knowledge and acquire technical know-how. They had to 'commercialise' themselves; this transformation into creatures comfortable (or at least competent and adroit) in a commercial world can be seen effectively as a process of re-acculturation. It is possible here to identify the way in which the NHS can be progressively opened up to greater penetration by capital and how a systemic shift towards the penetration of thitherto devalorised sectors by capital can be understood at the level of agency. Not only can practical skills, appropriate procedures and expertise be developed incrementally, thereby making further commercialisation easier to undertake, but so also can a changing consciousness on the part of managers and a changing perception of what is and is not acceptable within the NHS. It is the compulsory character of New Labour's public–private partnerships that makes this penetration over time difficult to avoid. Managers have to learn *how* to do it because they are not permitted to decide *whether* to do it.

By contrast, NHS managers gave no impression of believing that, apart from securing union recognition and valuable, but limited, concessions for transferred workers (Treasury Taskforce, 1998), they were attempting to alter the values and goals of the private companies they dealt with. Rather, they viewed the future as a period in which they expected service providers to minimise their own liabilities whenever possible. Indeed, rather than challenging the determinancy of the profit motive, some managers believed it was essential to accept it. In PFI, the public–private engagement radically alters the essential character of the public body; it has no such impact on the private corporation.

New Labour's description of PFI as a partnership appears to hang on its assertion of an 'absolute identity' of interest between the search for profit and the desire for good standards within the public body. By contrast, the Audit Commission (1998) defines PFI as a contractual arrangement, rather than a partnership, because goals are *not* shared but are merely compatible. Even this, however, is questionable. Some service providers may be able to make an acceptable rate of return only by cutting the quality of provision. One manager had been led by experience to suggest a direct link between the willingness and capacity of Trust managers to enforce standards and the profitability of service providers ("the service provider makes money *primarily* through their customers' management inertia"). He gave the impression that not only could such companies not be trusted to deliver on their own volition but that they could only be trusted *not* to deliver. To counter this, he suggested, the Trust must monitor vigorously and enforce penalties. Even here, the Trust might not win – it would depend on the precise details of the contract itself. For example, in hard FM, a maintenance company faced with substantial and costly repairs in the closing years of a contract might consider it preferable to incur financial penalties in a reduced payment stream from the Trust, rather than fund the repairs necessary to comply with the original contract. This would be influenced by the ownership arrangements at contract termination and the residual value, if any, of the asset at that point.

This potential scenario might explain why other managers fell back on an 'encouragement' approach. There are further reasons why managers might adopt a 'lighter touch' in contract compliance. As well as the expense involved, they might lack the information necessary for effective monitoring, as Coulson (1998) points out. Thus, the encouragement approach does not necessarily imply trust, but may in fact reflect relative powerlessness. Alternatively, the prospects of years and possibly decades in a contractual agreement might itself suggest that a 'constructive relationship' approach is the only sustainable way forward, as two managers believed. Again, this need not imply trust but an acknowledgement that the costs of relationship breakdown are high. This is not peculiar to 'partnership' but applies to other sorts of relationships also (Coulson, 1998) and appears to suggest nothing distinctively 'Third Way'.

Conclusions

Managers gave every impression of regarding the interests, values and goals of private and public sectors as, at best, distinct. They did not want to say that the profit motive was incompatible with good service delivery; to admit this would invalidate the deals they were trying to reach. However, many of their problems stemmed from the profit motive – 'pulling a fast one', evading and avoiding risk, allowing quality to fall. This seems to reflect a clash of philosophy and values; the public sector 'ethos' of service (to and for others) via balanced and fair agreements, versus the private sector reward for self (company profit) through maximising what is taken from others (price) and minimising what is given (cost). These major discrepancies in the values and goals of the respective partners negate one of the key conditions for successful partnerships (see Chapter Four). This is not the only approach to profitability but in PFI, with both its construction industry culture and the history of ferocious CCT cost (and quality) cutting, it may be the one that predominates. In this context, appeals to 'trust', 'sentiment' or 'partnership' were received by managers with scornful incredulity. The New Labour government might believe it is creating 'Third Way' partnerships, but these managers do not; they persist in viewing these deals as contractual.

It is important to understand that the 'partnership' between NHS hospitals and large commercial organisations is largely a forced one. All the managers alluded to the lack of any alternative route by which to procure a hospital, one manager going so far as to state that, outside the internal NHS private finance unit, no-one in the NHS would choose to adopt the PFI route (Ruane, 2000). However, the lack of an alternative, combined with the fact of the Labour Party's enthusiastic championing of PFI, has been decisive in compelling managers to bite the PFI bullet.

Provisions contained in the 2001 Health and Social Care Act relate to both the private development and ownership of NHS premises; the concordat with the private health sector establishes the planned and increasingly integrated involvement of commercial companies in the provision of 'NHS' healthcare; proposals in the 2001 Labour Party Manifesto promise, at the very least, the private management of 'NHS' units. The IPPR (2001) is strongly advocating an even more ambitious role for the private sector in the NHS. All this suggests a vision in which PFI will be only one of several models of public–private partnership, which together are likely to transform the character of the NHS.

References

Andersen, A. (2000) *Value for money drivers in the private finance initiative*, a report by A. Andersen and Enterprise LSE, Treasury Taskforce Guides to PFI Series 1, London: HM Treasury.

Audit Commission (1998) *A fruitful partnership: Effective partnership working*, London: Audit Commission.

Broadbent, J. and Laughlin, R. (2000) 'The role of the private finance initiative in the NHS: what is its role and can partnerships work?', unpublished paper for the second ESRC seminar on New Public Management, Cambridge.

Coulson, A. (1998) 'Trust: the foundation of public sector management', in A. Coulson (ed) *Trust and contracts: Relationships in local government, health and public services*, Bristol: The Policy Press.

DoH (Department of Health) (1997) *The purpose, organisation, management and funding of the National Health Service: A guide for the private sector*, London: DoH, March.

DoH (2000) *The NHS Plan*, London: The Stationery Office.

DoH (2001) *The NHS plan: Investment and reform for NHS hospitals*, (www.doh.gov.uk/investmentreform).

Farnham, D. and Horton, S. (1999) 'Managing public and private organisations', in S. Horton and D. Farnham (eds) *Public management in Britain*, Basingstoke: Macmillan.

Gaffney, D. and Pollock, A. (1997) *Can the NHS afford the private finance initiative?*, London: BMA Health Policy and Economic Research Unit.

Gaffney, D., Pollock, A., Price, D. and Shaoul, J. (1999) 'PFI in the NHS – is there an economic case?', *British Medical Journal*, vol 319, 10 July, pp 116-19.

Hastings, A. (1996) 'Unravelling the process of "partnership" in urban regeneration policy', *Urban Studies*, vol 33, no 2, pp 253-68.

HM Treasury (1997) *The Bates review of public–private partnerships*, London: HM Treasury.

IPPR (Institute for Public Policy Research) (2001) *Building better partnerships*, Report of the Commission on Public–Private Partnerships, London: IPPR.

Labour Party (2001) *Ambitions for Britain*, London: The Labour Party.

Mackintosh, M. (1992) 'Partnership: issues of policy and negotiation', *Local Economy*, vol 7, pp 210-24.

Mathiason, N. (2000) 'Beds crisis – in August?', *Observer Business*, 27 August.

Pollock, A. and Vickers, N. (2000) 'Private pie in the sky', *Public Finance*, 20 April, pp 22-3.

Pollock, A., Player, S. and Godden, S. (2001) 'How private finance is moving primary care into corporate ownership', *British Medical Journal*, vol 322, 21 April, pp 960-3.

Ruane, S. (2000) 'Acquiescence and opposition: the private finance initiative in the NHS', *Policy & Politics*, vol 28, no 3, pp 411-24.

Ruane, S. (2001) 'A clear public mission? Public–private partnerships and the recommodification of the NHS', *Capital and Class*, issue 73, spring, pp 1-6.

Treasury Taskforce (1997) *Partnerships for prosperity: The private finance initiative*, London: Treasury Taskforce.

Treasury Taskforce (1998) *Private finance policy statement no 4: Disclosure of information and consultation with staff and other interested parties*, London: Treasury Taskforce.

Treasury Taskforce (1999) *Technical note no 1 (revised): How to account for PFI transactions*, London: Treasury Taskforce.

FOURTEEN

Public–private partnerships in
pensions policies

Sue Ward

Introduction

> [The government's approach involves a] new public–private partnership
> building on the best features of state and private provision ... the share of
> national income devoted to pensions will increase, but a higher proportion
> will come from private, funded pensions.... Currently, about 60% of pension
> income is accounted for by the State and 40% by the private sector. As a result
> of the reforms set out in this Green Paper, the State's share is expected to fall
> to around 40% by 2050. (DSS, 1998, pp 30-1)

> Our reforms are designed to ensure that the UK pensions system remains one
> of the best in the world.... Occupational pensions are one of the greatest
> success stories of the 20th century. Funded pensions offer millions of people
> the best prospects of a decent and secure income in retirement. (Darling, 1999)

The rhetoric of 'partnership' has been prevalent for a long time in the field of
pensions in the UK. The 'partners' are seen as the state on the one hand, and
a mixed group of employers, insurance companies and financial institutions on
the other. Use of the term 'partnership', however, seems to be largely cosmetic.
The relationship could equally well be described as 'privatisation' or
'subcontracting'.

   The essence of the UK approach is that the pension provided through state
social insurance (or National Insurance), though close to universal, is very low
in comparison to other developed countries. Non-state providers are then
encouraged by generous tax advantages to 'fill the gap' and by further subsidies
(in terms of reduced National Insurance contributions) to take over a part of
the pension commitments the government would otherwise have carried. The
'partnership' has in the past also involved comparatively light regulation of
employers and the pension funds themselves (though the tax and National
Insurance subsidies have always come with generous helpings of red tape). In
recent years, regulation has been considerably tightened, but certain elements

are in the process of being relaxed again after complaints from the private pensions providers.

This chapter concentrates on the social welfare issues raised by 'partnerships' in pensions, rather than the economic issues. However, there is an equally interesting debate to be had about the way in which the state has worked with (and for) the vast financial power of the pension funds and insurance companies (see Minns, 2001).

The next section attempts to give a 'thumbnail sketch' of the UK's pension system, first as it stood before April 2001 when the first tranche of reforms was brought in, and then as it has changed and will change further as the reform programme as a whole comes into effect (see Ward, 2000b, for a more detailed explanation).

The current position

State pensions come in two main parts. There is a flat-rate basic pension, and an earnings related pension on top, commonly known as SERPS (state earnings related pension scheme). Cuts were made to the latter in 1988 and again in 1997, which are currently coming into effect.

Non-state pensions can be calculated in two main ways. In a 'final salary' (also called 'defined benefit') scheme, the pension promised is a proportion of final earnings, while contributions are variable to ensure that the promise can be met. In a 'money-purchase' ('defined contribution') scheme, the percentage contribution is fixed, but the eventual pension depends on the results of the invested contributions. Employers who offer a pension arrangement to their employees have traditionally done so through a final salary occupational pension scheme. However, it is now increasingly common to do this through a money-purchase 'group personal pension' (GPP), where the employer makes an arrangement for individualised 'personal pensions' (PPs), possibly with some additional benefits, to be sold by a commercial provider to the workforce. Individuals can also buy PPs for themselves in the financial retail market.

Until April 2001, the Inland Revenue did not allow anyone who was an active member of an occupational pension scheme to pay into a personal pension during the same tax year. It also required contributions to any kind of non-state pension to come out of taxable earnings.

Most members of occupational pension schemes are contracted out of SERPS. This means that both they and the employer pay lower National Insurance contributions. This rebate is intended to cover the costs of providing an alternative pension. Currently, around half the working population is in an occupational pension scheme. In the public sector, coverage extends to all levels of staff. In the private sector, however, the higher paid and those employed by larger firms are far more likely to have occupational pensions than are the lower paid and those working for small employers. Full-time workers are also more likely to belong to occupational schemes than part-timers, and men more likely than women. There are around 150,000 pension schemes; all but 700 of them have fewer than 1,000 members, and many of them are tiny

(Government Actuary, 2001, para 12.6). Around half of all self-employed people, and an unknown proportion of those in paid employment, are estimated to contribute to a personal pension. There are over 10 million personal pensions in existence, though many people will have more than one (DSS, 1998).

Historical overview

State pensions and means-tested benefits

The value of the basic pension hit its high point during the 1975-79 Labour government, when it was worth 25% of average earnings. Since 1980, it has been indexed only in line with prices, not earnings, and by 2001 had fallen to 17% of average earnings (Daykin, 2001). When SERPS was introduced in 1978, it had been expected that spending on means-tested benefits would by now be half, in real terms, of what it had been in 1978 (Altmann and Atkinson, 1981). However, this has not happened; in 1998, over a quarter of all pensioners were still estimated to be eligible for means-tested Income Support, though many do not claim (DSS, 1998, p 33).

Tax relief

Tax relief rules for pensions were first codified in the 1921 Finance Act and have been steadily developed – and become more complex – ever since. Sinfield (2000) has noted that the Organisation for Economic Co-operation and Development (OECD) calculated in the early 1990s that the cost of the UK's tax incentives for non-state pensions were the equivalent of 15% of personal income tax revenues. He also notes that over the 13 years of published figures "the cost of relief for both employers and employees to occupational schemes has doubled, increasing faster than the cost of living and almost in line with average earnings" (Sinfield, 2000, p 149). Inland Revenue estimates put the cost of tax relief on non-state pensions for 1999-2000 at £12.9 billion (Sinfield, 2000), but actuaries Philip Booth and Deborah Cooper (2000) have argued that the Inland Revenue is not measuring its costs correctly and that these are actually more modest.

Contracting out

Alongside the private pension tax relief is the 'contracting out rebate'. This is a reduction in National Insurance contributions granted to anyone who gives up rights to SERPS, in return for which they are expected to draw an occupational or personal pension.

The 1925 Pensions Act allowed employers with occupational schemes to 'contract out' of the state insurance pension arrangements, though requests to be able to do the same in 1946, within the new framework of National Insurance, were "confidently brushed aside" (Hannah, 1986, p 53). The Graduated Pension Scheme, introduced in 1959, was the UK's first attempt at a second state pension scheme. This allowed employers who could provide 'equivalent pension benefits' at a fairly minimal level to opt out of the Graduated Scheme. After several other attempts to bring in an earnings related state pension, what could be termed as the high point of partnership between state and private providers was reached in 1978, with the introduction of SERPS.

According to Barbara Castle, Secretary of State for Social Services at the time, the intention was that:

> ... the State scheme should work in partnership with occupational pension schemes which reach the standards we have laid down ... all employees will enjoy the advantages and benefits of the new and greatly improved State scheme. Those in occupational schemes will be able to draw some of the benefits through their own schemes instead, and earn still better pensions on top. (DHSS, 1975, p 1)

The Government Actuary, Chris Daykin, has explained in a recent discussion of the rationale for contracting out at that time that: "... it meant that SERPS could be introduced with much lower long-term costs than would otherwise have been the case, while providing encouragement to occupational pension scheme coverage" (Daykin, 2001, p 1).

SERPS and the contracting out arrangements were modified in 1988 and 1997 (1986 Social Security Act; 1995 Pensions Act). Each time, the guarantees required from the private pensions providers became less onerous. In 1988, money-purchase occupational schemes and personal pensions were permitted to contract out, on the basis of guaranteeing what contributions would be made, but with merely a hope that the resulting pension would be equal to, or better than, the SERPS that had been given up. In 1997, the guarantees were removed from final salary schemes also. No one now can know whether they will gain or lose from the decision to contract out of SERPS.

Regulation of pensions

The regulation of occupational and personal pensions (as opposed to that surrounding the granting of tax relief and contracting out status) has traditionally been fairly light. Occupational schemes grew up under the framework of trust law, while personal pensions developed as commercial insurance contracts. In 1991, following the Maxwell debacle, the Goode Committee was appointed and put forward proposals for a wide-ranging package of reforms (Pension Law Review Committee, 1993). In a modified form, their recommendations were carried through into the 1995 Pensions Act. Two important aspects of this legislation were:

- The creation of the Occupational Pensions Regulatory Authority (Opra), an agency that enforces the various obligations being imposed on trustees and employers. This has the power to fine and/or disqualify trustees and to fine employers for offences such as not having the scheme accounts duly

audited, or not passing over promptly the employees' contributions deducted from their pay.
• The introduction of the Minimum Funding Requirement (MFR), which imposes a common standard of financing for final salary pension schemes. This standard was to be phased in over a 10-year period.

The government's package of changes

The changes proposed by the new Labour government in its Pensions Green Paper (DSS, 1998) included:

• retention of the basic state pension, but to be increased in line with prices only;
• a Minimum Income Guarantee (MIG) for pensioners – that is, a renaming of current means-tested Income Support and its provision at a higher level than for non-pensioners;
• abolition of SERPS and its replacement by a State Second Pension (S2P) in two stages;
• provision of new, low-cost private pensions ('stakeholder pensions') on a money-purchase basis, for those not otherwise in a private pension scheme.

Since the Green Paper, there have been a number of changes to the proposed stakeholder pensions and the arrangements for contracting out of S2P, as a result of negotiations and compromises to get the deal through. Some further elements have also been added to the reform package:

• major changes in the way tax relief is given to individuals and for investment income;
• an extension of the scope of means-tested benefits through the planned Pension Credit;
• plans to abolish the MFR.

Two elements of the government's reform package came into effect in April 2001 – the new stakeholder pension and the changes in the tax rules.

In order to be registered as a stakeholder pension, pension arrangements must meet certain standards, of which the most important is a limit on charges to no more than 1% of each individual's fund. There is a general requirement on employers from 8 October 2001 to offer 'access' to a stakeholder scheme to their non-pensioned employees – that is, those who are not members of occupational schemes or personal pensions to which the employer is making a minimal contribution. However, exemptions from this general requirement are broad and cover small employers, short-term employees, those earning low wages and those who have been offered membership of the employer's scheme but turned it down. Employers are required to set up and operate payroll deduction arrangements, but not to make any contribution themselves.

The new tax rules break the historic link between taxable earnings and pension contributions. Anyone can now make contributions of up to £3,600 a year to a pension, regardless of the amount of their earnings and even if they have nil earnings. For non-earners, the tax relief then given represents a credit rather than a refund. Above the £3,600 limit, the same formula used for personal pensions, based on age and percentage of earnings (17.5% of earnings for those under 35, increasing to 40% of earnings for those over 60) is used to determine the maximum level of contributions that can be made. The arrangements for calculation of earnings for this purpose, however, have been very much relaxed. There is no lower age limit for stakeholder pensions, so it will be possible for a doting parent or grandparent to start paying into a scheme as soon as a baby is born.

In addition, any individual earning less than £30,000 can pay both into an occupational scheme, up to the current limits, *and* pay up to £3,600 into a stakeholder or personal pension scheme. This is described as 'concurrency'.

National Insurance pensions

The State Second Pension (S2P) is planned to replace SERPS in a two-stage process. In the first stage from April 2002, those on low earnings gain by the new calculation arrangements, in comparison to SERPS, but no one loses. Many carers and disabled people will also be credited into the scheme, where they would not have been under SERPS, although the definitions and eligibility criteria are narrow.

In the second stage, in 2006 or 2007, the government plans to convert S2P to a second, largely flat-rate, pension sitting on top of the state basic pension for those below a certain age, probably 45, at the time. At this stage, therefore, the assumption is that those earning little more than half national average earnings (£10,500 a year in today's terms) or more will be 'contracted out' through one or other form of non-state pension. Those earning more than this who choose to stay within S2P will then accrue less, year after year, than they would have done under SERPS. The National Insurance rebates, on the other hand, will continue to be paid as if stage 1 still applied, and people were giving up an earnings related benefit.

All those who do contract out will receive additional payments, either through an extra National Insurance rebate or through a special top-up benefit, to ensure that they do not lose by the change from SERPS to S2P.

State pensions and means-tested benefits

The Minimum Income Guarantee (MIG) was introduced in April 1999. A hint about the plans for a Pension Credit was given in the Pensions Green Paper (DSS, 1998, p 37). In November 2000 concrete proposals were published and legislation is now planned for the 2001-02 parliamentary session. The MIG is in reality a renaming of the current means-tested Income Support. It is set at £92.15 per week for a single person (2001-02 rates).

The Pension Credit will takeover from the MIG in April 2003. In effect, it will be a partial (40%) disregard of a band of income above the MIG level. It is not clear how the government plans to avoid the interaction with other means-tested benefits, which could mean an effective marginal tax rate of 91% (IFS, 2001). The government appears to believe that the low take-up of means-tested benefits, particularly by older people, can be solved by simplifying claim forms and using the tax system rather than the Benefits Agency to pay – despite the fact that only a third of pensioners pay tax.

It is intended that the level of the Pension Credit will rise broadly in line with earnings. Meanwhile, the basic pension is to continue to rise in line with prices only. According to the Government Actuary's calculations in 1999, this means that the basic pension would fall to 7% of average earnings for men by 2050 (PPG, 1999, p 48). SERPS, and the future S2P, are similarly planned to rise only in line with prices.

Increasing the basic state pension by only 75p per week in April 2001 was, Tony Blair has suggested, the biggest mistake of Labour's first term (*Observer*, 2001):

> The Government's argument that the low cash increase simply reflected low inflation did it little good. In the end, the low inflation-linked increase seemed to force the Government to offer a real increase in pensions in 2001. (Harley and Davies, 2001, p 24)

Discussion: the elements of partnership

As pointed out previously, the notion of 'partnership' between the state and private providers of pensions has a long, if rather poorly defined, history. Hannah (1986) quotes an insurance company source dated 1963, in which a distinction was drawn between the state as a *partner* (making basic provision and allowing non-state bodies to do the rest) or the state as a *competitor* (providing a state benefit high enough for people not to need additional provision). There were disputes in 1969 over the proposals for National Superannuation (never enacted) under one Labour government and in 1974-75 under another Labour government over SERPS (Hannah, 1986, pp 60-1). The opposition was led by occupational pension providers who believed that the new state benefits would discourage people from joining their schemes. It resulted in the framework of contracting out explained previously.

In 1985, the Conservative government proposed a 'new partnership', under which SERPS and contracting out were to be abolished (DSS, 1985). Instead, all employees would be required to take out personal pensions, unless they belonged to an occupational scheme. This was not carried through, however, primarily because the insurance companies were less than happy about being forced to deal with large numbers of low-paid workers. Instead, employers were forbidden to require employees to join their pension schemes as a condition of employment; and contracting out of SERPS, on a money-purchase basis and without any guarantees of the amount payable as pension, was allowed for the first time. Personal pension providers were not regulated as to the amount they could charge. The government also provided a specific 'incentive' from the National Insurance Fund, on top of the contracting out rebate, and allowed this to be backdated for a year. This incentive led to the personal pension mis-selling scandal, perhaps the largest in financial history, which is likely to cost £20 billion or more to put right (Ward, 2000b). The present government's reforms are essentially more of the same.

The argument made by successive governments has been that, by its relying on private rather than state benefits, the UK has escaped the 'demographic time-bomb' awaiting other European states that rely far more heavily on state provision. However, this is a myth, as members of the actuarial profession are currently anxious to explain to the public (IoA, 2001; Thompson, 2001). Increased life expectancy and reduced investment returns increase the costs of funded private provision just as they do unfunded state provision. It is a myth, however, that appears to be believed by the politicians.

One way of describing the state's relationship with non-state pension providers would be as a 'sugar daddy'. The state is enamoured enough of its partner to pay the bills, but does not get a very good deal in return. However, not all of Whitehall appears to want to act as a 'sugar daddy'. There is a plethora of policies emanating from different parts of the Whitehall machine, creating an incoherence that may lead to none of the government's aims being met.

State benefits

Low state pensions are reflected in a low level of direct public spending on state pensions – 5.5% of GDP (Government Actuary, 1999, para 1.18). This spending is expected to stay more or less constant as a proportion of GDP over the next 50 to 60 years, despite a 50% growth in the number of pensioners. It was originally expected to fall, but the costs have been increased by concessions made during the passage of the reform package (Government Actuary, 2000).

Once the second stage of S2P comes into effect, the state will have abandoned responsibility for providing any more than a tiny slice of retirement income for one part of the retired population – at least through a non-means-tested insurance benefit. The two-stage process of reform is probably a (successful) tactic to defuse political argument. The illustrative figures published by the government (DSS, 1998) treated the first-stage formula as if it would last 50 years or more, and almost all discussion has concentrated on this formula. It would perhaps be too cynical to think that the government hopes that, by 2006 or 2007, the original architect of SERPS, Barbara Castle, already well into her eighties, will no longer be in a position to protest about the effective destruction of her project.

Tax relief

The trade association for those running and advising on pension schemes, the National Association of Pension Funds (NAPF), argues that there is:

> ... logic in the State becoming a financial partner in the [mutual] insurance [provided by occupational pensions] through the tax system.... The State invests by forgoing taxes on the money flowing into approved pension funds in the form of contributions, investment income and capital gains. It then recovers its money and reaps a return on its investment through reduced expenditure on welfare benefits and increased revenue from the tax levied on the money flowing out as pensions on payments or as refunds on contributions and surpluses. (NAPF, 1998, p 12)

Paul Johnson has argued that the tax uncollected on pension contributions and investments is largely deferred, not forgone altogether (Johnson, 1999). Somewhat contradictorily, he also argues that "it is hard to imagine why anyone would voluntarily lock their money away into a pension fund rather than save it in another more flexible form – unless there were some *fiscal advantages* [my italics] in doing so" (Johnson, 1999, p 33). On the other hand, Gerald Hughes (2000) and Richard Minns (2000) have argued that the case for the efficiency of tax reliefs in this respect is by no means proven, while Adrian Sinfield (2000) has suggested that without greater transparency in this area, it is not possible to say whether the tax reliefs offer value for money. Agulnik (1999, pp 59-62) points out that the system is upwardly redistributive, since higher rate taxpayers benefit disproportionately from tax relief on their contributions. They are much more likely than the lower-paid to belong to a private pension arrangement and they can claim back tax at their marginal rate.

The pensions industry sets enormous store by tax relief, perhaps more than this government originally anticipated. In his 1997 Budget, Gordon Brown abolished the tax credits that pension funds used to be able to reclaim on companies' payments of Advanced Corporation Tax. This was described by the NAPF as "the biggest attack on funded pensions since the War" (Pensions World, 1997, p 9), while the Tory Party has repeatedly claimed that it is a 'stealth tax' on pensioners. However, their attempts to put forward this argument during the 2001 General Election seem to have had little effect on the electors, so Brown's short-term political judgement appears to have been vindicated. However, it meant that the new Labour government forfeited, within three months of coming into office, the goodwill of a powerful lobby.

Other tax initiatives on savings have also undermined the priority given to pensions, especially the very highly tax-advantaged All-Employee Share Ownership Accounts (AESOPs). There is now a view that the tax-privileged status of pensions has been eroded so that there is a 'fine balance' between contributing to a stakeholder pension or an individual savings account (ISA) (Thompson, 2001).

Contracting out

The second element in the 'partnership' between state and private providers is the system of 'contracting out' of the state additional pension arrangement (SERPS at present; S2P from 2002). A recent study of more than 170 countries described this as a form of voluntary privatisation. It noted that only Japan and the UK allow workers to reduce their social security contributions in return for participating in a funded, employer-provided plan, and only in the UK is contracting out to individual pension accounts also permitted. This is distinct from the full-blown privatisations in some Asian, ex-Soviet bloc, and Central and South American countries, of which the best known example is Chile (Turner, 2001).

The NAPF has described the relationship between government and occupational and personal pensions in the contracting out system as being "that of contractor and subcontractor rather than financial partners" (NAPF, 1998, p 12). Indeed, it is estimated that, in defined benefit schemes, every £1 of rebate paid out yields only 88p of saving on SERPS, while for personal pension schemes the saving is only 75p (PPG, 1999, p 86). The concessions made during the passage of the 1999 Welfare Reform and Pensions Act mean that contracting out under the new arrangements will be a net cost to the National Insurance Fund for more than half a century ahead, with 'savings' expected only in 2060 and beyond (Government Actuary, 2000, para 3.8). However, this is not a zero-sum game. As the Government Actuary has put it: "Giving more to the contracted out means charging more to those who are not contracted out" (Daykin, 2001, p 3).

No government since 1978 has managed to set the National Insurance rebate at a neutral level that is economic for the taxpayer. During the passage of the 1975 Social Security Pensions Act, an extra amount was added to the rebate and has been retained as a 'contingency margin' ever since. According to the Government Actuary: "This has always been rationalised as an additional rebate to make it attractive for a wider range of salary-related schemes to contract out, for example those with a higher than average age distribution" (Daykin, 2001, p 3).

Personal pensions were given extra rebates on National Insurance contributions as a deliberate 'incentive' (a major reason for the massive mis-selling scandal) from 1987 to 1993, and then on a smaller scale from 1993 to 1997. There have, though, been strong complaints from the pensions industry that the 2001-02 rates of rebate are not enough to make contracting out of the new stakeholder schemes economic (Professional Pensions, 2001a). It may be that the government is calculating that the industry is too wedded to contracting out to forego it, even if it does not make sense economically; or that it considers that the other concessions made on the launch of stakeholder pensions (discussed later) will be sufficient.

Regulation

The pensions industry, especially the NAPF, is accustomed to claim in response to almost every proposal for change that this is the 'last straw' and will lead to schemes closing down or changing their form. The government appears sympathetic to these pleas; according to the outgoing chairman of the NAPF in May 2001:

> ... tax rules that get in the way of pension provision are to be slimmed down. Regulations intended to provide consumer protection are to be reviewed since there is a real danger that if they remain unaltered, there will be no pension provision left to protect. Hopefully, the commitment to simplification will give rise to swift changes. If it does not, it may be too late. (Pickering, 2001, p 4)

An example: the minimum funding requirement

The MFR was brought in under the 1995 Pensions Act and was prompted in part by the Maxwell pensions debacle. It would be more logical to have a system of mutual insurance, as in a number of other countries. However, this is anathema to some of the very largest pension schemes, which see themselves as having to subsidise the smaller schemes. The government has emphatically stated that it is not prepared to act as guarantor for a commercial or mutual insurance system (DSS, 2001b). However, this means that each pension scheme has to carry its own risk of shortfall, rather than being able to pool the risk. This is "like a community denying itself a fire brigade", as one commentator has put it (Shuttleworth, 2001, p 3). Using the MFR mechanism to provide protection means that the protection itself can only be of a low standard. Even so, the pensions industry has complained that its investment freedom is being curbed by the mechanism.

The government has therefore been under pressure from both sides of industry to reform the MFR almost from the date it began to be phased in, in April 1997. The Chancellor took up the issue and announced in the 2001 Budget that the MFR would be replaced by legislation when Parliamentary time became available. In effect, this was a compromise between the NAPF, mainly representing large schemes, and the Treasury. Financial and investment goals appear to have taken precedence over social policy goals. Whether the new proposals are workable is not at all clear, nor whether they will satisfy European regulatory requirements (Pensions Board, 2001).

Personal and stakeholder pensions

With stakeholder pensions, the government is restricting the explicit charges, although there are additional hidden costs (Wynn, 2001). The system remains expensive by international standards, with the '1% of fund per year' maximum charge equating to 20% of the fund over a working lifetime (Murthi et al, 2001). However, there have been many complaints by potential providers that the restrictions are too severe and the system will not be viable.

It is too early in the life of stakeholder pensions for detailed figures to be available, but the evidence so far available suggests that the first purchasers have been comparatively affluent, topping up their occupational pensions or paying the maximum allowed contributions into pensions for their children and non-earning spouses. In effect, stakeholder pensions have been added to their portfolio of tax-sheltered investments. Lower-paid people do not appear to be buying stakeholder pensions, except when their employer offers to make a reasonable contribution on their behalf.

MIG and the pension credit

One of the reasons put forward in the 1998 Pensions Green Paper for reforming pensions was that: "By 2025, without reform, well over half of those reaching retirement age could have to rely on income-related benefits in their retirement" (DSS, 1998, p 14). It is odd, then, that the Pension Credit will bring half the pensioner population back within the ambit of means tests. This anomaly has sprung from the quite separate wish of the Chancellor to reform the tax and benefit system. As he told the Treasury Select Committee:

> I believe that this is a fundamental reform that has been long overdue in the country, to integrate tax and benefits; where we are going over time, as we are already doing in many instances, to eliminate a situation where people are paying tax on the one hand while receiving social security benefits on the other hand…. It is going to be a far more co-ordinated, cohesive and integrated approach…. We are doing what has been achieved in some areas such as America in integrating tax and benefits through the earned income tax credit as well. (Treasury Select Committee, 2001b, reply to question 339)

The argument for this reform put forward by the Minister for Social Security is that, by offering a partial disregard of a band of income above a minimum level, the Pension Credit ensures people always benefit from their savings and this will be enough to give low-paid workers an incentive to save (DSS, 2000). The problem with the Pension Credit, so far as the government's other pension reforms are concerned, is that both low-paid workers and those on quite reasonable incomes are being expected to behave irrationally if they take out a stakeholder pension. They will be forgoing current consumption in order to make investments on which they will receive low or negative rates of returns (IoA, 2001a). Thus, according to calculations by Jane Falkingham and Catherine Rake (2001), by 2060 the gap between the basic pension and MIG will be around £100 per week in constant terms. This will mean someone saving continuously from the age of 25 would need to put aside approximately £22 a week to achieve an income equivalent to that available via means-tested benefits. The required amount of savings rises to £62 a week for those who save for only 20 years.

Financial advisers say that it will be difficult for them to advise anyone with modest future income prospects that it is in their interests to buy a stakeholder pension, when they would risk losing 40% of their pension income to the Pension Credit means test. Moreover, it will be very easy to build up assets in other ways and still be eligible for the full credit. For example, no upper limits are planned on the capital that can be held while the Pension Credit is simultaneously claimed. Only actual investment income, rather than the current 'tariff' income assumed to be due from capital, will be taken into account in the calculation. These new conditions will create a 'deadweight' of people outside the intended target group, who understand – or have computer software that understands – how to obtain the greatest benefit from the system.

Does the rationale for the Pensions Credit lie in government plans for the future? Some commentators have suggested that the intention is to make it compulsory for all those earning above a certain level to contribute to one or other sort of private pension scheme (occupational, stakeholder, or personal). Certainly, the 1988 Pensions Green Paper contained in its appendices evidence of this possibility (DSS, 1998, p 105). Many in the pensions industry are taking it for granted that compulsion is on the agenda within the next few years (Professional Pensions, 2001b).

A more likely policy driver is the Treasury distaste for social insurance. According to the former Permanent Secretary to the DSS, Sir Michael Partridge:

> They [the Treasury] do not like National Insurance, they prefer means tested benefits which they can control because that comes from tax and you can put them up and down and people do not build up rights. They fought pension schemes tooth and nail and I think they fought them too far. (Treasury Select Committee, 2001a, answer to question 435)

Conclusions

To conclude, the evidence of the state's desire for 'partnership' with the private sector is strong. There is less evidence of the private sector having a similar desire, rather than just taking what it can get. However, different parts of the government – particularly the Treasury and ministers responsible for social security policies – are pulling in different directions and in turn making stated aims less achievable; the opposite of 'joined-up government'.

Certainly Sir Michael Partridge does not fill one with confidence. He told the Treasury Committee, in the contribution referred to previously, that the Chancellor tended to 'cook up' ideas and the (then) Department of Social Security was either told at the last minute or not told at all. There was no chance to work an idea through like a proper policy and ask whether it was feasible or practical, or what was the best way to do it. "If you do not have a strong Minister you can get a new policy put in, in the secrecy of the Budget" (Treasury Select Committee, 2001a, answer to question 435).

References

Agulnik, P. (1999) 'Pension tax relief and the green paper', in *Partnership in pensions? Responses to the pensions green paper*, CASE paper 24, London: London School of Economics and Political Science.

Altmann, R.M. and Atkinson, A. (1981) 'State pensions, taxation and retirement income, 1981–2031', in M. Fogarty (ed) *Retirement policy: The next fifty years*, London: Heinemann.

Booth, P. and Cooper, D.R. (2000) *The tax treatment of pensions*, Actuarial Research Report no 122, London: City University.

Darling, A. (1999) 'A new contract for pensions', Speech by Alistair Darling, Secretary of State for Social Security, National Association of Pension Funds Conference, May.

Daykin, C. (2001) 'Contracting-out: a partnership between public and private pensions', *PMI News*, Pensions Management Institute, July.

DHSS (Department of Health and Social Security) (1975) *Pensions: Britain's great step forward*, Leaflet NP 25, London: DHSS.

DHSS (1985) *Reform of social security*, Cm 9517, London: HMSO.

DSS (Department of Social Security) (1998) *A new contract for welfare: Partnership in pensions* (Pensions Green Paper), Cm 4179, December, London: The Stationery Office.

DSS (2000) *The pension credit: A consultation paper*, Cm 4900, London: DSS.

DSS (2001a) *Occupational and personal pensions: Simplification of contracting-out*, Consultation Document, London: The Stationery Office.

DSS (2001b) *Security for occupational pensions: The government's proposals*, London: DSS/Treasury, March.

Falkingham, J. and Rake, C. (2001) 'Pension posers', *The Guardian*, 16 April.

Government Actuary (1999) *National insurance fund: Long term financial estimates*, July 1999 edn, Cm 4406, London: The Stationery Office.

Government Actuary (2000) *National insurance fund: Long term financial estimates*, January 2000 edn, Cm 4573, London: The Stationery Office.

Government Actuary (2001) *Occupational pension schemes 1995*, 10th Survey by the Government Actuary, London: The Stationery Office.

Hannah, L. (1986) *Inventing retirement: The development of occupational pensions in Britain*, Cambridge: Cambridge University Press.

Hansard (1997) vol 297, col 508, 3 July.

Harley, E. and Davies, S. (2001) 'Low inflation: the implications for the FSA', in E. Harley and S. Davies, *FSA occasional papers series*, no 14, April.

Hughes, G. (2000), 'Pension financing, the substitution effect and national savings', in G. Hughes and J. Stewart (eds) *Pensions in the European Union*, Dordrecht: Kluwer, pp 45-61.

IFS (Institute for Fiscal Studies) (2001) 'Recent pension policy and the pension credit', London: IFS press release, 21 February.

IoA (Institute of Actuaries) (2001a) *Means-testing*, Position papers from Institute/ Faculty of Actuaries Pension Provision Task Force: February, available from www.actuaries.org.uk.

IoA (2001b) *Age of retirement and longevity*, Position papers from Institute/Faculty of Actuaries Pension Provision Task Force: February, available from www.actuaries.org.uk.

Johnson, P. (1999) *Getting older wiser*, London: IFS.

Minns, R. (2000) 'The control and centralisation of pension fund investment in the United Kingdom', in G. Hughes and J. Stewart (eds) *Pensions in the European Union*, Dordrecht: Kluwer, pp 71-81.

Minns, R. (2001) *The cold war in welfare; Stock markets versus pensions*, London: Verso.

Murthi, M., Orszag, J.M. and Orszag, P.R. (2001) 'The maturity structure of administrative costs – theory and the UK experience', in *Private pension systems, administrative costs and reforms*, Paris: OECD.

NAPF (National Association of Pension Funds) (1998) *Making pensions easy: NAPF's tax simplification report*, London: NAPF.

Observer, The (2001) 'We can be proud. But we must finish the job', interview with Tony Blair, *The Observer*, 12 May.

Pensions Board (2001) *Investment and occupational pensions*, London: Institute of Actuaries.

Pension Law Review Committee (1993) *Pension law reform*, Report of the Pension Law Review Committee (Chair: Professor Roy Goode), Cm 2342, 2 vols, London: HMSO.

Pensions Management (2001) 'Is the Myners review missing the point?', *Pensions Management*, February, London: Financial Times Publications.

Pensions World (1997) 'ACT: the Chancellor has stolen all the credit', *Pensions World*, August, p 9.

Phillips and Drew (2001) *Pension fund indicators 2001: A long term perspective on pension fund investment*, London: Phillips and Drew.

Pickering, A. (2001) 'Pensions and the workplace – a partnership worth preserving', Speech to IBIS conference, May.

PPG (Pensions Provision Group) (1999) *We all need pensions*, Report of the Pensions Provision Group, London: The Stationery Office.

Professional Pensions (2001a) 'Forced retirement', *Professional Pensions*, May.

Professional Pensions (2001b) 'Treasury denies hidden agenda on DB schemes', *Professional Pensions*, 24 May.

Shuttleworth, J. (2001) *Response to the MFR review*, London: Price Waterhouse Cooper.

Sinfield, A. (2000) 'Tax benefits in non state pensions', *European Journal of Social Security*, vol 2, no 2, pp 137-67.

Thompson, P. (2001) Speech by Peter Thompson, incoming Chairman of National Association of Pension Funds, NAPF Annual Conference, 18 May.

Treasury Select Committee (2001a) 'HM Treasury, Third Report, House of Commons', Minutes of Evidence, 9 November 2000.

Treasury Select Committee (2001b) 'Minutes of Evidence', Treasury Select Committee, House of Commons, 20 March 2001.

Turner, J. (2001) *Social security reform around the world*, Washington, DC: Public Policy Institute, American Association of Retired Persons.

Ward, S. (1999) 'Conference revelations', *Pensions World*, November, p 52.

Ward, S. (2000a) 'New Labour's pension reforms', in H. Dean, R. Sykes and R. Woods (eds) *Social Policy Review 12*, Newcastle: SPA, pp 157-83.

Ward, S. (2000b) *Pensions handbook*, London: Age Concern Books.

Ward, S. (2001) *Pension tension*, London: Industrial Society.

Wynn, S. (2001) *The stakeholder cap on charges; which charges?* (available on www.stakeholder.cwc.net).

FIFTEEN

Towards a theory of welfare partnerships

Kirstein Rummery

Partnerships and networked governance

In Chapter One, Powell and Glendinning discussed the significance of partnerships for the new Labour government in the UK, which was, at the time of writing, starting its second term of office. Notwithstanding the definitional difficulties of the concept of 'partnership' working within the welfare state, they asserted that the emphasis within New Labour rhetoric and policy on collaboration, partnership, cooperation and other associated terms (Huxham, 2000; Ling, 2000; Balloch and Taylor, 2001), meant that a critical focus on the theory and evidence of partnerships was necessary. One aim of this book was to establish whether what Newman calls "a powerful discourse of inclusion and collaboration which [is] central to Labour's attempt to forge a consensual style of politics" (Newman, 2001, p 104) can be reconciled with an arguably equal powerful pragmatic discourse underpinning New Labour's policies, the drive towards evidence-based policy (Davies, 2000).

This chapter will address some of the issues raised by the theoretical discussions and empirical evidence presented in the contributions to this book. Is partnership working a distinctive feature of New Labour policy and practice? What conclusions can be drawn from the evidence presented in Chapters Five to Fourteen about partnership working – is it possible to identify common themes that might take us towards a unifying, overarching theory of partnership working, or are there significant factors that differentiate between different types of partnerships? If so, what are these factors? Are they context specific or are there unifying themes that systematically and consistently characterise partnerships of different kinds? What is the relationship between partnership and the governance of welfare? And finally, what lessons can be drawn from the theory and evidence presented here about the development of partnerships and their role in the delivery of welfare in the 21st century?

Partnerships: new, distinctive, New Labour?

While it can be reasonably asserted that partnership working is at the heart of New Labour's ideology, there is a much less compelling argument to be made that it is particular to New Labour, or even, in some cases, a particularly radical departure from previous ideologies, policies and practice. All of the authors in Chapters Five to Fourteen cite evidence of long histories of effort towards collaborative working between the sectors described in their respective chapters, even if that previous effort had limited success. Arguably, one innovative feature of New Labour's partnerships is simply that they are now the focus of considerably greater policy and academic interest. Commentators on partnership working to date have fallen broadly into two camps: those who attempt inductively to theorise about partnership working and its ideological significance to New Labour; and those who attempt to deductively describe, analyse and account for the success (or otherwise) of partnership working in the delivery of welfare (see Chapter Two).

The rhetoric of partnership does, in principle at least, sit easily within a discourse of networked governance (Rhodes, 1997; Jessop, 2000; Stoker, 2000), characterised by a loosening of statist, bureaucratic forms of welfare delivery and the simultaneous recognition of the failure of markets or quasi-markets (Le Grand and Bartlett, 1993) to provide a viable and acceptable mode of welfare production and delivery. Such a mode of governance reflects the complex realities of welfare, which is delivered by a range of providers and characterised by dynamic, flexible and evolving methods of working that rely on horizontal, self-governing networks (Rhodes, 2000). Such networks reflect the diversity and pluralism of modern society (Rhodes, 1997). Partnership working, with its implicit rhetoric of trust, is said to be a defining characteristic of what Rhodes refers to as "governance: self-organising, inter-organisational networks" (Rhodes, 1997, p 53). A distinguishing characteristic of networked governance is that central government acts as an enabler, rather than coercing agents or organisations to act in a particular way (Stoker, 2000). While the British welfare state probably never exhibited 'pure' forms of either bureaucratic or marketised methods of governing, and is probably also unlikely ever to exhibit 'pure' forms of networked governance, in theory partnerships are to networked governance what contracts are to markets and command-and-control mechanisms are to bureaucracies: an essential element of that particular method of government. However, in Chapter Two, Powell and Exworthy make the point that "the search for greater coordination to solve 'wicked' or 'interconnected' problems has been a major feature of 'traditional public administration'". To a certain extent, therefore, the current emphasis on partnerships can be seen more as a feature of New Labour's drive towards 'evidence-based policy' (Davies et al, 2000; El Ansari et al, 2001), rather than an explicit loosening of the reins and a move towards networked welfare governance.

As Clarke and Glendinning remark in Chapter Three, "partnership is a word of obvious virtue (what sensible person would choose conflict over collaboration?)". However, they point out that until now, policy commitments to partnership working have not been accompanied by other significant features that would indicate the pursuit of networked governance. Drawing on the example of health and social care, which also features in several other chapters of the book, they assert that a deluge of accountability pathways accompanying the drive towards partnership working are designed to increase central government's ability to control the welfare state – more a case of overt steering rather than 'enabling' (Johansson and Borell, 1999; Newman, 2001).

Therefore, even before we consider the empirical evidence presented in the later chapters of this book, considerable doubt may be expressed a priori over whether partnership working reflects a new, distinctive, New Labour and 'Third Way' networked governance of welfare. Newman's assertion that New Labour's talk of the need for partnership "between those involved in the shaping of policy and those affected by its delivery" represents a considerable "paradigm shift" in policy and ideology (Newman, 2001, p 106) may be true. However, it is less clear that this constitutes an overt shift to a new 'Third Way' of welfare.

Theoretical and conceptual writing about partnerships has also concentrated on describing, categorising and analysing relationships between various partners in order to ascertain where a particular relationship is located on some kind of ladder or continuum of partnership activity (Hudson et al, 1997; El Ansari et al, 2001; Powell et al, 2001; Chapters Two and Four in this book). This is, at first sight, in keeping with the New Labour mantra of 'what counts is what works', a way of measuring partnership working in an instrumental and pragmatic way. In Chapter Four, Hudson and Hardy provide a particularly useful example of this based on analysis and evaluation of partnership working between health and social care agencies. However, useful as such tools are, they sidestep the issue of what partnerships might ultimately reasonably be expected to achieve: improved outcomes for welfare users. Although I have argued elsewhere that the process of welfare delivery is at least as important for service users as the outcome (Rummery, 2000), the lack of tangible evidence to date – that either networked governance or partnership working delivers tangible improvements in outcomes to welfare users – is of some concern (O'Toole, 1997).

The evidence of partnership working

The theoretical discussions outlined above do not really take us very far towards solving the definitional problem of partnerships. They may well be an essential feature of Labour policy (Hudson, 1999; Ling 2000), but that in itself leaves us with what Powell and Glendinning in Chapter One refer to as the 'Humpty Dumpty' issue: when someone calls something a partnership, by definition it *is* one. The evidence presented by the various authors in the subsequent chapters of this book add up to a complex and weighty empirical minefield.

A first step towards clearing this minefield is to adapt the 'Humpty Dumpty' analogy in a useful way. All of the relationships analysed in Chapters Five to Fourteen of this book constitute 'partnerships' in two important ways. First, while in many ways neither new nor particularly distinctive, all these partnerships are at least in part the result of explicit New Labour policies designed to support, encourage and on occasion enforce collaborative working within and between statutory and other sectors. Second, the partners themselves are explicitly engaged in a process designed to foster such collaboration, whether or not that is what they want to be doing. Therefore, from both an internal and external perspective, all of these relationships constitute self-defined partnerships.

While the complexity of the evidence would at first sight lead to the conclusion that there are as many different partnerships as there are situations and actors involved, it would be facile to suggest that there are no unifying characteristics or themes that can be deduced from the empirical evidence presented in this book. What emerges from the evidence is that at least two defining characteristics of partnerships are common to the various welfare relationships analysed here. First, the partners must experience a degree of interdependence in order for partnership working to be necessary. Second, unlike other methods of organisation or collaboration in welfare, partnerships are characterised by the existence of a certain degree of trust between the relevant partners. These two overarching and unifying dimensions of partnership working are discussed below.

Towards a unifying theory of partnerships

Interdependence: the purpose of partnerships

What appears to make partnership working necessary is a degree of interdependence between the relevant partners in achieving their own objectives. Without that interdependence there is clearly no need to engage in partnership working with an outside agency. As Hudson and Hardy put it in Chapter Four, "a prerequisite of partnership working is that potential partners have an appreciation of their interdependencies; without this appreciation, collaborative problem solving makes no sense". Given that partnership working may entail what can be quite significant losses as well as gains for the participating parties, any individual or agency engaging in a partnership that does not enable them to meet their own internal aims (which can include the goal of better collaboration) may waste a great deal of time and energy.

However, the evidence elsewhere in this book shows that the level of interdependence between the participating partners may not necessarily be the same or even equitable, and that this discrepancy may hold the key to whether or not a particular partnership is successful and sustainable. It may also therefore be a valuable indicator as to the appropriateness of partnerships within any given context, and thus may be a useful way of avoiding the trap of assuming that partnership working is a 'good thing' per se within the welfare state. Several relevant issues emerge from the evidence.

First, there appear to be significant differences in the nature and degree of interdependence between public–private partnerships and other types of partnerships. As was shown clearly in the examples of Education Action Zones (EAZs) (Chapter Twelve), the Private Finance Initiative (PFI) in the NHS (Chapter Thirteen) and pensions (Chapter Fourteen), the private sector does not appear to need the public sector to meet its own aims to the same extent as the public sector, within the present political climate, needs to work with outside partners to meet central government's objectives. In analysing public–

private partnership in the field of pensions, Ward argues in Chapter Fourteen that the private sector appears to be taking what it can get from the state, in contrast to the state's strong desire for partnership with the private sector: "The state is enamoured enough of its partner to pay the bills, but does not get a very good deal in return". Similarly, Dickson et al in Chapter Twelve argue that the incentives for private sector partners to participate in EAZs were comparatively weak (consisting largely of increased marketing and research opportunities), with the private sector having correspondingly less need to work with schools and local education authorities. The latter were under sustained pressure to apply for the additional central government resources that EAZ status would attract, so arguably needed to work with the private sector more than the private sector needed to engage with the public sector. In contrast, in Chapter Thirteen, Ruane presents evidence suggesting that in some circumstances the private sector can be argued to 'need' the public sector in order to meet its objectives. The degree of hard bargaining that the private sector was willing to engage in, in order to maximise profit, shows that where the public sector has something the private sector needs (in the case of PFI, money and long-term, secure contracts), it is more than willing to engage in partnership working. As Ruane remarks, "the goal of the consortium [the private sector] is to increase its long-term security by engaging with the new opportunities created by state policy to pursue new profit-making avenues opened up through public sector collaborations". Few private sector collaborations could offer the same long-term security as the NHS. An alternative view of the same evidence is that the partner with the less powerful need to work in partnership is placed in the more powerful bargaining position: they can usually walk away with much greater ease than the partner for whom the partnership is essential for being able to deliver on their core objectives.

Second, and related to the previous point, is the fact that the degree of interdependence experienced by partners will reflect the source of their individual internal objectives. The private sector is driven by the need to make and show a profit; the public sector is driven by whatever objectives government chooses to set it. As Clarke and Glendinning argue persuasively in Chapter Three, at the same time as being an alleged feature of networked governance, partnerships within the public sector come with a raft of incentives and punitive measures created by central government that have the effect of strengthening systems of vertical accountability. Rather than adopting a hands-off, enabling approach that would characterise true networked governance, Clarke and Glendinning point out that "both Labour governments since 1997 have produced a stream of policy guidance, legislation and moral exhortations (some of which are backed by substantial amounts of 'badged', or ring-fenced, funding) to develop partnerships between NHS and local authority organisations". The evidence presented by Davies in Chapter Eleven supports this view that partnership working has become a key feature of a more centralised control of welfare governance. He points out that his case studies "show how collaboration is driven by downward pressures, and how the internal dynamic of local collaboration between local authorities and the business sector remains weak".

Hughes and McLaughlin in Chapter Ten also highlight the intensified systems of audit and performance accountability that are supposed to sit harmoniously alongside local crime prevention partnerships. Indeed, for many sectors of the welfare state it is no longer an *option* to work in partnership with outside agencies; the exogenous pressures are overwhelming. In the drive to move partnership working from the margins to the mainstream of statutory agencies, it is in danger of becoming the *core* business. Arguably, however, government does not have the same degree of leverage over the private sector; it cannot set it objectives that make it *need* to work with the public sector in the same way that it can compel the public sector to work with the private sector. The comparatively weaker pressure that government can exert over the private sector (as illustrated by the somewhat ambivalent relationship of central government towards the private pension industry, as shown in Chapter Fourteen) does suggest that this relationship could perhaps be characterised as what Rhodes would recognise as 'governance', as opposed to the more overt steering of the public sector.

However, a third point that emerges from Chapters Five to Fourteen is that the state can exert *some* leverage over *some* sectors other than the public sector. Craig and Taylor argue in Chapter Nine that the third (voluntary and community) sector, as a relatively impoverished and less powerful partner, may risk becoming an even more unequal partner as a consequence of its engagement with the public sector, because the greater influence of the latter can distort both the aims and the independence of the former. Arguably, this engineered dependency could be construed as another form of enforced partnership which, as Craig and Taylor point out, could also lead to a diminution of the vital role the third sector plays in meeting the needs of some of the most marginal and disenfranchised communities. On the other hand, Clarke and Rummery present evidence in Chapter Five to suggest that the ability of a voluntary sector partner to adapt both its internal objectives and ways of working can actually facilitate closer partnerships (in this case with primary care, particularly GP practices) than an equivalent public sector partner (social services departments), because the latter's own objectives – many of which are prescribed by state and regulation – can act as an impediment to partnership working.

In contrast to the private and third sectors, the fourth point that emerges from earlier chapters is that organisations within the public sector often find themselves in the position of being unable to meet their objectives without the help of other, non-statutory agencies. Barnes and Sullivan point out in Chapter Six that a recognition of the social and other causes of ill health and health inequalities and, therefore, the role of sectors other than the NHS in improving the health of the population, was the driving force behind the setting up of Health Action Zones. Similarly, Hughes and McLaughlin point in Chapter Ten to the growing acknowledgement of the role of social and economic factors (which are outside of control of the police) in the rising crime rates of the 1980s, which drove the move towards crime prevention partnerships. In Chapter Five, Clarke and Rummery show how the realisation of their limited capacity to tackle non-medical issues affecting the health and well being of patients led GPs to be enthusiastic about working in partnership with social services and the voluntary sector. Davies argues in Chapter Eleven that pressure from central government made partnership working in the context of urban regeneration a necessity for local government, thus creating an interdependence and, he argues, furthering central government's control of local government. Arguably, the public sector now finds itself in the position where the prerequisite for partnership working, a degree of interdependency with one's partners, is becoming part of its core objectives.

These results may make sobering reading for a government committed to furthering the ideology and practice of partnerships in welfare delivery, particularly the facilitation of public–private partnerships. If an organisation or group does not *need* to collaborate with an outside agency in order to meet its own objectives, there may be no reason to engage in partnership working. While government can, using a variety of measures, control the core objectives of the public sector, it cannot exert a similar level of control over other sectors – particularly the private sector (see Chapters Twelve to Fourteen). In other words, the state can only partially create the conditions that necessitate partnership working (by setting the public sector's objectives), and it may therefore have difficulty in enforcing partnerships. Thus Ruane in Chapter Thirteen questions whether the core objectives of the private sector (in this case, the consortia of construction and facilities management companies that compete for contracts to build and maintain hospitals under PFI) were so divergent from those of the public sector that the relationship could hardly be characterised as a partnership at all. In Chapter Twelve, Dickson and colleagues argue that the objectives of the private sector partners led them to be particularly interested in schemes that promoted high achieving pupils, which contrasted with the objectives of EAZs to raise overall educational achievement and therefore has serious implications for the ability of EAZs to deliver on the government's wider social inclusion agenda. The limited scope that the public sector partners enjoyed in influencing the core objectives of their private sector partners was a significant factor in the inequitable distribution of costs and benefits intrinsic to such partnerships.

Trust: the distinctive characteristic of partnerships

While all of the contributors to both the theoretical and empirical sections of this book have carefully avoided committing themselves to a single definition of 'partnership', it is nevertheless apparent that trust is an important defining characteristic. What makes partnerships distinctive from other methods of working, at least in the eyes of the participants and their academic observers, appears to be that the parties involved are engaged in *trusting* the other parties to deliver on jointly held objectives.

Trust appears to have many dimensions. Hardy and Hudson note in Chapter Four that a history of successful collaborative working engenders trust between the relevant participants and thus facilitates future partnership working. Where relationships are based on trust, the evidence suggests that it is easier for the individuals and organisations involved to develop and, crucially, where necessary adapt and change their goals and methods of working to accommodate the achievement of the partnership's objectives. In Chapter Six, Barnes and Sullivan argue that within Health Action Zones it was necessary to build the capacity for collaboration; and where there was no history of partnership working, there was no foundation of trust on which to build that capacity. Conversely, in Chapter Eleven, Davies points out that the pressure from central government towards formalised partnership structures under urban regeneration policy in some cases actually undermined local partnerships that had developed trust-based relationships. Davies therefore argues that the policy drive towards partnership working is not evidence of a move towards network-style governance, but a further extension of statist bureaucratic control.

In a similar vein, where partnerships can be seen to have failed, either to sustain themselves or to deliver on their objectives, they are characterised by the *absence* of trust. Daly and Davis show in Chapter Seven that a failure to demonstrate the legitimacy of representation on various community forums led to a breakdown in trust between the local authority and community. Craig and Taylor in Chapter Nine, and Alcock and Scott in Chapter Eight discuss how local voluntary organisations can be marginalised in various local government activities, such as local government reorganisation, because they lead to the fragmentation and severance of the key relationships necessary to engender and maintain trust. While perhaps not an intended outcome, it would appear that government can undermine partnership working by putting in place contrary policies and objectives that have the result of destroying the vital element that distinguishes partnerships from other types of relationships. Trust cannot be mandated and attempting to do so can be the death knell for partnership working.

In Chapter Two, Powell and Exworthy note that trust is a characteristic of networked governance (Rhodes, 1997, 2000). They argue the case that issues such as quality and trust are accorded greater significance within networked governance than, for example, the significance accorded to price, which would predominate in a market-led form of governing. If this analysis is correct, the absence of trust as a key feature of a relationship would signify not only that such a relationship was not characterised by networked governance, but also that it would not constitute a recognisable partnership. In her analysis of PFI in the NHS in Chapter Thirteen, Ruane argues that such 'partnerships' are in fact contractual relationships rather than true partnerships. Contracts bind the parties into behaviours that they would not otherwise engage in. If a partnership needs to be 'enforced' through a contractual relationship, can the relationship be said to be a partnership at all? Is it not simply another manifestation of the operation of the market, or more accurately a quasi-market?

A degree of caution is required before it can be asserted that contractual relationships are not built on trust and therefore partnerships and contracts are mutually exclusive. Even if it is accepted that trust is a defining characteristic of partnerships, it does not necessarily follow that contracts play no role in facilitating successful partnerships. As Hardy and Hudson argue in Chapter

Four, a lack of clarity over objectives is not conducive to a successful partnership. However, contracts have the advantage over less specific agreements of making aims, objectives, penalties and rewards absolutely clear and unambiguous. They can offer protection against the breakdown of trust that results from one or both parties failing to deliver expected results. Moreover, the process of contract negotiation can itself *engender* trust, by giving the relevant parties a chance to work together and overcome inter-professional or inter-organisational mistrust (Rummery, 1998). While the NHS managers in Ruane's study of PFI reported feeling bruised after hard-hitting negotiations with the private sector, they also reported a greater understanding of the values that drove the private sector, which could lead to a greater sense of trust that they would deliver on the objectives.

Trust is therefore a defining characteristic of partnerships; it is what distinguishes them from other inter-organisational and inter-professional relationships. Trust is the result of experience of joint working and flourishes in an atmosphere marked by the successful achievement of goals. As the earlier discussion of interdependence showed, it can be easier to develop and maintain trust where an organisation or individual's values and goals are similar, and difficult to attain and sustain trust where values and goals are highly divergent. However, like interdependence, it is clear that the partnerships discussed in this book were characterised by very different levels of trust, depending on a number of factors. This is further evidence of the caution needed in embracing public–private partnerships in particular, where the evidence suggests that levels of interdependence and trust are lower than in public–public and public–third sector partnerships (although the latter also arguably have weaker interdependence and trust than public–public partnerships). The following section lays out some of the lessons to be learnt from the evidence of inter-sectoral differences in partnership working.

Towards a sectoral theory of partnerships

While interdependence and trust may be what makes partnerships distinct from other forms of working, as the previous section shows, these characteristics are not particularly well developed or robust in all the examples discussed in this book. In fact, what divides partnerships is at least as interesting as what unites them. There are clearly several areas in which the partnerships discussed in this book diverge significantly from each other. The important question is whether, in the midst of these divisions, there can be said to be any elements that characterise particular clusters or types of partnerships. As the theoretical and conceptual arguments discussed in the earlier part of this chapter show, partnerships can be categorised using a variety of mechanisms, whether that be on a continuum similar to Arnstein's ladder of participation (Arnstein, 1971); a framework such as that used by Powell and Exworthy in Chapter Two or by Powell and colleagues to evaluate measures to reduce health inequalities (Powell et al, 2001); a deductive pragmatic tool like the one developed by Hardy and Hudson in Chapter Four; or similar tools designed to reduce the complexity of inter-sectoral collaboration to an instrumental measurable outcome (El Ansari et al, 2001). Such mechanisms have the advantage, in a pragmatic and outcome-focused policy discourse, of being able to measure 'success' and 'failure' in partnership working and so are a useful way of analysing (and sometimes predicting) the outcome of any individual partnership within the welfare state. However, rather than simply applying them to the evidence presented in this book, it is also useful to compare partnerships across a range of sectors to establish what characteristics distinguish them from each other. What are the key elements to be aware of when critically analysing partnership working?

The distribution of power and benefits

Perhaps one of the most compelling characteristics that divide partnerships between the public and 'third' (voluntary and community) sector from partnerships involving other sectors is the inequitable distribution of power. In summarising partnerships between local government and the voluntary and community sectors (Chapter Nine), Craig and Taylor maintain: "Organisations that are well-resourced in human and financial capital, have expected ill-resourced community groups and relatively poorly-resourced voluntary organisations to engage with them on equal terms…. This engagement appears tokenistic and oppressive to many voluntary and community organisations". Rather than addressing this power imbalance by ensuring a more equitable distribution of the costs and benefits of partnership working, engaging in partnership working with the public sector can have significant costs for the third sector, with the public sector reaping most of the benefits (because it is meeting the centrally set goal of 'working in partnership' with its local community). Attending 'partnership' meetings is in the job description of many public sector managers: it is a deviation from their core, often under-resourced, business for many voluntary and community sector workers.

Indeed, addressing this power imbalance would possibly entail significant losses for the public sector. In their analysis of partnerships with the voluntary sector in Chapter Eight, Alcock and Scott point out that "power is a positional good and, for partnership working to be based on redistribution of power between partner agencies, then some have got to lose in order for others to gain". Moreover, Alcock and Scott question the capacity and willingness not only of the public sector but also the voluntary and community sectors to tackle this power imbalance; with power comes responsibility, but there are serious questions about the third sector's current capacity to cope with the responsibility that comes with engaging in partnership working with the public sector.

Unequal power is also starkly evident in the analysis of public–private partnerships. Ruane's note of caution that the public sector can sometimes be in a relatively powerful position in negotiations with the private sector may be true. Nevertheless the costs and benefits of partnership working appear disproportionately to benefit the private sector. Ward, in Chapter Fourteen, states that "the evidence of the state's desire for 'partnership' with the private sector is strong. There is less evidence of the private sector having a similar desire, rather than just taking what it can get". Again, this should be a sobering conclusion for a government committed to furthering public–private partnerships.

Major imbalances of power are less evident in public–public or inter-statutory partnerships. As Hughes and McLaughlin point out in Chapter Ten, participants in partnerships between local authorities and the police are "remarkably uncritical, in public at least, of what is a highly prescriptive top-down approach". Perhaps because engaging in partnership working has become such a central feature of New Labour policy, public sector organisations are less likely to lose any appreciable power to other public sector organisations that are under similar pressures to work in partnership. It is more of a 'win–win' situation for both parties. Moreover, performance indicators that reward public–public partnerships serve further to legitimate the power held by those organisations. A public sector organisation can increase its own power and legitimacy by meeting the government's targets; the process of engaging in partnership working becomes, in itself, a benefit for the organisations concerned.

Partnerships entail some kind of reciprocity: there need to be gains, or benefits, for all partners in order to make the process worthwhile. The evidence in this book suggests that where power is unequal at the outset of the partnership, the most powerful partner will also get the greatest benefits and the least powerful partner is likely to bear a disproportionately high burden of the costs. It would appear that only in public–public partnerships is this balance likely to be more equitable.

The setting and achievement of goals

There also appear to be marked differences between different types of partnerships in how goals are set and whether these are achieved. Whether objectives or targets are set horizontally or vertically appears to make a significant difference to whether or not partnership working is feasible for the parties concerned. Clarke and Glendinning argue in Chapter Three that the use of targets, incentives and 'badged' funding to foster partnership working between health and social care were ways for central government to steer and direct the actions of those care agencies, rather than ways of enabling them to cooperate to meet local needs. Hughes and McLaughlin observe in Chapter Ten that: "It is becoming increasingly obvious that 'success' in the reduction of crime and disorder is, in the short-term, largely synonymous with what can be counted, audited and easily targeted". Davies also argues persuasively (Chapter Eleven) that vertical targets act as significant barriers to the achievement of targets set locally, across horizontal networks. He points out that: "If [government] wishes to pursue regeneration by increasing its influence on local politics, it is arguable that current approaches are working. But if, on the other hand, it wants to generate strong, self-sustaining local partnerships to lead the regeneration process, it is failing".

Davies' point is sustained by evidence from most of the other inter-sectoral partnerships discussed in this book. The strong element of central control, as epitomised by the setting of what Davies calls 'exogenous' targets designed to increase vertical accountability, is inimical to enabling the horizontal sharing of goals that would empower local networks to work together effectively in partnership. In fact, the only example of partnerships in this book where there was a considerable degree of flexibility in setting of goals, one of the key factors that Hudson and Hardy note in Chapter Four is vital to the success of partnership working, is that described by Clarke and Rummery in Chapter Five between GPs, primary care and voluntary workers in the WellFamily service. It was precisely the lack of centrally driven and defined targets that enabled GPs, as independent contractors with relatively large amounts of freedom, and voluntary sector workers with similar freedom to negotiate their own service goals, to work together successfully. The fact that this relationship was built on strong flexible horizontal networks meant it could respond successfully to local needs. However, it is debatable in the present climate of centrally dictated mechanisms in the NHS (such as the National Institute of Clinical Excellence and National Service Frameworks) and moves to control the behaviour of GPs more effectively through clinical governance, Primary Care Trusts and practice-based contracts, that such freedom to set local objectives will persist.

Where this is not an issue is of course when partnership working in itself becomes a goal. There is significant evidence that this is happening in public–public partnerships. As Chapters Two, Three, Four and Six point out, partnership working is no longer an optional, marginal activity for health and social care agencies in the UK, but is becoming part of the mainstream, core activity for these agencies. Indeed, there is a danger of partnership working becoming an end, rather than a means of welfare delivery. Partnership by central *diktat* is an increasingly common feature of relationships between public sector agencies. What does this imply for the role of partnerships in the governance of the welfare state?

Partnerships and the governance of welfare

There are two main questions concerning partnerships and governance that arise. First, can partnership working deliver government objectives? Second, what is the role of partnership within the governance of welfare? Are they really a feature of New Labour, 'Third Way' delivery of welfare?

Clearly the centrality of partnerships to New Labour's current policy rhetoric shows that the state has a vested interest in the success of partnership working to deliver welfare. Davies argues in Chapter Eleven that, in the case of urban regeneration, the internal dynamic of collaboration between local business and local government remains weak and overridden by the external (that is, centrally driven) pressure to work in partnership. He points out that the 1999 Local Government Act actually increased central government's power to intervene in the event of the perceived failure of partnership working and that pressures to push participants into formalised partnership working sapped local energy, leaving little room for local autonomy (a point echoed by Clarke and

Glendinning in Chapter Three). Arguably, this increase in the state's control over the functions of public bodies is evidence of a continuing hierarchical, bureaucratic statist form of governing, rather than an extension of Third Way, networked governance.

In Chapter Ten, Hughes and McLaughlin point out that the New Labour move away from the Conservative 'prison works' regime in crime reduction towards the promotion of community-based crime prevention partnerships has not been accompanied by a loosening in statist control of police functions. On the contrary, they show how the drive towards performance management (in the shape of SMART targets) is evidence of a top-down approach to partnership dominated by technical risk assessment and discrete measurable outcomes. This has the effect of what Davies (Chapter Eleven) refers to as strengthening vertical linkages at the expense of horizontal networks. In other words, there appears to be a danger in over-prescriptive encouragement of partnership working from central government; the audit trail necessitated by such an approach undermines the kind of reflexive, adaptive working methods that are the hallmark of successful partnerships.

In the drive towards 'evidence-based policy and practice', another New Labour mantra (Davies et al, 2000), systems of auditing and measuring results have become important governing mechanisms in the facilitation (or otherwise) of welfare partnerships. However, targets and audit trails risk skewing partnership activity away from the production of better welfare services and towards the meeting of certain discrete, measurable objectives. Dickson and colleagues argued in Chapter Twelve that the case of EAZs showed that partnership working with the private sector was often targeted on bringing key groups of students (those who were just under standard) up to the standards necessary to pass examinations. Both public and private sector partners were most interested in supporting the aspirations of the most able (and therefore most employable) students. This alliance of targets, while useful for meeting short-term, measurable objectives, was at odds with the need for schools and LEAs to raise standards of education for all students, and arguably diverted funds and attention away from more inclusive and equitable initiatives.

It would appear that the overt drive to measure and account for partnership activity reflects a lack of trust between central government and public bodies. However, in the case of public–private partnerships, the private sector may appear to benefit more than the statutory partners and may therefore be trusted less. Arguably when the state has the least control over the internal aims and objectives of the participating parties (as in the case of the private sector), it appears to tighten control over other areas where it can, using hierarchical, command-and-control type methods commonly associated with bureaucratic statism.

However, the state can only do this with public sector bodies; it does not appear, at least under New Labour, to have a similar predisposition for governing the private sector through bureaucratic audit and other accountability mechanisms. The evidence from this book suggests that where partners enjoy a degree of freedom in adjusting the way they work (their values and objectives), this facilitates both the operation of the partnership and its enhanced success in delivering improved services (see Chapters Five and Seven). This 'hands-off' approach to partnership working, characterised by a lack of bureaucratic audit, is perhaps the most closely akin to Rhodes' vision of networked governance (Rhodes, 1997).

It is clear, however, that the state does not just control partnership working in welfare delivery through bureaucratic or governance systems. New Labour has happily continued the quasi-markets approach of endorsing financial and other incentives, often to the extent of forcing public sector bodies to compete against each other for resources. This can lead to extra resources going to those areas and organisations that are the most competent in putting together partnership bids, which are not necessarily the areas with the highest level of need. Such competitive bidding can lead to 'partnership-itis', particularly among participants for whom partnership working is less necessary for them to achieve their internal goals (that is, the private sector).

A further danger arising from the overt steering of partnership working, whether through statist, bureaucratic controls or market-type incentives, is that the effort of the participating parties is almost exclusively drawn into the mechanisms of partnership working itself. Resources and attention become focused on the structures of partnership working – the partnership boards; systems of accountability; appointment of key managers and liaison officers; setting up of committees and teams and systems – rather than on the actual delivery of welfare services. Many of the systems of audit and control put in place by central government in the examples used in this book measure such processes. This inevitably risks less attention and fewer resources being devoted towards the actual delivery of welfare services – which are arguably the core objectives of welfare agencies.

We have been here before, at least in health and social care. The requirement during the 1980s for local authorities and the NHS to jointly plan services led to time and energy being spent on servicing the joint planning structures, with little evidence of joined-up services on the ground (Nocon, 1990). What role do partnerships play in the actual delivery of welfare? If the efforts of the partners, and their rewards, are focused and dependent on the mechanics of partnership working, rather than on delivering improved welfare outcomes, does this really constitute an improved system of delivering welfare? There is little evidence in this book to suggest that partnership working delivers improved services to users. In fact, some of the writers are remarkably sceptical about the potential for partnerships to improve welfare outcomes. Dickson and colleagues argue that the gains for schools and LEAs in working with the private sector in EAZs were negligible, and possibly outweighed by some of the losses. Their points are echoed forcefully by Davies in his analysis of urban regeneration partnerships, where he points out that partnership working can have a *negative* impact on welfare delivery. Are there any indications that users might benefit from partnership working in the welfare state?

Partnerships: who benefits?

It is clear from the evidence presented in this book and discussed in this chapter that partnerships, per se, are not necessarily features of networked governance of welfare. In some cases, partnership working appears to be a remarkably effective means of ensuring that the state retains, and in some cases strengthens, its powers over some sectors (particularly the voluntary and community sectors). Moreover, partnerships New Labour-style appear to embrace a mixture of quasi-market-style incentives with bureaucratic, statist controls; only in some, rare, cases does the state adopt a laissez-faire enabling approach that might signify a true commitment to a 'Third Way' networked governance.

In some cases, the state is a clear beneficiary of partnership working; it can achieve its aims *and* dictate the aims of the other partners, thus furthering its own power and legitimisation. In the case of public–public partnerships, the state can achieve its aims by dictating them; partnership working becomes an aim in itself, so by working successfully in partnership with other public sector agencies, the public sector organisations and managers legitimise their own power and performance. In other partnerships, the private sector clearly benefits from its engagement with the public sector in gaining access to new markets, security and profit-making possibilities, while reducing its own risks and costs. These gains may be at the cost of the public sector.

There is little evidence so far that users of welfare benefit significantly from partnerships. Indeed, in some cases, such as the public–voluntary sector partnerships discussed in this book, they may bear significant *costs* as a result of working in partnership, because both the public sector's power to dictate the terms of the partnership and its need to show vertical accountability to central government can overwhelm the voluntary and community sector's capacity to pursue its own objectives. There is little evidence that users or communities can be empowered by partnership working, unless the public sector is willing to divest itself of some of its power and there is very little evidence that New Labour is willing to do that.

Partnership working New Labour-style benefits powerful partners. Such partnerships reinforce power inequalities that are already in existence, placing central government in a relatively powerful position vis-à-vis local government, the private sector in a relatively powerful position vis-à-vis the public sector and the public sector in a relatively powerful position vis-à-vis the voluntary and community sector. They divert resources away from the core business of welfare service delivery and they do relatively little to empower users or local communities. Yet who could possibly object to partnerships as a concept?

The evidence in this book suggests that while central government may be reasonably sure of achieving its goals by fostering public–public partnerships, its aims of securing social inclusion by fostering public–third sector partnerships is questionable; and its aim of securing improved welfare delivery by fostering public–private partnerships should, at best, be approached with a significant degree of caution. The private sector cannot be controlled within the present political climate by central *diktat*, and any claims that improved welfare outcomes can be achieved by public–private partnerships should be treated with scepticism. After all, if what counts is what works, partnerships don't necessarily always work.

References

Arnstein, S. (1971) 'A ladder of participation', *Journal of the Royal Town Planning Institute*, vol 57, April, pp 176-82.

Balloch, S. and Taylor, M. (eds) (2001) *Partnership working: Policy and practice*, Bristol: The Policy Press.

Davies, H.T.O. and Nutley, S.M. (eds) (2000) *What works?: Evidence-based policy and practice in public services*, Bristol: The Policy Press.

El Ansari, W., Phillips, C.J. and Hammick, M. (2001) 'Collaboration and partnerships: developing the evidence base', *Health and Social Care in the Community*, vol 9, no 4, pp 215-27.

Hudson, B. (1999) 'Dismantling the Berlin Wall: developments at the health–social care interface', in H. Dean and R. Woods (eds) *Social Policy Review 11*, Luton: SPA, pp 187-204.

Hudson, B. Hardy, B., Henwood, M. and Wistow, G. (1997) *Inter-agency collaboration: Final report*, Leeds: Nuffield Institute for Health.

Huxham, C. (2000) 'The challenge of collaborative governance', *Public Management*, vol 2, no 3, pp 337-57.

Jessop, B. (2000) 'Governance failure', in G. Stoker (ed) *The new politics of British local governance*, Basingstoke: Macmillan.

Johansson, R. and Borell, K. (1999) 'Central steering and local networks: old-age care in Sweden', *Public Administration*, vol 77, no 3, pp 585-98.

Le Grand, J. and Bartlett, W. (eds) (1993) *Quasi-markets and social policy*, Basingstoke: Macmillan.

Ling, T. (2000) 'Unpacking partnership: the case of health care', in J. Clarke, S. Gewirtz and E. McLaughlin (eds) *New managerialism, new welfare?*, London: Sage Publications.

Newman, J. (2001) *Modernising governance: New Labour, policy and society*, London: Sage Publications.

Nocon, A. (1990) 'Making a reality of joint planning', *Local Government Studies*, March/April, pp 55-67.

O'Toole, L. (1997) 'Treating networks seriously: practical and research-based agendas in public administration', *Public Administration Review*, vol 57, no 1, pp 45-52.

Powell, M., Exworthy, M. and Berney, L. (2001) 'Playing the game of partnership', in R. Sykes, C. Bochel and N. Ellison (eds) *Social Policy Review 13*, Bristol: The Policy Press and the SPA, pp 39-62.

Rhodes, R. (1997) *Understanding governance*, Buckingham: Open University Press.

Rhodes, R. (2000) 'The governance narrative', *Public Administration*, vol 78, no 2, pp 345-68.

Rummery, K. (1998) 'Changes in primary health care policy: the implications for joint commissioning with social services', *Health and Social Care in the Community*, vol 6, no 6, pp 429-38.

Rummery, K. (2000) 'A citizenship and social exclusion issue? Access to health and social care for older people under New Labour', presented at the *Social Policy Association Annual Conference*, University of Surrey at Roehampton, July.

Stoker, G. (2000) 'Urban political science and the challenge of urban governance', in J. Pierre (ed) *Debating governance: Authority, steering and democracy*, Oxford: Oxford University Press.

Index

see also Education Action Zones;
Private Finance Initiatives; private
sector

C

Cabinet Office 26, 27
capacity building *see* collaborative
capacity
Capital Prioritisation Advisory Group
200
care management 35
Care Trusts 37, 40, 43
Castle, Barbara 216, 220
centralised government control 43, 45,
46, 230-1, 239-40, 240-1
Health Action Zones 95
influence on Compacts 122, 125
inhibits regeneration partnership 167,
168, 178-9, 232-3, 236
limited influence over private sector
233-4, 238-9, 243-4
see also accountability; compulsory
partnerships; performance
management; regulation
Challis, L. 2, 7, 10, 23, 25
champions of change 19, 25, 27, 59
see also reticulists; social entrepreneurs
change
HAZs as agents of 82
theories of change approach 88-95
see also champions of change
Chartered Institute of Public Finance
and Accounting 21
citizen capacity 88
City Challenge initiative 169, 173, 185
City Pride Partnership, Birmingham 102
City Technology Colleges 185
civil society involvement 20, 43-4
in Health Action Zones 82, 86, 87-8,
90-1, 92-3
in local governance 97-110
mechanisms for 100
and voluntary sector 114-15
see also community involvement;
voluntary sector
Clarence, E. 26, 124
Cole, A. 178
Coleman, J.S. 114-15
collaborative advantage 7
collaborative capacity 55, 133
in Health Action Zones 86-95, 236
types of 88
collaborative governance 16

Commission for Health Improvement
(CHI) 26
commitment to partnership 56-7
communication in partnership 73
communitarianism 114, 132, 156, 157,
162
community capacity 88
community care 35, 67-8
limits of reforms 38, 68
voluntary sector involvement 118
Community Empowerment Fund 133
community initiatives 20, 86
community involvement
autonomy of community 131
collaboration in HAZs 84, 85, 86, 87-8,
90-1, 92-3, 94
Compact agreements 137-8, 143
consultation 43-4
in Education Action Zones 188,
189-90
excluded from anti-poverty work 135,
136-7, 141-2
lack of resources 140-1, 142, 144
legitimacy challenged 140, 236
in local governance 97-110, 238
barriers to 106-9, 116, 117, 134-5,
140-1
Birmingham case study 103-5
mechanisms for 100
policy for 132-3
regeneration partnerships 133-5, 139-
40, 167
representation of community 106-7,
135, 141-2, 187-8, 189-90, 236
and voluntary sector 114-15, 131-44,
234
see also neighbourhood renewal
programmes; regeneration
partnerships
community nurses 69, 70, 72, 74, 75
Community Plans 102, 105
community policing 153-4
Community Safety initiatives 115, 154-5,
159-60, 162
Compact agreements 10, 113, 117-27,
131, 143
background to 117-19, 132
constitution of 119-21
evaluation of 119, 137-8
organisational complexity 120-1, 134
in practice 121-5, 138
problems 119, 126-7, 138
complexity theory 51
Comprehensive Community Programme
184-5